ACADEMIC LEADERSHIP

ACADEMIC LEADERSHIP

JOUNI KEKÄLE

Nova Science Publishers, Inc.
Huntington, New York

Senior Editors:	Susan Boriotti and Donna Dennis
Office Manager:	Annette Hellinger
Graphics:	Wanda Serrano and Dorothy Marczak
Information Editor:	Tatiana Shohov
Book Production:	Cathy DeGregory, Kay Seymour, Jennifer Vogt and Lynette Van Helden
Circulation:	Ave Maria Gonzalez, Ron Hedges and Andre Tillman

Library of Congress Cataloging-in-Publication Data
Kekäle, Jouni
     Academic Leadership / Jouni Kekäle.
         p.   cm.
     Includes bibliographical references.
     ISBN 1-56072-899-X
     1. Educational leadership -- Finland -- Case studies. 2. Education, Higher -- Finland --
Case studies. I. Title.

LB2944.F5 K45   2001
378.1'01'094897 -- dc21   2001018725

Printed in the United States of America

CONTENTS

Preface   vii

Chapter 1   Introduction   1
1.1. Key Concepts   3
1.2. The Structure of the Thesis   7

Chapter 2   Historical Background   11
2.1. The Finnish Higher Education System   11
2.2. The Expansion of Higher Education in Finland   11
2.3. The Tides of Finnish Higher Education Policy   14
2.4. Increasing the Power of Individual Leaders   26

Chapter 3   Leadership Theories and Academic Context   31
3.1. Theoretical Perspectives on Leadership   31
3.2. Academic Institutions as a Leadership Environment   42
3.3. Finnish Studies on Academic Leadership   55

Chapter 4   Methodology and Data   61
4.2. Research Methods   71
4.3. The Choice of the Departments to be Studied   72
4.4. Access   74
4.5. The Phases of The Study   76
4.6. The Interviews and The Respondents   76
4.7. Coding and Analysis   79
4.8. A Note on Credibility of Interpretations   81

Chapter 5   Disciplinary Cultures and Academic Leadership   87

5.1. Becher's (1989a) Frame   88

5.2. Interpretations of Disciplinary Perspectives and Values   90

5.3. Schools of Thought and Intellectual Divisions   107

5.4. Choice of Specialisms and Mobility Between Them   110

5.5. Disciplinary Differences and Leadership Issues   113

Chapter 6   Leadership Cultures in a Historical Perspective   119

6.1. The Levels of Culture   119

6.2. The Formation of Departmental Leadership Cultures   121

6.3. Some Remarks on the Departments Studied   125

6.4. Eight Case Studies   127

Chapter 7   Conclusions   159

7.1. Types of Leadership Cultures   161

7.2. Diverse Leadership Contexts   166

7.3. Leadership and Cultural Change; Does Leadership Matter?   169

7.4. A Note on Power, Leadership and Academic Work   171

7.5. Concluding Remarks   173

References   177

Index   193

PREFACE

This study of academic leadership can be seen as one link in a chain of studies of higher education carried out in the department of psychology at the university of Joensuu. My supervisor, Professor Yrjö-Paavo Häyrynen, started his studies on educational climates in the late 1960s at the University of Helsinki. This line of research was continued as a longitudinal study by (currently Associate Professor) Hannu Perho in Joensuu in the 1970s. In 1989, Professors Häyrynen and Perho embarked on a broad study on the educational atmospheres of 57 departments at 12 Finnish universities. My own career as a researcher originates from this project: I carried out a few qualitative departmental casestudies, which provided an approach complementary to the broad survey study. The resulting Master's thesis provoked my interest in cultural values and assumptions, which - when I concentrated on these issues in my Licentiate's thesis - eventually directed my interest towards leadership issues in university departments. I am indebted to Professor Häyrynen and to Professor Perho for offering me an initial opportunity to work in the field of higher education studies, and grateful for their helpful guidance and comments concerning my study.

I wish also to acknowledge the help of several other scholars in Finland and abroad. First, I would like to express my gratitude and respect to three leading scholars who have made major contributions, among other things, to cultural studies in the context of organizations or higher education. Professor Edgar Schein (MIT, USA) helped me to embark on this study by providing a recommendation and some clarifying answers to my questions. His support and encouragement greatly contributed to my motivation in the critical starting phase of the study. His work has had a considerable impact on my intellectual development. I also wish to thank Professor Emeritus Burton Clark (UCLA, USA) for his positive attitude and reassurance, which he has expressed whenever we have met during the past three years, and for the intellectual stimulation I have gained from his books and articles. I am especially indebted to Professor Emeritus Tony Becher (University of Sussex, UK) for his intellectual leadership, help and contribution. During the three years in which I have worked on this research, his continuous support, comments and criticism have had a considerable impact on my thinking, writing and work motivation. I have been privileged to work under his supervision at the university of

Sussex for the whole calendar year of 1996. During this year, I finished the dissertation and wrote it in English. Professor Becher has read and commented on numerous drafts of the chapters. I am appreciative of the friendly mentorship he has provided during this project.

I would also like to thank the following scholars whose research interests include, or focus on, the area of leadership and management in higher education and in other types of organization. Dr. John Dearlove has acted as my second academic tutor at the University of Sussex. Despite his demanding job as the Dean of the School of Social Sciences, he has always welcomed me to discuss issues with him. His suggestions concerning my research have been very useful. I am further indebted to Ms. Robin Middlehurst of the UK Higher Education Quality Council, who commented on a preliminary version of chapter 3, dealing with leadership theories and academic institutions as a leadership environment - topics which are directly connected to her own specialism. In addition, I have received useful and interesting materials from Professor Ingrid Moses (The University of Canberra, Australia), Professor James Hearn (The University of Georgia, USA), Professor David Dill (The University of North Carolina at Chapel Hill, USA), Professor Mark Peterson (Texas Tech University, USA), and Associate Professor Barbara Sporn (Wirtschaftsuniversität Wien, Austria), among others. I wish to thank all of them.

Numerous Finnish researchers have contributed to this research. I would like to express my gratitude to Academician, Professor Emeritus Erik Allardt (University of Helsinki), who read a preliminary version of the study and provided me with useful comments which I have tried to incorporate into the analysis. I recently received a manuscript of his speech for the 10th Anniversary of the Finnish Academy in 1980. I was surprised at the relevance of his speech to my research; not only had he discussed many of the issues I have dealt with in this study, but his viewpoints often came close to mine. I need also to acknowledge Dr. Seppo Hölttä and Professor Kyösti Pulliainen from the University of Joensuu, as well as Professor Isto Ruoppila and Dr. Tapio Aittola from the University of Jyväskylä, who have helped me in diverse ways during the past years.

In 1994 and 1995, my research was made financially possible by the Finnish Ministry of Education. My stay in England in 1996 was sponsored by the University of Joensuu, and by the Department of Psychology and the Faculty of Social Sciences of the same institution.

I have studied academic leadership in diverse disciplinary communities (history, sociology, physics and biology) at two Finnish universities. The views of the scholars representing these different areas have turned out to be distinctive in many ways, as have their basic tasks and the intellectual territories they occupy. In all four disciplinary areas I much enjoyed my discussions with these sharp-witted and committed people, and I wish to cordially thank them for their participation in this study.

I have received assistance in practical issues from Assistant Professor Pentti Sinisalo and Mr. Kari Tahvanainen in the department of psychology at the University of Joensuu. Dr. Jopi Nyman (University of Joensuu) has checked the translations of the titles of the Finnish books and articles included in the list of references. In England, Ms. Margaret Ralph (EDB, University of Sussex), Mr. Hugh Turner, Ms. Sue Petri, Ms. Val Flanagan and Mr. Dave Flanagan have offered kind assistance when I have needed it. My parents have supported me in various ways during my studies. Finally, I wish to thank my wife Leea for her understanding and support during these three years, for being tolerant of my absences, and, most of all, for sharing this time with me.

Jouni Kekäle

Brookside, Kingston, 31. November 1996

Chapter 1

INTRODUCTION

This is a study of how Finnish professors lead their university departments. It deals with leadership in the context of different disciplinary and departmental cultures during an era when budget funding for universities has been declining and the power of individual leaders increasing. It is a comparative study involving eight university departments, which represent four distinct disciplines - *history, sociology, biology* and *physics* - at two Finnish universities (section 4.3.). All the departments studied were established around a single chair. Within them faculty members are trained, teach, and have common backgrounds in the same basic discipline.

When I started this research, I had worked for three years as a researcher in a project developing university teaching. Eight departments participated in the project. I and my colleague visited the departments regularly. Perhaps the most striking aspect of these visits was to find out the great differences between the units. For example, in some departments clear guidelines concerning teaching were expected, whereas in some others such advises were obviously not welcomed nor tolerated. It was as if the staff in the latter case would have seen such (well-intended) suggestions as indicating that they could not handle their teaching tasks by themselves.

In early 1994, I encountered the departmental differences again as I started to negotiate my access to the departments under study in order to carry out the empirical part of this dissertation. I visited first a department of *biology*. I found researchers gathered informally in their large coffee room, as they always do at certain times during the day. The atmosphere was very casual and friendly. Somebody told jokes; others discussed in pairs. I described the outline my study to staff and they readily agreed to participate in the study. We decided that I would contact certain members by phone so that times and places for the proposed interviews could be arranged.

Next, I visited a department of *physics*. As in other cases, I had phoned the head of department first. The head had called several researchers into a meeting room. The discussion was much more formal than in the department of biology. Although there were many researchers present, it was obvious that the head would make the decisions about their participation in the study. He listened to my description and apparently found the research interesting; he noted that this had been his impression on the basis of my initial phone call. Then he made sure that each of the researchers present, one by one, found suitable time for the interviews during the following week.

In department of *history*, the head remarked at the beginning of my visit that the historical truth is that university departments cannot be led. Leadership in the academic context was shortly discussed, on a general level, by those researchers who had attended the meeting. After a while, the staff agreed to participate in the research.

I then moved ahead to visit a department of *sociology*. I met them in their meeting room. As in the previous cases, I described the purpose and the general outline of my study and asked them to consider their participation in the research. Unlike the previous cases, some members of the faculty seemed to be suspicious and critical about the study. They wanted to know more about the research. One researcher asked to see my application for funding in order to get to know the 'real' purpose of my research. The discussion about their participation did not proceed. We agreed that I would phone the head afterwards in order to find out what they had decided. About a month later, after some further negotiations, most of the researchers decided to participate in the study.

Already these short descriptions of my initial visits to the departments give some clues about the diverse ways in which the issues of leadership may be viewed and handled within academic departments. The broad theme of academic leadership and management is actual, controversial; and it obviously provokes strong emotions and interests. The head of the department of history is hardly alone in his faith that academic departments cannot - or should not - be led at all.

However, the fact remains that the actual importance of the issues of academic leadership has been increasing. In early 1990s, there has been a large-scale public discussion about the suitability of the recently introduced doctrine of Management by Objectives in Finnish universities. Quite a lot of decision-making power, which had been firmly in the hands of collegial councils in the 1970s and 1980s, has recently been delegated to individual leaders: rector, deans, department heads (Höltttä & Nuotio 1995). The increasing emphasis on individual leadership is by no means a Finnish curiosity (see Middlehurst 1995). Miller (1995, 167) maintains that the explicit reference to 'managers' in universities is a relatively new phenomenon, which has developed in the western world in the 1980s. Clark (1995, 7) notes:

> In the United States, efforts to restructure universities entail hard questions of how to establish change-oriented leadership, focus comprehensive institutions, and translate an overall sense of direction into management at the operational levels of school and department.

Middlehurst (1995) identifies several trends (such as political and economic pressures, increasing size and scope of university business, and increased demand for accountability), which suggest that "management and leadership have become necessary" in the academic context. Hogan et al. (1994) maintain in their article "What We Know About Leadership" that the management of creativity is one of the most important problems of the future. This practical problem is faced daily by academic leaders such professors and leaders of research projects at the level of academic departments. However, Hogan et al. (1994, 500) conclude that

> we know very little about different ways of leading and managing teams whose primary tasks are problem solving and the developing of new knowledge, methods, and products.

Even more striking is the fact that most of the papers and studies on academic leadership seem to deal with the issue on a rather general level. Little attention has been paid to academic leadership in the contexts of different disciplinary or departmental cultures, although it is often noted that managerial criteria and the psychology of management can never be universally valid, in that they are always connected to the given situation, and the branch or culture within which they have been produced (e.g. Juuti 1989, 196; Lahti-Kotilainen 1992, 29).

Studying departmental and disciplinary cultures alone would seem worthwhile. McNair (1993) concluded in his summary speech at the EHE conference (Edinburgh, November 1993):

> We still have rather poor maps of the many cultures of higher education, of where shared values cluster and conflicting ones separate.

In this study, I shall focus on the relationships between academic leadership and the culture of discipline/specialism on the one hand, and leadership and the organizational culture of the department on the other. I shall try to understand the backgrounds and contexts of departmental leadership by concentrating on the following initial and interrelated questions: What is (are) the main function(s) or tasks of departmental headship in different departments? What kind of leadership patterns can be found in the studied departments and which of these patterns have been effective in supporting the academic work in different disciplines? How is 'good' academic leadership seen in different disciplinary and departmental contexts? How (and in which circumstances) are the heads of departments and informal leaders able to embed and reinforce the organizational cultures of their departments - if they lead this culture at all? I am especially interested in the 'informal' leadership cultures and practices of the departments: How are important decisions actually made in different departments? What kind of disciplinary and departmental values, practices, patterns and assumptions are connected to the issues of leadership, management and decision-making in the studied departments?

1.1. KEY CONCEPTS

The concepts of *leadership* and *management* are complex and open to numerous definitions and interpretations (Birnbaum 1989, 22; Middlehurst 1993, 7; Bush 1995).

Leadership and management can be seen as two complementary aspects or systems of action (Middlehurst 1993). A loose conceptual distinction is often made between them, where management refers to orientation towards results and goals, organizing tasks and systems, while leadership alludes to orientation towards human relations and organizing people. For example, management can be seen as

> a matter of running an organization so that the variety of people who want something out of it will go on supporting it in such a way that it is able to continue its existence into the future (Watson 1994, 10).

In her discussion of leadership in an academic context, Middlehurst (1993, 129) notes that leadership and management functions have been closely integrated at the departmental level. She distinguishes several popular conceptions or aspects of leadership, which highlight separate facets of the subject (aspects of both leadership and management), and demonstrate an implicit or explicit focus on five 'Is': integrity, initiative, influence, inspiration and imagination (Middlehurst 1993, 183-184). First, leadership is often associated with providing a vision and direction for others. Second, leadership is commonly linked to the authority of position and to taking charge. This legitimates the exercise of influence over others, which is also based on consent. Third, the leadership position is connected to 'initiative' both as a quality and as a responsibility for action. Leadership is also linked to achievement and to successful outcomes of action. These aspects are connected to each other:

> Together they provide a complete circle of responsibility and expectation: from origination to conclusion of task, a vision, or some individual or collective purpose (Middlehurst 1993, 183).

Fourth, leaders are set apart from others, as exceptional individuals, as an example for others, or as persons able to attract voluntary followers. Finally, leadership may also carry strong moral or ethical connotations, which relate to symbolic aspects of leadership such as representation of collective values, interests or aspirations (Middlehurst 1993, 183-184).

When these popular conceptions are all put together, a picture of quite strong and influential leaders is formed. It may be possible to find leaders (also in academic contexts) who can be characterized by all the aspects mentioned (for example, experienced, powerful, leading experts). But the conceptions of strong management and heroic leadership may not always apply very well to bottom heavy university organizations[1]. Middlehurst and Kennie (1995, 128) argue that traditional perspectives on

---

[1] In this study, I use the term *organization* to refer to existing functional systems and groups of people which systematically try to pursue certain broad aims, have developed some kind of internal hierarchy, division of tasks, and distribution of information (see Allardt & Littunen 1984, 261-269). The term (academic or university) *institution* is used here as a synonym to university organization. Depending on the context, the terms academic institution and university organization

leadership, which start from the assumption of a unilateral relationship between "a visionary, charismatic or autocratic leader and a group of obedient or submissive followers", is wholly inappropriate in the context of academic institutions[2]. Birnbaum (1989, 3-4) even speculates that universities are successful perhaps just because they are "poorly managed, at least as management is often defined in other complex organizations". Becher (1989a) points out fundamental differences between disciplines. On that basis, he argues against false managerialism which tries to force disciplines into same mould, or impose crude accountability and over-simplified indicators of performance, which are, however, not well suited to the nature of academic work.

My working assumption is that common leadership and management functions and conceptions such as 'being in charge', 'providing direction, purposes, visions and goals for the future', or 'being first or foremost' (Middlehurst 1993, 8-11; Bush 1995, 1-2), may have different meanings and practical outcomes in different disciplinary and departmental contexts. Moreover, I assume that leadership functions may be arranged in a variety of ways in different conditions. Because of this, I start with a loose definition of leadership and try understand - by means of qualitative research - the actual position and (potential) influence of those persons who are in a leading or decision-making position in the departments under study: that is, (especially) professors and heads of departments, or other researchers who essentially take care of the leadership functions.

Consequently, I will use the term *academic leadership* in a broad sense, in both the meanings of leadership and management, although the main emphasis will be on the human relations (leadership) aspects. By the term leadership I will also refer to both organizational leadership (arranging times, funds and facilities) and intellectual leadership (provided by respected researchers) as identified by Griffith and Mullins (1972, 961). I share Clark's (1983, 4-5) view that this kind of "relaxed approach" and definition "better accommodates to the peculiarities of academic tasks and work". As will be seen, diverse aspects of leadership (and management) are highlighted in different leadership cultures. Consequently, a narrow definition would not do justice to the complexity of the phenomena of academic leadership which I intend to describe and understand. A relaxed approach is also in line with the nature of a qualitative study, where the key concepts may evolve and develop during the course of the research.

Another key concept of this study, namely *culture*, has numerous meanings as well. As Aaltio-Marjosola (1991) and Sackmann (1991, 8) have pointed out, Kroeber and Kluckhorn already in 1952 identified hundreds of different definitions of culture. Many attempts have been made to simplify this multiplicity of meanings (e.g. Smircich 1983 and Gagliardi 1986).

---

refer to university as a general ideal typical type of organization, or to a concrete individual university.

[2] However, according to Middlehurst and Kennie (1995, 127) the purpose of leadership in professional organizations remains similar to its purpose in any other organization: "making it happen, deciding and articulating what 'it' is, and taking people with you individually and corporately"

In the context of higher education, the concept of culture has been used in studies focusing on organizational cultures[3] and in studies concentrating on disciplinary cultures (Maassen 1996, 155). Gagliardi (1986, 126) claims that the term culture is used in the field of organizational culture research, often indiscriminately, in two different meanings. First, it refers to the coherent system of assumptions and basic values distinguishing a group and directing its choices. Second, it refers to a group's distinct set of features or traits, which does not only mean its basic values and assumptions, but also its beliefs, models of behaviour, technology, symbols, and artifacts. These two definitions, one being much broader than the other, might cause some confusion. In disciplinary culture studies, the term is usually used in the broader (second) sense. For example, Huber (1990, 241) notes that the term culture has offered "a concept sufficiently wide and complex to cover all the relevant traits from everyday life to cognitive and social structures in the disciplines".

In this study, I shall use the term culture in its broader sense. By the term *(leadership) culture* I refer to a group's distinct set of (leadership) patterns, features and traditions as well as the values and assumptions on which these patterns have apparently been based. I do, however, agree with Gagliardi (1986) and Schein (1985; 1991b) that some cultural elements, namely deeply held values and basic assumptions, tend to be more enduring and profound than others[4].

I assume that the issues of leadership and culture are intertwined in a circular process: academic leaders may contribute to the formation of the culture in their department, and the established culture, in turn, may start to limit and direct also their own action (Schein 1985; Kekäle 1993 a). I also assume that departmental leadership more easily affects local culture within the department, while some broader disciplinary

---

[3] Schein (1985, 8) maintains that the word culture can be applied to "any size of social unit that has had the opportunity to learn and stabilize its view of itself and the environment around it its basic assumptions". From this perspective, any set of people with some common history and shared experiences, including personnel in university departments (at least the permanent staff) and their work - the construction and deconstruction of knowledge, world-views, and assumptions - can be seen from the point of view of organizational culture research (Kekäle 1995b).

[4] A value can be seen as "an element of a shared symbolic system which serves as a criterion or standard for selection among the alternatives of orientation which are intrinsically open in situation" (Parsons 1951). Basic assumptions, which are stressed by Schein (1985; 1991b) as the core of culture, are unconscious, taken for granted beliefs, habits of perception, thought and feeling. Thus, they are often even more powerful in guiding behaviour; other alternatives are not even taken into account (Kekäle 1992; 1993a). However, a sharp distinction between conscious values and unconscious basic assumptions is not always appropriate, especially in the academic context. For example, commitment to background assumptions of different scientific paradigms may be a conscious or unconscious act, but in any case such assumptions seem to distinguish different schools of thought from one another (e.g. Guba & Lincoln 1994; chapter 4). I share Sackmann's (1991, 25-26) view that it is not necessarily fruitful to start from universal a priori dimensions of basic assumptions (e.g. nature of human nature or nature of time and space; see Schein 1985) to be scrutinized in different organizational settings. Instead, I shall concentrate on values and assumptions which seem relevant for the purposes of my study on the basis of my data and research literature which deals with the specific disciplines under study.

values and perspectives usually act as a loose framework for departmental leadership and action. Clark (1983, 75-76) notes, cultures of institutions and disciplines are

> powerful sources of belief, working locally in the department and the subfaculty, as well as in the university or college as a whole, and producing the more specific set of beliefs that academics live by.

On the other hand, academic tribes (Becher 1989a) also have their chieftains, scholars who are more influential than others in affecting and directing the disciplinary culture in question, or even academic culture in general (Ylijoki 1994). Research is human action, and it is not foreign to the phenomena of leadership.

1.2. THE STRUCTURE OF THE THESIS

A central starting point in this study has been that current cultural features and leadership patterns can be understood against their historical background. Throughout the book, some underlying themes may be identified. These include ambiguity and fragmentation vs. integration and cohesion of values and practices, local vs. universal 'truths', and the dynamics between stability and change.

In cultural studies, comparisons are often fruitful, since they bring out the diverse features of the cultural units (Heiskala 1990, 248-249; Alasuutari 1994, 190-191). In this research, I shall make comparisons between cultures of disciplines and specialisms in order to bring out some of their 'inherent' cultural values and aspects which seem to affect academic leadership in their context. In this respect, the relevant framework for interviews was derived from Becher's (1989a) study. The departments studied were chosen to represent different disciplinary cultures (or basic disciplines - history, sociology, physics and biology) on the basis of the same study (Becher 1989a). I have also compared the leadership cultures and their local historical backgrounds in the eight studied departments. This part of my study stems from organizational culture studies, and the basic framework for interviews was received from Schein's (1985) and Tierney's (1988) work. I have conducted altogether 56 interviews by using this basic framework (see appendix 1). The layout of the forthcoming chapters is the following:

> In *Chapter 2*, I shall concentrate on relevant features and on the history of the Finnish higher education system in order to provide the reader with background information against which the departmental leadership practices can be viewed. A short overview of the Finnish higher education system, its expansion and of the historical changes of higher education doctrines is provided. Although I point out that Finnish higher education system has changed in pace with the systems of many European countries (Kuoppala 1995) - or rather slightly after them - I shall not try to systematically compare different national systems or their changes in this chapter (see Clark & Neave 1992). However, I believe that the information

on Finnish higher education may be particularly illuminating for the foreign readers, who are perhaps not familiar with the specific national background. The discussion is also useful for the purposes of my analysis: in the forthcoming chapters, I shall frequently connect this general background (and the tensions which distinctive eras in higher education seem to have generated or reinforced) to the leadership issues under discussion.

Chapter 2 also aims at pointing out the fundamental changes in the steering and funding of higher education, which had taken place during the early 1990s, just before the time when the 56 interviews of this study were carried out (in 1994 and 1995). By 1994, all Finnish universities adopted budgeting by results. As already noted, the changes in steering policy have underlined the power of individual academic leaders. Another dramatic change is the decline of resources for higher education. The resources had increased continuously for decades, but in the mid 1990s, the worst recession of the century strained universities and affected moods within the departments.

In *Chapter 3*, I shall discuss different theoretical perspectives on leadership. It is useful to give a brief consideration to the main approaches to leadership, in that these approaches help to demonstrate the different scholarly conceptions and views on leadership and they also throw light on different aspects of the phenomenon under study. The discussion gives some guidelines about the development of leadership theories and studies. It also helps to pinpoint the main areas of focus (and the strengths and weaknesses) of the main theoretical frame(s) used by researcher(s). In this study, my main theoretical approach has been the broad cultural frame. As will be seen, this orientation overlaps with many other major theoretical perspectives on leadership. Chapters 5 and 6 deal with my findings from the cultural perspectives.

After the theoretical orientation in chapter 3, I continue by discussing academic institutions as leadership environments in order to consider the applicability of different conceptions and models of management and leadership in academia. I will specify the organizational level I will be focusing on in this study (basic units), and reflect some of the general features of leadership environment at this level in comparison with the more often analyzed institutional level. Relevant Finnish studies on academic leadership will be examined as well.

Chapter 4 deals with methodology and data. I start by discussing different paradigms of qualitative research on the basis of Guba and Lincoln's (1994) model in order to reflect my own assumptions concerning epistemological, ontological and methodological matters. This is followed by sections dealing with the research methods used, with the detailed description of research process, the respondents and the data base, and finally with the coding and analysis of the empirical data and the credibility of my interpretations.

Chapter 5 starts with a discussion of Becher's (1989a) theoretical frame, on basis of which the departments studied were chosen to represent different enough disciplinary cultures. On the basis of my empirical data and research literature, I focus on some basic features and value-orientations of the disciplines and specialisms under study, which seem to affect and direct the issues of academic leadership. My argument is that epistemological and social features of disciplines and specialisms, among other things, provide a relevant framework for leadership. Conclusions are provided in the end of the chapter.

Chapter 6 deals with departmental leadership cultures. The chapter starts with a theoretical orientation which derives from studies on organizational culture. This is followed by empirical case studies of the leadership cultures of the eight departments studied. The chapter is the longest one since it deals with the largest part of my empirical data. It is noted that the leadership cultures and values concerning leadership may diverge in different disciplinary and departmental contexts because of local social processes, leadership history and influence. In some cases they diverge from one to another even in departments representing the same basic discipline. The discussion highlights psychological and social psychological processes within the departments, and aims at describing and understanding the current leadership cultures of the departments and their historical backgrounds.

In *Chapter 7*, I shall make concluding remarks about the study. The perspectives on leadership in the context of disciplinary and organizational culture study are compared. I shall also discuss the main types of leadership cultures in the light of my initial research questions. Especially disciplinary and departmental cultures and the general background discussed in chapter 2 will be highlighted in the analysis of departmental leadership. Academic leaders' role in cultural change, and the limits of their power in academic context are considered.

Chapter 2

HISTORICAL BACKGROUND

2.1. THE FINNISH HIGHER EDUCATION SYSTEM

According to Jolkkonen (1985), the typical features of the Finnish higher education system include an exceptionally large number of higher education institutions in relation to the overall population; decentralized location of universities; co-existence of general and specialist institutions (which all share the tasks of research and instruction) with relatively equal status; (generally speaking) their small size; and the privileged position of the university of Helsinki. Kivinen (1989, 93) has compared the Finnish and American systems of higher education in the late 1980s. The following characteristics of the Finnish system were added to the list by him: centralized allocation of resources; rather restricted competition which is directed towards budget funding, not towards the business world, potential students or markets; inability of higher education institutions to take initiatives; and a lack of entrepreneurship.

In principle, the Finnish higher education system has been based on the German university model (Jolkkonen 1985, 9; Hölttä 1995, 21). In practice, the professional education of civil servants has been a major task of higher education (Jolkkonen 1985, 9). The Humboltian ideal (unity of research and teaching, autonomy of research and the priority of civilization) has been increasingly replaced by an emphasis on technological applications, and by an interest in strengthening the competitive edge of the economy (Kivinen et al. 1993, 252). Although the Finnish higher education system has become more market- and competition oriented during the 1990s, the general features pointed out by Jolkkonen (1985) still remain.

2.2. THE EXPANSION OF HIGHER EDUCATION IN FINLAND

The oldest of the Finnish universities is *the university of Helsinki*. It was established over three hundred and fifty years ago (in 1640) in the time of Swedish rule in Turku (Kivinen et al. 1993, 16; Hölttä 1995, 21; *Helsingin yliopisto* 1970). By 1828, the Academy was transferred to Helsinki and reopened as the Imperial Alexander University of Helsinki (Finland was an autonomous Grand Duchy of Russia at that time; see *Higher Education* 1996, 29). The university of Helsinki was the only institution of higher education in Finland for over two hundred and sixty years. The Helsinki Institute of Technology was given university status in 1908. In 1917 and 1920, around the time when Finland achieved independence (1917), the higher education system started to expand as two universities were founded in Turku (*Higher Education* 1996, 29-30). The background of the expansion of the Finnish higher education system in the beginning of the century can be observed, among other things, in the growth of the (comprehensive) school system (Elovainio 1974), in the nation's economic growth and in the consequential increase of offices and posts, and in the development of public health care services (Jolkkonen 1985).

Finland experienced a post-war expansion of higher education simultaneously with most Western European countries (Pesonen 1982, 365). After the 1950s, the Finnish system expanded rapidly in terms of the numbers of professorial staff (see Kivinen et al. 1993, 215-216), in terms of increased student enrolment and increased numbers of other teaching staff, and in terms of the growing network of university institutions in the country (Kuikka 1992). Student numbers tripled, the number of professorships doubled (from 340 to 720) and the total number of university teachers quadrupled (from 1000 to 3900) between 1950 and 1965 (Pesonen 1982, 366).

This rapid expansion can be seen in relation to society's changing educational needs and its demands on the workforce. Jolkkonen (1985) has identified three waves of expansion of higher education in Finland: *the education wave in the 1950s, the welfare-state wave in the 1960s* and *the technical-economic wave since the mid 1960s*. These waves do not merely portray the growth in the numbers of students: they also reflect the changes in major orientation of the new universities founded at different times, and the opportunities for study in different disciplinary fields. During the educational wave, for example, the growth was most rapid in the humanities, mathematics and the sciences, when many graduates found their jobs in education. During the 1960s, the growth was rapid in law and the social sciences in response to the tasks needed by the welfare-state. During the third wave, academic schooling grew rapidly in technical and economic fields (Jolkkonen 1985; Kivinen et al. 1993): several specialized business and technical institutions had been founded in the fifties and sixties in response to the increasing demands of industry and the business sector (*Higher Education* 1996).

Especially from the 1960s onwards, political interests and the increase in population also seem to have affected the expansion of higher education. The Finnish higher education system was still fairly narrowly based and concentrated in the south of Finland, until the rapid regional development and expansion which took place during the 1960s and 1970s (*Higher Education* 1996). The rising interest in regional politics was channelled in attempts to level off the obvious differences in population, employment and industrial production between the developed and developing areas of the country. It became politically impossible simply to keep on developing the existing major southern universities (Nevala 1983, 17; see Kivinen et al. 1993, 190). More student places were needed also because of the increased number of potential applicants from the large post-war generation (Kivinen et al. 1993, 52-55; see Pesonen 1982).

As a result, new universities were established and the number of permanent posts within universities grew rapidly. During the 1960s and 1970s, altogether 420 (full or associate) professorships were established in five relatively young universities in Oulu, Tampere, Jyväskylä, Joensuu and Kuopio, while the three older universities in Helsinki and Turku received altogether over 360 professorships (Aaltonen 1993; quoted in Kivinen et al. 1993, 216). In 1994, altogether 1199 full and 842 associate professors worked in Finnish universities, while the total number of teaching staff was 7735 (*Higher Education* 1996, 109). In nearly all regions of Finland, student numbers increased continuously as well: the only exception was during the depression in the 1970s, after which the growth stopped in most universities for a few years (Kivinen et al. 1993, 212-214). In 1940, about 10 000 students studied in the then existing universities (Jolkkonen 1985, 13), while in 1995, the total number of university students was 135 000 (*Higher Education* 1996, 31).

Today, there are twenty universities in Finland (the total Finnish population is about 5 million people). The current network of higher education institutions is extensive, covering the whole country, including the sparsely populated eastern and northern regions. Ten of the institutions can be categorized as general, multidisciplinary universities. Six are specialist institutions (half of which are schools of economics and business administration, while the rest are universities of technology). The remaining four are art academies. All the institutions are State-run and engaged in education and research (*Higher Education* 1996; *An Introduction* 1994). There are two Swedish language universities in Finland. The university of Helsinki is bilingual, while in all other universities the main language of teaching is Finnish (Hölttä 1995, 23)[1]. The current student enrolments in Finnish universities vary from 32 500 (university of Helsinki) to 200 (Academy of Fine Arts). Five institutions have around 10 000 - 12 000 students each, but the typical size of the rest of Finnish universities varies between two to six thousand students (see *Higher Education* 1996, 31). About 45 percent of students are enrolled outside the southernmost (Helsinki and Turku) area of Finland (Hölttä 1995, 25).

Despite the rapid expansion of higher education, the university of Helsinki has kept its privileged position. In 1950, the majority (almost 2/3) of university students studied there; 46 % of the established full professorships were located there; and nine out of ten of the published doctoral dissertations were produced at the university (Kivinen et al. 1993, 19). In 1995, the university of Helsinki still remains by far the largest university in the country with its share of 24% of all students, 22,9% of the total teaching staff and 25% of the total budget for higher education in Finland (*Yliopistot* 1995, 52).

---

[1] In addition to this, Finland is building up a non-university sector of higher education, which currently consists of 28 polytechnic institutions (so called 'ammattikorkeakoulut') offering 15 000 starting places. The reform will be completed by the year 2000, when there will be 24 000 places for school leavers, and a further 8 000 places for degree programmes for adult students (see Kuoppala & Marttinen 1995, 276-282; *Higher Education* 1996, 79-86).

2.3. THE TIDES OF FINNISH HIGHER EDUCATION POLICY

The historical periods of the Finnish higher education system can be examined from the point of view of changing higher education policy and doctrines[2]. Kivinen et al. (1993, 15-158; 192-195) have identified three higher education doctrines on which the official Finnish higher education policy has rested: *the academical-traditional doctrine, the development doctrine, and the doctrine of management by results*. Roughly speaking, the main emphasis of official higher education policy has shifted from autonomy of universities, to centralized control and administration by the Ministry of Education (aiming at democratization of education), and further towards Management by Objectives and increasing demands on efficiency and cost-effectiveness (Kivinen et al 1993; Nevala 1991; see Kaukonen 1990, 30-39).

Because of the slow change in policy and practice, there is a considerable overlap between the different doctrines. The allocation of resources and the planning of higher education policy do not go hand in hand either. The allocation of resources in annual budgets follows the actual changes in political atmosphere and economic situation of the state more rapidly than do the long term plans of qualitative development of higher education. Moreover, a new development doctrine does not necessarily change resource planning or practices at once: indeed, the delay may be of several years (Kivinen et al. 1993, 193-196).

According to Hovi et al. (1989, 245), the justification of Finnish educational policy as a whole has been based on an "internationally institutionalised cultural model for the development of national educational systems":

> At the heart of this model is the doctrine of the national state, of citizenship and of national progress: the better the citizens of the state are educated, the more effectively they can be mobilized to serve the goal of national progress (Hovi et al. 1989, 245).

The changes in Finnish higher education doctrines have generally reflected the broader trends which can be identified in the Western World (*Higher Education* 1994, 50; Kuoppala & Marttinen 1995, 118-120).

---

[2] *Higher education policy* consists of those actions and endeavours through which the state and other actors in society have attempted to affect - or have affected - the tasks, direction, resources, structures, processes, outputs and content of higher education. *Higher education doctrine* consists of the principles, tasks and legitimation of the higher education system as expressed by the state through planning, steering, law-making and drafting, and by the political and ideological legitimation of these actions (Kivinen et al. 1993, 10-14). I shall concentrate here mainly on the official higher education policy of the state and on its legitimation and guiding principles (the higher education doctrines) as identified by Kivinen et al. (1993).

2.3.1. The Academical-Traditional and Development Doctrines

The first higher education canon, *the academical-traditional doctrine*, lasted until the 1960s. A central feature of this period was the independent position of professors and the autonomy of universities. Academic traditions were respected and the direction of higher education policy was determined mainly by the universities (Kivinen et al. 1993); no nationwide policy plan or unified guidelines was provided by the state (*Higher Education* 1996). To a degree, however, the state was interested in higher education policy. For example in 1938, Hannula, the Minister of Education of the time, asked the university of Helsinki to consider means to shorten university studies, and to develop students' talents and thinking so that the demands of practical tasks and those of academic work were both kept in mind. However, the university of Helsinki, rather than the Ministry of Education, decided the direction of higher education policy for decades (Kivinen et al. 1993, 18-19). Nowadays, all the institutions of higher education still have their autonomy guaranteed by law for the administration of their internal affairs (Kuikka 1992), but the scope of 'internal affairs' seem to have become narrower.

The development doctrine - the steering of higher education on the basis of legislation - started in 1966 with the Act on the development of Higher Education 1967-1981, and lasted until the 1980s[3]. The period was characterized by the expansion of higher education and a guarantee by the state continuously to increase the resources for higher education institutions. During this period research carried out by young scholars became a paid labour, since grants were awarded also for non-established researchers. At the same time it was demanded that administration, research and teaching should become more efficient. In other words, universities received more money, but in return fewer drop-outs, faster graduation and more societal relevance in research and education were expected by the Ministry of Education[4] (Kivinen et al. 1993, 41-133). The purpose of the Act was also to

> give a larger proportion of each age group a chance to study at university, to balance the regional distribution of higher education, to shift the sectoral distribution of student places towards technology and the natural sciences, and to promote research in universities (*Higher Education* 1996, 32).

The reforms expected in exchange for increased resources did not seem be realised well enough when their practical implementation was delegated to universities. As a reaction, the Ministry of Education (which had been re-organized in 1966, and had grown in personnel during the decade; Pesola 1982, 367; Kuoppala & Marttinen 1995, 271) took

---

[3] For the background of the law, see for example Kivinen et.al. 1993; Allardt 1995a, 145-148; Kuoppala & Marttinen 1995.

[4] Sundin (1996, 29-30) notes that the idea of science as an investment - as something that produces utility - is of recent origin when compared to other legitimation of research (Beauty, Reason, God, Civilization). He sees the Manhattan-project, which produced the first atomic bomb, as the origin of the ideal of "Big Science" and of the conception that anything is possible if enough resources are provided.

a more active role in the steering of higher education. particularly when the administrative and educational reforms of Finnish higher education were carried out (Kivinen et al. 1993, 82-133).

These reforms turned out to be a major incident in the history of Finnish Higher education. They took place when most of the departments I have studied were still relatively young. Because of this, it seems fair to say that they provide a critical event and meaningful background for the leadership cultures to be discussed in this study. At least in some cases they - and the era they represented - seem to have had a long-standing impact on the relevant leadership and departmental cultures. Next, I shall briefly discuss these reforms, and the closely related issue of student radicalism. The doctrine of Management by Objectives, which represents a new era in official steering policy, will be discussed after these topics.

Administrative and Degree Reforms

In 1969, the Ministry appointed a commission (led by office manager Jaakko Numminen from the Ministry of Education) which subsequently published its suggestions concerning *the reform of internal administration of universities*. The commission stipulated that the principles of democracy, efficiency, adequacy, economy, legal protection and planning should guide administrative reform in Finnish higher education. According to Vartola (1980, 14), especially democracy and planning were stressed by the committee and by many other parties in society at that time.

Universal and equal suffrage in university administration - the issue of 'one man-one vote' (Ketonen 1971; Pesonen 1982) - became the question which dominated the discussion of administration reform in Finland. Professors had traditionally enjoyed most of the formal decision-making power in the universities. It was now proposed that university councils should be elected by all the members of the university community (including students), and that other groups of teachers and students should be allowed to participate in university government alongside professors (Pesonen 1982, 370-371). The professors and the political opposition (among others the right wing Coalition Party) were mainly against the principle of one man-one vote, while the government (especially the Centre Party, partly the Social Democrats) and the majority of the student movement were for it (Vartola 1980, 14; Kivinen et al. 1993, 86-99).

During the next few years, the Finnish government made three attempts (the so-called Lex Virolainen, Lex Itälä and Lex Sundqvist) at a new frame law laying down the principles of university government. All the bills included somewhat compromised versions of the principle of universal and equal suffrage: for example, according to the bill Lex Virolainen, the democratically elected Rectors would still have had the final decision-making power within universities (Kivinen et al. 1993, 98). The bills were either rejected in Parliament or dissolved even before they reached it. As a result, the conflict remained unresolved throughout 1970s, and the frame law and total reform in Finnish higher education administration appeared unattainable.

However, the dispute resulted in partial and 'temporary' reforms which were drafted separately for individual universities. In 1980, the reforms affected the administration of ten universities (Vartola 1982). The new administration followed the triple-parity-scheme at each level of organizational hierarchy (university, faculty and departmental levels) according to which one third of the members of all administrative bodies were professors, one third of them were other teachers, and one third were students (Pesonen 1982, 371-372; Kivinen et al. 1993, 82-106; Hölttä 1995, 27). The seemingly 'temporary' solution (which was not based on frame law) was not satisfactory from the point of view of student organizations or the ministry (Kivinen et al. 1993, 103-104). But since the talks were at deadlock, the 'temporary' solution became relatively permanent. Most of the remaining Finnish universities carried out the administrative reform in this form during the 1980s; the last one - the university of Helsinki - completed the process in 1992 (Kivinen et al. 1993, 104).

According to Vartola (1980, 25) and Kivinen et al. (1993, 104-105), the implications of the administrative reform process were far-reaching. The process reflected, and probably also reinforced, the strong political passions of the era. As a result, universities became a field of political struggle and the ideological interests were institutionalized. For example, the appointments to committees of Finnish Academy and to University Council became connected to party politics. Political interests played a greater role in competition for and in allocation of resources, whereas the impact of scientific interests on such decisions declined (Kivinen et al. 1993, 104-105). The issue of collegial/democratic vs. individual/professorial decision-making and leadership - a continuum according to which, as will be seen, the studied leadership cultures can be classified - was strongly linked to polarized ideologies of the political Left and Right[5].

The political passions had not calmed down in the mid-1970s, but the major interest in administrative reform diminished due to increasing academic unemployment, the recession, and the lack of rapid progress in the reform (Vartola 1980, 26). The *degree reform* - which was carried out during the years 1975-1981 - had by that time become the contentious issue (Vartola 1980, 26).

The process of degree reform had started, again, with a committee. The Ministry of Education had set up (in 1969) a commission whose task was to prepare the degree reforms in the philosophical and social sciences. The FYTT commission was led by Yrjö-Paavo Häyrynen, one of the most influential Marxian scholars in the Finnish educational planning of the 1970s (Kivinen et al. 1993, 110-111). It has been often claimed that the basic ideas of the reform were modelled after the education system of DDR (e.g. Häikiö 1977; Kuoppala & Marttinen 1995, 289). However, Kivinen et al. (1995, 114) maintain that most of the influences of the FYTT commission came from the new British universities, especially from the University of Sussex. The commission's recommendations were published in 1972.

---

[5] During my interviews, this connection to politics was still emphasised in the departments of sociology. This is not a surprise, since the radical movement of the political Left of the era affected especially the departments of sociology (Allardt 1995a, 116-117). Häyrynen et al. (1992a, 71-73; 1992b, 92-97) have noted that the political activity of the students and their interest in higher education policy had decreased remarkably by the late 1980s, when compared to the situation in 1969 and in 1973. However, their longitudinal survey studies did not deal with the political attitudes of the teaching/research staff.

Another commission, consisting of the civil servants of the Ministry, was set up in 1973 to consider the implications of the FYTT report. The goals of the resulting degree reform were derived from the FYTT report, but they also became simplified. The principles of educational reform included the following: connection of education to the political goals and problems of society; broad basic studies; better integration of theoretical and practical knowledge from different disciplinary fields; increased relevance of schooling from the point of view of practical professions and tasks; faster graduation (within four years) (Häyrynen 1974, 7-8; Kivinen et al. 1993, 110-123; Kuoppala & Marttinen 1995, 289). The principles of democracy, collectivism and open discussion were stressed in the implementation of the reform (Häyrynen 1974, 13; Koho 1974, 2-3).

The degree reform was largely resisted, especially at the large and old universities (Häyrynen et al. 1992b, 11; Kivinen et al. 1993, 122). To a degree, professors and students "found each others" again (Vartola 1980, 26). In the beginning of the administrative reform process, the student organization had allied itself with the Ministry of Education in order to break the professorial rule in universities. Now many student leaders turned to defend the autonomy of universities against the power of the Ministry of Education, and to resist the process of degree reform (Vartola 1980; Pesonen 1982, 375; Silvonen 1990). Despite of the resistance from the students and universities, the reform was pushed through.

Recently, it has been claimed that the actual degree reform distanced itself from its original principles and materialized mainly in changed rhetoric (Häyrynen et al. 1992b, 114-115; Kivinen et al. 1993, 122-123). It has also been maintained that the degree reform further strengthened the trend, which had started already during the administrative reform, by bringing the cliquishness of political parties into the universities, and by increasing bureaucracy (Kuoppala & Marttinen 1995, 289-290).

The interpretations are in line with Aittola's (1987) observations. According to him, both administrative and degree reform failed to meet their targets. Instead, they have increased standardization, Taylorism and bureaucracy within universities, while professional autonomy has decreased. The reforms forced all the departments and disciplines into the same mould; they resulted in practices which only seemed to be democratic, but which were actually based on administrative bureaucracy (Aittola 1987, 101-103, 135). Bachelor's degrees, which were removed during the degree reform, have currently been re-established as a part of the degree system (*Higher Education* 1996, 35).

Student Radicalism and The Ideal of Democratic Education

One clear trend during the decades of *the development doctrine* is that the ideal of democratic education was brought into the forefront of Finnish higher education policy, although other values and priorities were also emphasised[6]. According to Kuikka (1992,

---

[6] Another typical feature of the (educational) policy of the period was a strong belief in centralized planning (Hölttä 1995, 25; Kuoppala & Marttinen 1995, 70-71). "Radical rationalism", which was characteristic of Finnish and Swedish educational policy of the 1970s and 1980s, represented a

210), the principle of equal education emerges clearly in the regional distribution of universities from the 1960s. Hovi et al. (1989) have studied the justification of higher education policy in Finnish educational committee reports. Within the period of 1975-1986, values like democracy and societal equity, public interest and international competitiveness were used to legitimate policy much more often than before. The democratic ideal in education, the ideal that knowledge and civilization - as well as participation in decision-making - should be everybody's right, was not new per se. Rather, it was considered as one of the "classic" goals which had not yet been achieved (Häyrynen & Hautamäki 1976, 22-28; Antikainen 1986, 133-141).

It is possible to identify some broad political, economic and social trends which have affected this emphasis in higher education policy. For example Vartola (1980, 2) distinguishes the following main reasons for the crisis in higher education in the 1960s: the economic growth after the second World War; the rapid structural change in society from agricultural to industrial and post-industrial production; the scientific-industrial revolution and the idea that science and education are central forces in increasing production; the increased demand for starting places in higher education due to the rapid growth in the numbers of (potential and actual) students; the lack of facilities and teachers which led to 'mass higher education'; the broader social background of university students; the radical student movement resulting from both the (objective and subjective) worsening of the position of students, and from the examples set by student movements in other countries; and the inability of the universities to re-organize their internal structures. In short, there was a social need to educate more people, a need for more money to do that (which was available due to economic growth), and a large population who wanted to become educated and to get better, previously unmaterialized, profits and positions within society.

The general political atmosphere of society had changed, too. Democratization became a popular theme in the whole society during late 1960s and onwards (Kivinen et al. 1993, 100). According to Pesonen (1982, 376), the Parliamentary election of 1966 was a significant turning-point in Finnish politics: "For the first (and only) time the political Left received the majority of votes cast in Finland". One background factor in the change in university politics was that the voting age was lowered from twenty-one to twenty years in 1970. Between 1962 and 1966 the net growth in the Finnish electorate had been only 85 000 persons, whereas from 1966 to 1970 the increase was 294 000. The young post-war generation now added its weight: it was "large, visible and vocal" in a way which political parties had not quite faced before, and which was impossible to ignore (Pesonen 1982, 380).

The 'populistic' administration reform can be viewed as a part of political game of the time, and also as an attempt to damp down student radicalism (Kivinen et al. 1993, 94-97). After the French student radicals staged their 'revolution' in Paris in May 1968, some Finnish students occupied the Old Student House in November of the same year. The occupation caused only minor - if any - damage, lasted only twenty-four hours and

---

faith in final solutions and societal plans of action which - it was believed - could be achieved by applying a scientific approach (Allardt 1995a, 144; Kuoppala & Marttinen 1995, 272).

involved no more than a thousand students. However, the incident received much publicity and promoted the previously discussed student participation in university governments and councils in the 1970s (Pesonen 1982; Kivinen et al. 1993, 85).

As noted, the student organizations of the early 1970s demanded equal suffrage in universities. Until the mid-1970s they increasingly emphasised the need for improvements in student housing, study loans and other support received from the state budget (Pesonen 1982, 385; see Silvonen 1990, 10). The demand was in line with the policy of Nordic welfare states followed by Finland: to guarantee increased well-being and a higher standard of living for all parties in society. As a whole, student radicalism had turned from a general student movement towards a much narrower activity of Marxism-Leninism[7]. Throughout the decade, the radical movement stayed alive mainly in social sciences, and affected especially the departments of sociology (Allardt 1995a, 116-117). During the 1980s, party politics lost much of its previous appeal among university students (see Häyrynen et al. 1992a, 73; Silvonen 1990).

However, the political consensus concerning the ideal of educational and regional equity has remained strong for much longer. The ideal has been cherished by the long-time (1956-81) Finnish President Kekkonen, by the political Left, by the Centre Party and other Agrarian Parties, and even by the right wing Coalition Party in the 1960s (Kivinen et al. 1993, 188). After the oil crisis in the 1970s, higher education policy was connected tightly to the political goals of society and to regional politics: during the recession of the 1970s, more resources were allocated to the new regional universities than to the old ones (Kivinen et al. 1993, 196-197).

The official doctrine of educational policy started to change towards that of Management by Results only during the 1980s as the President changed, as the Coalition Party entered Government after a long period in opposition, and as other changes in politics and society took place (Kivinen et al. 1993, 188-189). Despite the shift in doctrine, it can be said that different views and political ideals concerning higher education co-existed and that they still do. Kuikka (1992, 210) maintains that the ideal "to promote equality among the population and to provide all young people with appropriate knowledge and skills", which requires "an even distribution of schools and other educational facilities throughout the country" still remains the generally accepted goal of education in the 1990s. The 'ammattikorkeakoulu' experiment represents an outgrowth of the same "basic tenets of the educational reforms carried out over the last few decades" (*Higher Education* 1996, 17).

2.3.2. The Doctrine of Management by Results

The third period of official higher education policy - as identified by Kivinen et al. (1993) -is *the doctrine of management by results*, which started in 1980s and continues

---

[7] According to Silvonen (1990, 8) the movement fragmented rapidly into conflicting groups of radical Left.

into the present. The Ministry of Education had noted that the rapid expansion of university system had had "some undesirable side-effects". Among other things:

> Studies suffered from bottlenecks and inadequate resources. Rapidly growing industries and services were short of labour, while graduates in the humanities and social sciences had difficulty finding jobs... Graduation was tending to last even longer, and the drop-out rate was high. Many domestic and international assessments noted that post-graduate education was poorly organized in this country. University management was beset by structural and functional inadequacies... (*Higher Education* 1996, 31-32).

In 1986 came the new Higher Education Development Act as well as the Government decision on higher education development (see Kuikka 1992, 214). The objective was, again[8], to "guarantee stable resource development for the universities until the mid 1990s and to prepare the ground for internal reform" (*Higher Education* 1996, 32). For most part, the annual growth of resources was expected to be no less than 15 per cent in real terms (*Higher Education* 1996, 74).

Kivinen et al. (1993, 187-188) view the essence of transition in policy as reflecting the view that the development of society has become unpredictable, turbulent and difficult to control. Given that the major projects of societal planning in different countries appeared largely unsuccessful[9], the aim of the new policy was to reward promising and competent researchers working in fields which were considered as particularly important (Kuoppala & Marttinen 1995, 272-273). Centralized societal planning was abandoned and the responsibility for decision-making and problem-solving concerning the "visionless future" was delegated to the universities (Kivinen et al. 1993, 187-188).[10] The long-standing ideal of social and regional equity as the core of higher

---

[8] Kivinen et al. (1993, 201) have noted that the problems, to which different educational and political solutions have been sought, have remained largely unchanged during the decades.
[9] In Finland, administrative and examination reforms did not proceed in a predictable way. Educational policy and growth in available starting places in higher education did not result in a more democratic education when parents' education and socio-economic status was taken into account: the majority of university students still came from academic families (Antikainen 1986; Nevala 1990; *Taustaraportti* 1993). However, the regional equity and equal opportunities to study in universities for both sexes have progressed: since the early 1980s, the majority of students have been female (Kivinen et al. 1993, 141; *Higher Education* 1996, 60).
[10] *Self-regulation* as a steering strategy for higher education is widely used in the western world today. As Hölttä (1995, 15) notes:

> Governments in industrialized countries have learned that the comprehensive planning model covering all aspects of inputs of universities and centralized control of degree programs and educational processes does not work effectively in a rapidly changing world characterized by the unexpected and turbulence. To an increasing degree, they have transferred initiative and autonomy to the universities. Instead of giving most attention to resources and processes, they have directed their interest to the quantity and quality of outputs.

However, Immonen (1995, 35-36) claims that the conception of increased autonomy of universities is misleading. According to him, the policy of Management by Objectives has given

education doctrine was largely replaced by the steering of market forces: the new era placed an emphasis on innovativeness, flexibility and the universities' ability to react to external changes (Kivinen et al. 1993, 13; 187-192).

The new steering policy can be characterized as a shift from regulations to objectives (*Higher Education* 1996, 32). Universities were expected to compete for their resources. The introduction of international and domestic assessment about the results and costs of research, and the consideration of performance in allocating new funds were part of the policy changes. Universities were also expected to prepare regular performance reports. Undergraduate and postgraduate instruction should became more efficient, enabling most students to graduate within four to five years, and to complete their doctorates after four years of full-time study (Kivinen et al. 1993, 199-200; *Higher Education* 1996, 32-33). The growth of resources was made conditional on increasing efficiency. The trend received additional support as a result of the collapse of socialism, and due to the severe recession in 1990s, which ended the continuous growth of resources for higher education.

Recession and Decline of Resources

Finnish universities are financed mainly by budget funding. Since the universities do not charge tuition fees, private funding accounts for only three per cent of the current total university education budget (*Higher Education* 1996, 74). Sustained by legislation, the higher education budgets (and the numbers of students and academics) grew steadily up to 1992 (*Taulukoita* 1994; *Higher Education* 1996, 73). For example, the increase of resources during the period 1986-1991 was 50 per cent in real terms (Linna 1992). At around that time, Finland ranked eighth in the world in terms of national income per capita (Kuikka 1992, 209).

In the early 1990s, severe problems in the Finnish economy began to appear: adjudications of bankruptcy almost doubled from 1990 to 1991; exports to the Soviet Union collapsed; unemployment rose; the gross national product declined rapidly and the country began to run into external debt (Härö et al. 1993). The most serious recession of this century forced[11] the Government to cut higher education budgets. The actual budget cuts in higher education were 16 per cent within the period 1991-94 (*Higher Education* 1996, 73), while the estimates of cuts until 1995 varied from almost 20 per cent (Höltä 1993, 3) to as much as 30 per cent (Willner 1995, 98-99). At the same time, however, budget funding channelled through the Ministry of Trade and Industry was rapidly increased (Kivinen et al. 1993, 225; Kuoppala & Marttinen 1995, 285-288).

In the mid 1990s, when the empirical part of this study was carried out, recession and budget cuts represented a dramatic threat within a system used to increasing funding.

---

the Ministry of Education and the Finnish Academy more power than ever before in the steering of research and higher education policy: in order to maintain their scope for discretion, universities now have to fulfil the goals and expectations which are largely set by the Ministry (see Kivinen et al. 1993, 240).

[11] As Kuoppala (1995, 62-63) has pointed out, budget cuts are consequent upon political decisions: for example, Sweden has continued to increase higher education budgets despite its economic problems in the 1990s, while the higher education systems of Denmark and the Netherlands experienced budget cuts well before Finland.

Hölttä (1993, 3) estimated that the real budget cuts of 20 per cent equalled the total budgets of the eleven smallest universities in Finland. Kivinen et al. (1993, 225) noted ironically that an alternative way to reach the savings would be to discontinue 150 departments or to dismiss the whole professorial staff of Finnish universities. Naturally, the allocation of scarce resources and dramatic budget cuts became the crucial issue within the university sector: which units and functions should be given priority if there were not enough resources to maintain the whole network of higher education institutions?

The savings hit the general operating expenditure the hardest; purchasing by libraries was cut drastically and purchases of equipment had to be postponed (*Higher Education* 1996, 74). But it was clear that the implementation of massive cuts would also result in a reduction of personnel costs, which form about 80 % of the total budget of higher education (Hölttä 1993, 3). Discontinuance of posts, departments and even universities was frequently and openly discussed in the main Finnish newspapers as a one potential solution to the economic crisis in higher education (e.g. Kivinen & Rinne 1992; Latomaa & Vilén 1992; Lounasmaa 1993).

However, the "structural developing" of higher education by closing down units proved to be difficult to carry out (Vanttaja & Ketonen 1995). The universities reacted by playing for time. The general pattern has been to cut the resources of each unit on an equal basis. In practice, this means that the temporary posts of young scholars are the first in line when cuts are implemented. By 1995, structural reforms had advanced most within the medical sector, but even there the discontinuation of units had touched only the faculties of dentistry in Kuopio and Turku (nonetheless, the University of Kuopio received compensation). At the other faculties of medicine, savings were to be achieved mainly by cutting the budgets of each faculty in 1995-1998 (Saarinen 1995; Vanttaja & Ketonen 1995).

By 1996, the economic future of universities did not look much brighter, although the decline of budget resources "came to halt in 1995, and a slight increase is expected for 1996" (*Higher Education* 1996, 73). Restructuring, rationalization and assessment of productivity will remain part of normal activity within the universities (Saarinen 1995). A general aim is to widen the financial base of higher education by increasing private funding and other financing not channelled through the Ministry of Education. The Government and the universities have agreed on a reallocation of about FIM 200 million between 1994 and 1998; the resources will be tied to the universities' development projects and areas of focus (*Higher Education* 1996, 74)[12].

Management by Objectives - Increasing Competition

The policy characterized by Management by Objectives and demands for increasing efficiency was not only a reaction to economic crisis; as noted, the policy had started well before the recession. According to the Ministry of Education, the development

---

[12] In late 1996, however, a decision was made to provide an additional FIM 1,5 milliard for temporary research projects during the next three years. A lions share of the considerable additional funding will be channelled to applied research in technology (Liiten 1996b).

programme based on the 1986 Law "was implemented with good results" at a time still characterized by "extremely favourable progress in higher education funding" (*Higher Education* 1996, 33). However, Kivinen et al. (1993, 158) have claimed that the extent of the implementation of the 1986 Act remained unclear during the 1980s, since the Act did not specify norms concerning the resources of individual institutions. Only a minor part of the budget money was allocated on the basis of measurable results during that decade (Kivinen et al. 1993, 158). The Ministry of Education saw that "rewarding cost-effectiveness has a powerful incentive effect even if the appropriation allocated in this way" was small in the beginning. The cost-effectiveness criterion helped to "draw attention to results considered significant" and induced "universities to develop cost-effectiveness criteria of their own and to reward their top units" (*Higher Education* 1994, 61).

All Finnish universities had adopted budgeting by results by the beginning of 1994 (*Higher Education* 1994, 60). In mid 1990s, the basic funding has covered c. 90 per cent of the operating costs of the universities, while the share of performance-based funds and project funding has been 5 per cent each. Only professorships, associate professorships and certain administrative posts are specified in the budget. On top of that, a university and its departments receive a lump sum which each "may spend as it wishes, treating personnel as a resource on par with others" (*Higher Education* 1996, 75).

In 1996, the basic funding will be determined by graduation and degree targets agreed between the university in question and the Ministry of Education; bonuses will be distributed on the basis of the results and quality of operations. A working group appointed by the Ministry of Education examined the procedures and principles of Management by Objectives (*Higher Education* 1996, 74-75). The working group proposed that the agreements on basic funding and result targets of the universities should be made for periods of three years at a time (Liiten 1996a).

Reactions and Discussion

The 1986 Act and the principles of Management by Objectives have caused much public discussion and criticism (e.g. Myllynen 1992; Koski 1993 and 1994; Alestalo 1995). The criticism has sometimes materialized in unexpected ways: Numminen (1987, 61-62) has pointed out that the academic elite was at first against, or sceptical about, the development Act of the 1960s when it was introduced, but when the new development Act in 1980s saw the light of day, the same persons demanded strongly that the official policy should be continued on the basis of the previous Act.

An often expressed, modest criticism of Management by Objectives warns against pushing things to extremes. For example, Allardt (1992) maintains that universities are responsible for promoting civilization and education in society. Such objectives are extremely difficult to measure. The goals of universities are never static and there is no exact consensus about them. Rather, some kind equilibrium about these issues can be reached through a critical discussion between scholars. Indicators can be used in this discussion, but definite conclusions cannot be drawn on the basis of statistics alone (Allardt 1992). In a similar vein, Kivinen et al. (1993, 220-221) admit that the achievement of results is important. However, they maintain that oversimplified measurement of results is not a satisfactory basis for the allocation of resources in universities.

Indeed, quality may be more important than quantity. In physics, for example, a scholar (Kenneth Wilson) who had not published anything for some years was appointed to professorship after he published his theory on critical indexes; by that time he had only three publications. Soon he was also awarded a Nobel prize (Byckling 1996, 24). But low quantity does not guarantee high quality, either. Although measurements of results are problematic, it can be argued that a certain measure of quantity is essential in academic work. A researcher who does not produce anything, or who does not make his/her work known by publishing, cannot win a Nobel prize, nor contribute to the research in his/her field.

With this in mind, four Finnish academics (Aarnio, Ylikangas, Kanniainen and Kekkonen 1995) have provoked discussion about the scientific activity of professors. According to the writers, some Finnish professors can be considered as 'state officers' who have only published one noteworthy publication: their own dissertation. The writers note that lack of performance indicators supports precisely the interests of 'state officers'. However, some quality and quantity in scientific work should be expected from professors in exchange for their salary[13]. The current situation affects also the motivation of those who would be willing to carry out research and to increase their competence. Therefore: bonuses and extra resources should be allocated to scholars willing and able to contribute to scientific work, while the 'state officers' should get only a minimum pay. "Clearly", the latter group is the one to be laid-off, should this became necessary due to the difficult economic situation (Aarnio et al. 1995).

Many of the commentators on the provocative text have agreed in principle. It has also been suggested that many professors' weakness is a low interest in teaching and supervision, rather than a lack of publications (Mustajoki 1995); that a free description - rather than quantitative measurements - might reflect better the actual scientific activity of a scholar (Mustonen 1995); that the debate is likely to increase the unhealthy competition and dubious measurements of efficiency within universities (Cronström 1995); and that simple sanctions for inefficiency may be easily circumvented as 'lazy professors' start to add their names to the publications of younger scholars (Valkonen 1995).

In any case, the current reward structures in universities are not democratic and fair as far as the different generations of researchers are concerned. In that respect, the situation is not very different whether the ideal of fair allocation of resources is approached through the social equity norms of the development doctrine (i.e. same opportunities for everybody), or from the ideology of Management by Objectives (i.e.

---

[13] A professor is an unquestionable authority and part of elite in his/her own field. The particular feature in the Finnish system is that this authority seems to be connected to the (permanent) post rather than to the person. When the President appoints somebody as a professor, his/her authority no longer depends on his/her actual deeds; and the salary remains the same despite the actual outcomes of his/her work. This aspect of reward systems of university professors has been highlighted, in addition to Aarnio et al. (1995), by Ahonen (1995), Airaksinen (1987), Kanniainen (1995), Kivinen et al. (1993, 235-236), and Wiberg (1995).

rewarding those who produce more or better quality than the rest). The rhetoric of 'equal opportunities' and 'rewarding efficiency' are dubious insofar as the salaries from tax-payers' money are, in practice, guaranteed to some scholars regardless of their actual scientific output or contribution. In higher education, young researchers have become the de-facto payers of the recession: most of them live in the permanent insecurity of the risk society and compete for the short-term jobs which may be available - again, largely in spite of the quality of their actual output[14]. In the studied departments the budget cuts have affected the temporary personnel first. The same situation is reflected throughout the public sector: the average age of employees within the sector was around 41 years in 1995 (Helenius 1995). In the 1990s, more and more graduates have become unemployed. The majority of young female members of the central trade union AKAVA (which incorporates all academic professional associations) were working on temporary jobs in 1993 (Helenius 1995, 25). The unemployment rate in Finland is currently 19 %; in the mid-1990s it was over 20 %.

However, despite of the decline in resources, the tasks of universities (research, instruction and the education of new researchers) are seen, perhaps more than ever before, as a vital part of contemporary developed societies (Kivinen et al. 1993, 221). The Ministry of Education states:

> Education and research are crucial to Finland's strategy for the future, which aims at the well-being of its citizens, cultural diversity, sustainable development and prosperity... Every effort will be made to provide the operating conditions necessary for high-quality basic research and researcher training (*Higher Education* 1996, 33).

According to the Ministry of Education, the development of research and education in the late 1990s will focus on, among other things, the principle of lifelong learning; internationalization; strengthening the status of evaluation as an integral part of steering and development policy, with an emphasis on quality; and continuing to reward centres of excellence and to upgrade the training of researchers (*Higher Education* 1996, 33).

2.4. INCREASING THE POWER OF INDIVIDUAL LEADERS

In this chapter, I have discussed some general trends in the Finnish higher education system as a background to the coming analysis of departmental leadership. One trend still

---

[14] Those young scholars who are efficient and show good quality in their work have probably better chances to carry on their academic careers. However, this is by no means guaranteed due to the lack of resources. The existing resources are first allocated towards established and permanent costs. After that, the large (increasing) population of non-established researchers compete for the remaining excess funds, which have so far declined. As noted (footnote 12), from 1997 onwards *temporary* project funds for postgraduates (especially in hard applied disciplinary areas) will increase, but also more doctorates (around 1000 a year in the whole country) are expected to take their degrees.

deserves closer attention, since it is closely related to the issue of academic leadership: namely the changes in the position of individual academic leaders, and especially their seeming increase in power.

In the 1970's and 1980's - the era of the development doctrine - individual academic leaders did not have much formal *administrative* authority in Finnish universities. In practice they acted as chairpersons of the decision-making bodies (collegial councils) which were established after the administration reform (Hölttä & Pulliainen 1992, 9; section 2.3.1.). During the past few years, however, the formal authority of individual administrative leaders (such as rectors, deans and department heads) has increased remarkably (Hölttä & Pulliainen 1992, 9). The principles emphasised in the new service regulations of the university include flexibility, academic leadership, administrative expertise, accountability, and broadly based decision-making. At the level of basic units, departmental heads are made officially responsible for the allocation of budget funds and for administrative decisions: collegial councils now act as forums for discussion. The head is also responsible for the performance of the department to the dean and rector (*Yliopiston* 1993).

Today, it is usual for one of the doctors or (full or associate) professors to be elected to the post of head of department for a period of two to four years at a time. The heads of departments are now officially and formally responsible for the allocation of the (diminished) budget funds for research and teaching within their departments. As noted, there are permanent costs (salaries) specified in the budget. The departments receive a lump sum, which they may spend as they wish - after the permanent costs are taken care of (*Higher Education* 1996, 75). Decisions concerning the appointment of non-academic staff have also been shifted from councils to individual academic leaders (Hölttä & Pulliainen 1992, 34).

According to Rekilä (1994), the de-regulation of administrative procedures has widened the potential scope of, and the need for, individual leadership within universities - both in terms of decision making and in terms of providing emotional security during the recession. Faculty or Dean appoints departmental heads on the basis of the proposals of departmental councils. Rectors are elected rather than appointed. This emphasises the continuing collegial control of scholars over them. Kivinen et al. (1993, 237-240) maintain that because of this, the academic leadership of Finnish university rectors has been, as a rule, weak "consensus-leadership". According to them there is a need for stronger academic direction, which would promote the necessary changes and distinctive policies even against the interests of established groups within universities. Kivinen et al. (1993) have not been alone in suggesting the need for more power for academic leaders (e.g. Jääskeläinen 1994; Kettunen 1994; Sallinen 1994; for counter-arguments, see for example Kuoppala & Marttinen 1995, 273-275; Willner 1995, 102). The possibility of using professional leaders in universities has been raised, but has not been taken up (Kuoppala & Marttinen 1995, 274-275).

As far as departmental leadership is concerned, it is important to distinguish between the position of professor and departmental head. On the basis of my preliminary research (Kekäle 1994b), it would seem that the formal and traditional academic authority connected to the chair and professorship has been quite strong, while the position of the heads of departments has usually been rather weak. The permanent full professorship has generally required a strong academic contribution, while for the most part headship of department has been an undervalued and unwanted administrative post (Kekäle 1994b)[15]. According to Clark (1983, 111) the personal rule of professors has many sources:

> ...it has historical roots in the dominance of the master in the early academic guilds. It is ideologically supported by doctrines of freedom in teaching and research, which in practice have been interpreted to mean that senior professors in particular should be free to do largely as they please. It is functionally based in expertise and the need for conditions that would promote criticism, creativity and scientific advance.

Kivinen et al. (1993, 235) note that the large number of departments with just one full professor in Finnish universities has automatically strengthened the professorial rule. The first holder of the chair can be considered as the founder of the department, around which the departments have been originally built. This position as a founding father of the department has given the original professor a remarkable authority and power both in administrative and scientific aspects. During the past decades, the full professors of small departments of Finnish universities have often also carried out the tasks of head of department, although recently the rotating headship has become common[16].

The departments of young Finnish universities are only few decades old, and many of the founders are still working there. Consequently, the impact and the position of some of the full professors (the founders) is likely to be stronger in the studied departments; at least when compared to departments of old universities, the current situation is a special case. It seems that despite the changes in higher education policy the impact of the leadership of the professor/head is likely have remained significant from the point of view of the development of the department: s/he is, and has been, in the best position to start new research projects, to acquire funds for them, to make strategic choices, and to

---

[15] Nearly all the interviewed researchers noted that the post of the head of department is not valued or desired. Only two or three admitted that they considered the post to be at least partly interesting. Most of the interviewed heads of departments also expressed their readiness to leave their post. We can identify several reasons for the undervaluation of departmental headship. Generally, research was seen psychologically and also - at least below the professorial level - economically to be more rewarding. In financial terms, the headship is not particularly rewarding since in some universities the head earns only a few hundred Finnish marks net (around £60) extra per month. The administrative tasks of the head have to be carried out along with other duties including teaching and research. No obligatory training for the administrative tasks was provided when the interviews were made. When applying for professorships, it is mainly the applicant's research merits that are taken into account. Recently, however, some universities have been experimenting with teaching portfolios (Seldin & Annis 1991; Kekäle 1994a), which would allow teaching merits to be considered as well. Nevertheless, so far someone has always accepted the invitation to occupy the post of the head of department. Some professors stressed that there have always been willing and competent candidates available. Senior researchers may feel an obligation to take on the post in their turn, and the headship may also provide a route to a higher position within the university administration (deanship; or even possibly rectorship).

[16] For the positions of departmental heads and professors in different countries, see Moses (1992).

supervise post-graduate students. As noted, the changed legislative basis currently offers a stronger position for the head of department as well.

In the forthcoming chapters I shall discuss the theoretical and methodological background of the study, followed by an analysis of leadership cultures and practices on the basis of my empirical cases. As will be seen, the changing higher education policies have provoked different reactions in different disciplinary and departmental communities. Departmental differences are interesting, since the changing higher education doctrines have in general treated different disciplinary fields and departmental units on a uniform basis. During the development doctrine, the 'right' way for decision-making at all levels of the university hierarchy was considered to be democratic discussions in collective councils, whereas the doctrine of Management by Objectives re-established the power of individual leaders in all disciplines and at all levels of hierarchy. As will be seen, the empirical cases in this study suggest that different styles of leadership and decision-making may be considered good and valid in different disciplinary and departmental contexts: in this sense there is no one 'best buy'.

Chapter 3

LEADERSHIP THEORIES AND ACADEMIC CONTEXT

3.1. THEORETICAL PERSPECTIVES ON LEADERSHIP

According to some estimates over one hundred different schools or theoretical orientations can be identified in the field of leadership/management studies (Temmes 1990, 15; see Lumijärvi 1985). It would be inappropriate to discuss these multiple approaches in detail here. In any event, scholars such as Bensimon et al. (1989), Birnbaum (1989), Middlehurst (1993) and Bush (1995), who deal specifically with leadership and management in academic settings, usually identify a limited number of theories relevant in that context. Bensimon et al. (1989), Birnbaum (1989, 23) and Middlehurst (1993, 13) single out five to six basic approaches: 1) trait theories, 2) behavioral theories, 3) contingency theories, 4) power and influence theories, 5) cognitive theories and 6) cultural theories. In this study, my main approach will be the *cultural* one. However, I believe that it is useful to give brief consideration to the other main approaches to leadership, and to offer some illustrative examples of each, since these different approaches help to demonstrate scholarly conceptions and views on leadership, and so to throw light on different aspects of the phenomenon under study (chapter 1).

1) *Trait theories* seek to identify specific characteristics that contribute to a person's ability to function successfully in a leadership position (Birnbaum 1989, 23). According to Middlehurst (1993, 13), trait theories are based on the following assumptions: a) leadership is a personal quality, natural endowment or characteristic; b) there are certain qualities which set leaders apart from other people; c) these special characteristics contribute to the power and influence which leaders are able to exert over others; d) if these special qualities of good leaders could be isolated, then potential leaders could be identified through a selection process within organizations. Such a standpoint is obvious, in a quite extreme form, for example, in the writing of Frederick Taylor at the beginning of the century:

> Therefore the workman who is best suited to handling pig iron is unable to understand the real science of doing this class of work. He is so stupid that

the word "percentage" has no meaning to him, and he must consequently be trained by a man more intelligent than himself into the habit of working in accordance with the laws of this science before he can be successful (Taylor 1970).

However, decades of research have been unsuccessful in providing general and universal qualities or abilities of good and successful leaders (Bensimon et al. 1989, 8). The notion of personal traits represents a somewhat static and unidimensional view and is therefore not an adequate explanation of the dynamic phenomenon of leadership. The heyday of trait theories lasted until the late 1940s, although some kind of comeback in a more sophisticated form (associated with cognitive theories) can be identified in recent years (Middlehurst 1993, 13-14).

2) *Behavioral theories* focus on activity patterns, leadership roles and behavioral categories, and pay attention to what it is that leaders actually do (Birnbaum 1989, 23). The idea that leaders can be 'made' challenges the previous notion that some people are born with suitable leadership qualities while others are not. Roughly speaking, the prime focus of attention moved to leadership behaviour during the period from the 1940s to the late 1960s. In line with the emergence of the 'human relations' approach, the potential importance of informal leadership, as well as group-related leadership functions, was recognized and stressed (e.g. Roethlisberger & Dickinson 1970). Two aspects or orientations of leadership were identified in large research programmes of the era: orientation towards tasks and orientation towards relations with people (Middlehurst 1993, 14-16). This distinction forms the basic dimensions of Blake and Mouton's (1964) famous managerial grid as well as Hersey and Blanchard's (1982) subsequent model of situational leadership. Nowadays, this broad conceptual distinction is often made by separating *management* (orientation towards tasks, systems and results) and *leadership* (orientation towards human relations and organizing people) (e.g. Eklund 1992, 82; Middlehurst 1993, 44; see section 1.1.).

3) *Contingency theories.* The two previous theoretical approaches had basically attempted to find a universal 'one best way' to lead. For example, in the managerial grid (Blake & Mouton 1964 and 1982) this best way was conceptualized as calling for both a high concern for people and a high concern for tasks (while the tactics for achieving this goal could be highly variable). Moreover, classical management and organizational theories had been based essentially on a *closed system* approach, that is, one which is self-contained and deterministic.

Contingency theories emphasize the importance of situational factors, such as the nature of the task, the external environment, and the abilities of the followers, in effective leadership (Birnbaum 1989; Middlehurst 1993). Some of these approaches view organizations as *open systems*, which are in a constant and complex interaction with their environments through input-output cycles. The system remains dynamic, not static; it may seek multiple goals, and there is always an expectation of uncertainty (Katz & Kahn

1974; Richman & Farmer 1974, 4-6). Leaders may face diverse, complex and changing demands in different contexts[1]. Consequently, as Smith and Peterson (1988, 156) put it:

> In a certain sense, once the notion of One Best Way of Leadership is discarded, all subsequent leadership theories must be contingency theories. That is, they must make some statement about what are the circumstances which affect the behaviour and effectiveness of leaders.

According to Middlehurst (1993, 20), these theories are based on at least three assumptions: a) different circumstances require different qualities or patterns of behaviour for a leader to be effective; b) leadership is not unidimensional: the dynamic interaction between leader and context will inevitably shape the nature of leadership; c) context and circumstances place different demands, constraints and choices on leaders. I shall lean on these assumptions in this study.

Contingency theories have remained influential from the late 1960s to the present (Middlehurst 1993, 13). The previously mentioned Hersey and Blanchard's (1982) situational leadership model is a well-known example of contingency theory. According to the model, a leader's style should correspond to subordinates' "maturity" and encourage its development. Leadership styles should vary from directive (when subordinates are immature, unwilling or insecure in relation to the task at hand) to more supportive (as their confidence increases) and further to a delegating leadership style (when subordinates are very mature) which allows subordinates to exercise considerable autonomy (Hersey & Blanchard 1982). A straightforward implication of this model would be that academic experts and other professionals do not need to be led in a traditional sense - or, in other words, that the leadership style should be mainly delegative.

On the other hand, Richman and Farmer (1974, 289-336) start from a contingency and open systems approach and end up stressing the increasing external pressures for strong leadership, improved efficiency and clearer goals in academic institutions. An organization which constitutes an open system is continually dependent upon inputs from the environment; the inflow of materials and human energy is not constant (Katz & Kahn 1974, 156). Focusing primarily on goals or outputs of the system and inputs (economic resources) into the organization, Richman and Farmer (1974) call for effective leadership and management which would act as a "buffer" between different, conflicting interest-groups, and would steer academic institutions away from economic crisis. According to them, a key task of management is to "structure the goal system in ways that maximize advantages and minimize disadvantages to the institution" (Richman and Farmer (1974, 331).

---

[1] In universities the leadership environment may vary for example according to disciplinary field, personnel and the organizational level an academic leader is responsible for (i.e. department, faculty, or the whole university). I shall discuss this complexity of academic context further in the forthcoming sections.

Thus, these two perspectives seem to stress views similar to those already expressed in the previous chapter. But it is not fruitful to argue whether a strong leadership or a delegative style is better, since contingency approaches stress that good leadership depends on contextual factors. If the main responsibility of the leaders and managers is to keep things going and keep the organization working, one good way to achieve this is to make the followers more independent, to facilitate commitment and reflective *self-management* (Hersey and Blanchard 1982; Smith and Peterson 1988; Sims and Lorenzi 1992). However, when serious problems or times of crisis arise and the self-management skills of the members of staff are tottering - or if a severe disintegration threatens the organization, or when the organization's needs otherwise require it - leaders may have to contribute more actively to the process by providing support, advice or even a more direct leadership (Hersey and Blanchard 1982; also Birnbaum 1989).

Middlehurst (1993, 26) concludes that the broad theoretical approaches discussed so far start from similar frames of reference in two senses: 1) that leadership can be discovered through rational and objective analysis, and 2) that ideal leadership exists, in that the search is generally set in the context of effectiveness. However, the models fail to take satisfactorily into account leader-follower interactions, followers' influences on leadership, differences in leadership at various organizational levels and the contrasts between different leadership influences. In more recent theories, which will be discussed next, the impact of power and cultural influence, subjectivist perspectives, and the idea of leadership as process are examined more closely (Middlehurst 1993, 26-27).

4) *Power and influence theories* look at the source and amount of power available to leaders and the ways in which leaders exercise influence over followers through unilateral or reciprocal interactions with them (Birnbaum 1989, 23). The concept of power has been subject to continuing debate (Tucker 1993; see also Hoy 1986). A typical dictionary definition of power states that power is an ability of an individual (or of a group) to effect change in someone's behaviour - a change that might not otherwise occur (Tucker 1993, 44).

Based on the work of Lukes (1974) as well as that of Bachrach and Baratz (1962), Walford (1989, 144-145) discusses the phenomena of power in universities. He concludes that the previously mentioned definition of power is one-dimensional in a certain sense. A two-dimensional view would acknowledge that power is not only concerned with direct confrontation, but is also present when individuals and groups are able to create and reinforce social values and institutional practices in a way that limits the scope of what may be discussed and considered within the political process. A third dimension of power consists of influencing the very wants of others by shaping their perceptions, cognition and preferences so that they view their role as unchangeable, natural and beneficial (Lukes 1974; quoted in Walford 1989, 144-145). Walford (1989, 145) notes:

> Those with power are able to exploit the elements of a collegial or bureaucratic model, for example, on different occasions to achieve their ends.

It seems to me that although the conception of the third dimension may highlight more subtle, deeper and hidden forms of power, it also opens the door for endless speculation about unnoticed or subconscious influence, even 'bewitchment'. It also becomes problematic to distinguish a pure voluntary agreement or followership from manipulation and false consciousness, since the model implies that even subordinates cannot tell the difference. If we cannot take people's own judgements seriously, it becomes easy to label any aims and practices - especially those which are not in line with the observer's own values or political goals - as a result of ideological indoctrination or a hidden and an unnoticed influence exercised by the rulers. Moreover, this third dimension - like all the other discussed dimensions of power (Walford 1989) - stress only one direction of influence, since they consider only leaders' or rulers' impact on followers.

As far as leaders' influence on others is concerned, we can distinguish different types of legitimate authority on which a leader's power can be based. According to Weber (1974, 5), the validity of claims to legitimacy may be based on *legal authority*, which rests on "a belief of 'legality' of patterns of normative rules" or regulations on which a leader's formal position is grounded; *traditional authority*, which rests on an established belief in traditions on which the status of leaders is based; and *charismatic authority*, which rests on the devotion to the "exemplary character", powers or "heroism" of an individual person or leader (Weber 1974, 5; also Middlehurst 1993, 30).

Tucker (1993, 44-45) has presented a more modern version of forms of authority in the context of university departments. He speaks about the power of a chair as deriving from formal authority, which gives an individual a right to command resources or to enforce policies or regulations, position power, which comes from having an appropriate title or from being in an important position, and personal power, which rests on peers' respect and commitment to the chairperson (Tucker 1993, 44-46). In his turn Bush (1995, 80-82) discusses different forms of power relevant to schools and colleges. Middlehurst (1993, 31) comments that although such classifications "are useful in identifying the sources of power that may be available to leaders (the most likely sources of power for academic leaders being expert and referent power), they do not fully explain the nature of the leadership process", since "insufficient attention is given to the ways in which power is received (or perceived) by followers".

Middlehurst (1993, 28-36) also discusses those power and influence theories which concentrate on a mutual influence between leaders and followers. Examples can be found in social exchange theories (e.g. Blau 1974; see also Birnbaum 1989, 23-24; Middlehurst 1993, 32-36). According to Birnbaum (1989, 23) and Middlehurst (1993, 32), exchange theories are particularly well suited to higher education, where group and individual autonomy are strong and authority and power widely spread across different interests groups. Blau (1974) maintains that the dilemma of leadership is that it requires both power over others and their legitimating approval of that power. Collective approval of a leadership position must be earned. Leadership requires a use of power, which may have - at least in the beginning - a frustrating effect, and may not yet be approved by the followers. Moreover, the rewards individuals obtain in social associations tend to entail costs to other individuals. Blau writes:

The satisfaction a man derives from exercising power over others requires that they endure the deprivation of being subject to his power. For a professional to command an outstanding reputation in his field, most of his colleagues must get along without such pleasant recognition, since it is the lesser professional esteem of the majority that defines his as outstanding[2] (Blau 1974, 127).

But this does not mean that most social relations should be viewed as zero-sum games. To different degrees, interests and benefits may also be mutual, and some social associations can be intrinsically rewarding. According to Blau (1974), members of a group will follow a leader's suggestions if they believe that they will gain something valuable in exchange, i.e. if they believe that they will "benefit from doing so more than from following the suggestion of someone whose abilities are less respected" (Blau 1974, 135). In the long run, an individual's outstanding abilities to contribute to subordinates' welfare makes him/her a particularly strong and respected leader. And conversely, the maintenance of a leader's power and authority - his/her ability to stay in a leading position - is contingent on his/her continuing capability to fulfil followers' expectations (Middlehurst 1993, 32). Of course, followers' views on leadership may change: a currently unpopular leader can, with time and hindsight, be regarded as effective.

Leaning on Baldridge's (1971) study of a crisis which faced New York University, Walford (1987, 134-145) views complex organizations such as universities as political systems. Walford (1989) draws together the assumptions behind Baldridge's (1971) model of political process and slightly modifies some of them in the following manner:

> 1. Prevailing uncertainty and fluid participation. Most people do not participate in the policy-making most of the time. Instead, they will only become active when the issues are of direct interest to them. On the other hand, Walford (1989, 144) also comments that some members of the senior management team will be present in decision-making on a permanent basis, and will thus potentially influence decisions more;

---

[2] On the other hand, complete equality would probably be also frustrating. To quote Clark (1983, 260):

> As Ralf Darendorf has noted, equality has a built-in frustration effect. Behind the demand for equality is the wish to extend opportunity: how can more people enjoy more life chances? But many life changes defy continuous extension, since to increase them past a certain point is to destroy them. The acquisition of a degree increases one's chances in life as long as the degree has some special value in the eyes of others. To be valuable, it cannot be possessed by all. As soon as most persons can have it, it adds little or nothing to life chances... It is a bitter irony for those who vigorously pursue the equalization of access, treatment, and outcome in higher education that the end result, if achieved, would be relatively worthless. Everyone would have the same thing, but be worse off... Justice in academic systems must be varied and specific, attached to contexts that promote different competencies and, in their aggregate, widen the play of liberty.

2. Decisions are usually made by those who persist and invest the necessary time in the process.

3. Universities are fragmented into interest groups with different goals and values. The interest-groups will only engage in a minimal conflict when resources are plentiful and the environment harmonious. However, when resources are tight, they will mobilize and fight to influence decisions in their favour.

4. Conflict is normal and may be a sign of health rather than a breakdown in the academic community.

5. The formal authority of a bureaucratic system is severely limited by the political pressure that interest groups can generate. These interest groups may be both internal and external.

6. External interest groups exert a great deal of influence over the policy making process (Walford 1987, 134-135).

According to Walford (1989), this model acknowledges only direct and visible use of power (the previously discussed 'one-dimensional' conception of power; Walford 1989). However, it seems to acknowledge the mutual or reciprocal influence of different interest-groups and agents. It has been argued that a crisis would call for transformational leadership[3]. But at the same time, we may also expect (according to the described model) a rising concern for, and a higher participation in, decision making by different and conflicting coalitions and interest groups. Thus, during difficult times and crises, practising transformational leadership may become more important, but also much more complicated as various interest groups attempt to influence decisions.

5) *Cognitive theories and* 6) *Symbolic and cultural approaches.* Birnbaum (1989, 24-25) connects the cognitive approach strongly to the cultural approach, whereas Middlehurst (1993, 36-42) discusses them as separate groups of theories. There are indeed some similarities and connections. Consequently, I shall discuss these theories here in connection with each other. According to Middlehurst (1993, 39), both approaches concentrate on the ways in which meanings are created in the social context. However,

---

[3] A *transactional leader* meets the followers' expectations and needs and emphasises means, while a *transformational leader* stresses ends and taps or builds on the motivations of followers in order to support change and to lead them to new and better values (Birnbaum 1989, 23-24; Middlehurst 1993, 32-36). Transactional leaders may be needed in a steady situation where no pressures of change are present, but they may not be suitable in times of crisis, which tend to call for transformational leadership (Middlehurst 1993, 33). Viewing transformative leadership in higher education from a critical perspective, Tierney (1989, 145-146) calls for "transformative leaders who are centrally concerned with issues of social justice and empowerment, whose overriding commitment is on behalf of the disadvantaged and silent".

cognitive theories place more emphasis on social attribution - that is, the explanations used by persons to find meanings for shared events. Seen in this light, leaders are believed to have caused events. In my view, however, cultural approaches do not necessarily see leadership as merely a social attribution, but stress that it may - at least potentially - be one force influencing, not only the meanings, values and assumptions of the members of an organization, but also the outcomes of organizational action (Kekäle 1995b). Leadership may also, more or less profoundly, contribute to the functioning of an organization (Schein 1985; Middlehurst 1993). Middlehurst (1993, 39) highlights this difference between the theoretical perspectives in the following manner:

> cultural and symbolic approaches stress the role of leaders in 'inventing' the reality for followers, while cognitive models emphasize the importance of followers in 'inventing' leaders.

Cognitive approaches have been applied to leadership studies since the 1980s (Middlehurst 1993, 13). However, in a cultural sense, leadership as a social attribution is also an interesting phenomenon, which probably reveals something about the culture in question. In that way, too, leadership can have cultural functions by providing a target for the hopes and projections of the followers. Anyhow, critical academics are hardly the first to attribute hero-like properties to their leaders without any reasonable grounds (chapter 1).

Smith and Peterson (1988) and Birnbaum (1989) link cultural and cognitive approaches closely together in their analyses. It has already been stressed that leadership is not a one-way process of influence. Smith and Peterson (1988) have suggested that a fruitful approach would see the leader as "the hub of a network of people", all responding and contributing to the specific culture of the organization. What works or does not work in any attempt to influence others cannot, they argue, be analyzed exclusively in terms of styles of leadership. Effective leadership depends upon the agreed meanings which members of the organization attribute to particular behaviour. They further contend that the leader's environment is by no means a fixed and static entity. Leaders may construe it in a variety of ways, depending upon such things as the degree to which their attention is engaged by it, the reasons they invoke for what they perceive as happening, and their own particular motives at the time.

Smith and Peterson (1988) have developed a model of event management. The model is not directly open to empirical testing. Instead, its function is a heuristic one, suggesting aspects of leadership which need fuller exploration. They believe that it is important to develop the skills of diagnosing and using the differing tactics which constitute appropriate responses to events that occur in each cultural or organizational context. The event management model can be summarized as a series of six propositions. Smith and Peterson (1988, 159) put it in the following manner:

> 1. Sources of event meaning direct the leader's attention towards or away from various aspects of the work situation, thereby affecting what is seen

and not seen, the conscious construction of events, and the tacit context which frames those events.

2. Sources of event meaning provide alternative schemes within which the leader can interpret events and link them to other events, in the past, present and future.

3. Sources of event meaning affect the relative salience of attitudes or schemes which determine the meaning placed on events.

4. Sources of event meaning determine the relative weight given to the elements used for explaining the causes of events and what information will be sought about those events.

5. Sources of event meaning determine the behavioral choice processes by which leadership actions are selected.

6. Sources of event meaning provide the context-rich vocabulary within which leadership actions are expressed.

The term *culture* became fashionable in organization research during the 1980s and the 1990s. Even before the surge of interest in the subject during the 1980's, it had been proposed fairly frequently that organizations as such have cultures (Allaire & Firsirotu 1984, 194). For example, Burton Clark's 1970 study on organizational saga in higher education (Clark 1987a) is among the first actual studies on organizational culture (Hatch 1993, 657); Clark introduced cultural studies on higher education institutions as well (Middlehurst 1993, 38). Later on, cultural analysis has been increasingly applied also to higher education (e.g. Becher 1984, 1989a; Becher & Huber 1990; Tierney 1988). Cultural models of leadership emphasize the informal aspects of organization rather than its official elements. They focus on the practices, meanings, values, norms and beliefs of the members of the organization. A background assumption is:

> Leadership operates within this complex social and psychological system by offering a way of finding meaningful patterns in the behaviour of others and by helping to develop common understandings about the nature of reality both within and outside the organization. Such common understandings may reflect existing circumstances or a new set of understandings, developed in response to change (Middlehurst 1993, 37).

Heads and principals have their own values and beliefs which arise from many years of successful professional practice (Bush 1995, 130-138). It is often held that the leaders of an organization have the main responsibility for developing and sustaining its culture and communicating its core values and beliefs to its members and to external stakeholders. Since this issue deals with my main theoretical approach and with one of my initial research questions, I shall return to it in chapter 7. I shall discuss relevant cultural theories and models in more detail in the forthcoming chapters dealing with my empirical data (chapters 5 and 6). Background assumptions of my approach will be considered in chapter 4.

3.1.1. Multi-Perspective Approaches

Birnbaum (1989, 209) has suggested that academic leaders should be aware of various conceptual models of organization and leadership and seek to understand their institution by drawing on multiple rather than single frames:

> Simple understandings lead to general rules to be applied in all situations; complicated understandings suggest that situations differ and that reliance on experiences of the past may prove dysfunctional (Birnbaum 1989, 209).

Following the seminal analysis by Morgan (1986), many scholars in higher education have discussed different organizational images, such as collegial, bureaucratic, professional, political, anarchical or ambiguity, and cultural models or perspectives (Walford 1987; Birnbaum 1989; Middlehurst 1993; Bush 1995; Hölttä 1995). It seems that each of the theoretical perspectives on organization and leadership highlights particular aspects of phenomena under study, while other aspects are left in the shade (Lockwood 1985; Morgan 1986; Tsoukas 1994; Bush 1995). Consequently, Bush (1995) speaks for conceptual pluralism and tries to achieve an eclectic synthesis between different theoretical frames. Morgan (1986, 321-322) stresses 1) the importance of a diagnostic reading of the situation being investigated, and of using different metaphors to identify or highlight key aspects of the situation, and 2) the need for a critical evaluation of the significance of the different interpretations resulting from analysis. He maintains:

> Any realistic approach to organizational analysis must start from the premise that organizations can be many things at one and the same time. A machinelike organization designed to achieve specific goals can simultaneously be: a species of organization that is able to survive in certain environments but not others; an information-processing system that is skilled in certain kinds of learning but not in others; a cultural milieu characterized by distinctive values, beliefs and social practices; a political system where people jostle to further their own ends; an arena where various subconscious or ideological struggles take place; an artifact or manifestation of a deeper process of social change; an instrument used by one group of people to exploit and dominate others; and so on. Though managers and organization theorists often attempt to override this complexity by assuming that organizations are ultimately rational phenomena that must be understood with reference to their goals and objectives, this assumption often gets in the way of realistic analysis. If

one truly wishes to understand an organization it is much wiser to start from the premise that organizations are complex, ambiguous, and paradoxical (Morgan 1986, 321-322).

I agree that multiple perspectives can provide a richer and probably a more realistic picture of leadership and organization under scrutiny. Such a multi-perspective approach may indeed help managers and researchers to be more flexible and creative in their thinking, and to capture organizational and administrative complexity in a fruitful way (Bensimon et al. 1989, 70).

However, I also see some problems in this kind of broad approach. Bush (1995) and Birnbaum (1989) believe that multiple perspectives can guide educational managers to better practice. But to what extent is the application of multiple perspectives possible given the limits of human understanding, time and other resources? The application of multiple perspectives may be held to result in a highly complicated view of the situation under study. In practice, academic leaders may have to choose from the different interpretations when they are called upon to take concrete actions. If the starting point is that each perspective is equally important, on what basis can the final choice be made between the conflicting interpretations? It is probable that among the multiple situational factors, (cultural) values and assumptions as well as the power of different participants are likely to come into play when the key decisions are made.

Similar problems can be expected to arise when researchers are carrying out empirical studies. While an attempt to adopt a multi-frame approach may be fruitful, no research is likely to be able to take everything into account. As Becher (1989a, 4) puts it: "Any piece of research which does not aspire to be encyclopedic and all-embracing must start from a particular perspective". In the same spirit, Alvesson (1995, 12) reminds us that attempts to employ numerous perspectives and metaphors in advanced analysis can easily result in superficiality. However, he also notes that the metaphors employed (espoused) by the researcher will not always illuminate the researchers' basic view of the phenomenon under study: "Complex understanding is perhaps more often derived from a synthesis of different metaphors than from a single sharp-profile picture" (Alvesson 1995, 13). Indeed, the distinctions between different approaches to leadership are somewhat arbitrary, since there is a considerable overlap between them[4].

My main theoretical perspective, the cultural frame, overlaps especially with the contingency and the cognitive models of leadership, as well as the power theories. It even resembles the behavioral theories by revealing certain leadership patterns when cultural meanings are connected to concrete behaviour. However, the notion of one universal best way of leadership, the idea of organizations as closed systems, as well as the unidimensional view of leadership influence are rejected in cultural models. Chapter 5

---

[4] However, it is useful to differentiate these approaches for the sake of clarity (Middlehurst 1993, 28).

deals with academic leadership in the context of disciplinary cultures, while chapter 6 views leadership from the perspective of organizational culture research[5].

3.2. ACADEMIC INSTITUTIONS AS A LEADERSHIP ENVIRONMENT

The foregoing has indicated that during the past decades leadership studies have produced different theoretical perspectives which can, more or less appropriately, be applied to the context of higher education. It has been argued that leadership models and theories developed in the context of other organizations are not applicable in the academic context because of the unique features of higher education institutions (e.g. Birnbaum 1989). But how do universities differ from other types of organizations? What are their unique features? I shall first present some arguments about such unique features, and then assess these views critically.

Attempts have been made to identify the basic characteristics of higher education institutions, which affect the issues of leadership and (strategic) management in academic settings (e.g. Lockwood 1985; van Vught 1988; Maassen and van Vught 1992). The following basic features of universities singled out by van Vught (1988, 7-8) and Maassen and van Vught (1992, 1486) stress the importance, power and authority of the professionals at the basic operational level:

> 1. The handling of knowledge is the most crucial activity in universities (Clark 1983).
>
> 2. The knowledge areas (disciplinary departments) form the basic building blocks of a higher education organization; consequently, the typical organizational structure of universities is fragmented and its specialized cells are only loosely coupled.
> 3. Decision-making power is spread across a large number of units and actors.
>
> 4. Innovations in universities mainly have a "grassroots" character. Sudden and major changes are rare and extremely difficult to effect because of the diffusion of power and the fragmentation of tasks (Clark 1983).
>
> 5. Authority is located at the lower levels of the organization (with academic professionals), while the institutional authority in higher education institutions (of continental Europe) is rather weak.

---

[5] In a forthcoming paper, I shall discuss departmental leadership from various theoretical perspectives (Kekäle forthcoming; Kekäle 1995d).

These basic characteristics of bottom-heavy university organizations to a large extent limit "the capacity of institutional planners to steer the professional experts in traditional bureaucratic ways" (van Vught 1988, 16).

Lockwood (1985) notes that there are differences between universities, and that institutions of higher education share common features with many other types of organizations[6]. However, according to him there are also specific features of most higher education institutions: complexity of purpose; limited measurability of outputs; mixture of autonomy and dependency in relation to society; diffusion of authority; and internal fragmentation (Lockwood 1985, 31-32). The evolution and history of universities has given rise to some basic socio-cultural attitudes which affect most academic institutions (e.g. expectations of objectivity in research, of high standards in teaching), and some basic features which are commonly built into their internal milieu (e.g. the ideal of academic freedom):

> Those attitudes and milieu have helped to create in-built resistance to management control, and thus they limit the influence of the institutional and corporate management upon the basic activities in the institution (Lockwood 1985, 26).

Indeed, the ideal of academic freedom limits the power of academic leaders, as the researchers have the right to make their own decisions on issues dealing with research and to test and question received knowledge, as well as the right to put forward new, sometimes even controversial and unpopular ideas "without losing their jobs or privileges" (Russell 1993).

It has been a popular view that vision and mission distinguish leaders from mere managers (Sims & Lorenzi 1992, 118). But providing a common vision and mission does not seem to be an easy task in academic settings because of the complex, fragmented and loosely coupled nature of the university organization which has been highlighted by many writers (e.g. Cannon 1983; Van Vught 1989; Birnbaum 1989). Cohen and March (1974, 195) stress the multiplicity, ambiguity and complexity of goals of a university. According to them, attempts to clarify purpose or to generate normative statements of the goals are, for most part, "well-intentioned exercises in social rhetoric, with little operational content", which tend to produce goals that are "meaningless or dubious". Because of broad and ambiguous goals,

---

[6] According to Lockwood (1985, 29) universities possess, among other things, the following features common to most forms of organizations: a university exists to accomplish something; it has a purpose - although the purposes seem to be more unclear than in many other organizations (Clark 1983; Cannon 1983). Moreover, a university consists of people and other resources, and it exists in a changing environment in which it interacts with other organizations.

there is no way that anyone can assess the degree of goal achievement. No one even knows if any or all these goals are accepted by significant groups within system, and with what priority (Clark 1983, 19).

One outcome of anarchistic features such as complex and unclear goals and means is that it is difficult to maintain management and leadership at universities in the traditional sense of administration (Cohen & March 1974; Järvi et al. 1990; section 1.1.). The list of legitimate university missions tends to be a lengthy one, too (Allen 1988; Birnbaum 1989, 11)[7].

These broadly accepted basic characteristics of universities seem to underline the difficulties of applying hierarchical or traditional management in academic settings. As for example Birnbaum (1989, 22) notes, there is often a strong resistance in higher education to leadership understood in the context of "followership" - to the way in which leadership is usually seen in hierarchical business and military organizations. While I consider that these aspects are partly relevant, and that they should be taken into account when leadership in academic settings is discussed and practised, I do not think that they make all kinds of leadership in the academic context impossible or irrelevant. First, many of the features mentioned seem to be changing (or may change with time) in different countries; at least there have been strong external pressures for such a change (e.g. Middlehurst 1995; chapter 1). Second, it can be argued that faculty members carry out a number of leadership and management roles when, for example, they have responsibility for resources, finance, staff, curriculum, or supervision of students. Consequently, academics who initially reject a managerial label "take too narrow a definition of the term" (Gordon et al. 1994, 9). I agree with Hearn and Anderson (1996, 8), who acknowledge that universities are not entirely like other organizations, but who also note many general similarities, most of which seem to apply to European universities:

> Colleges and universities are not immune to the universal patterns and forces of organizational life: a mission is stated in written, albeit often vague, terms; hierarchy among employees is formally recognized; there is a clear division of labour with horizontal and vertical differentiation; norms and values emerge and socialization occurs; various kinds of inequalities are noticed and important; conflicts occur; procedures and

---

[7] Because of ambiguities in goals, Cohen and March (1974, 2) have even stated: "the presidency is an illusion". In contrast to this, Allen (1988) argues strongly for more discussion and research about the goals of universities, as well as for more effective use of mission statements:
> It can be argued... that it is naive to expect complex organizations to produce simplistic statements of aims. It can be equally well be argued that it is naive to suppose that they can go on expecting to receive large sums of public money without being prepared justify their existence to laymen... In a period when universities are once again suffering a reduction in resources, the continued failure to address the question of purpose, with the same rigour as other intellectual issues are addressed in universities, seems positively perverse (Allen 1988, 158-159).

Richman and Farmer (1974, 32) have expressed a similar kind of criticism of the garbage-can model.

standards are established and reformed; some people move up in the organization more quickly than others, largely on the basis of expertise; turnover is endemic; authority relations exist; problems are solved in patterned ways; and so forth. Although research and theory from other settings must be employed cautiously, that research and theory can indeed be useful in aiding our understanding of academe.

Furthermore, the picture of the 'basic features of a university' becomes more complicated when we take into account the closely interrelated issues of the frame of reference of the interpreter/researcher and the level of analysis applied.

3.2.1. Application of Theoretical Frames of Reference

It has already been noted that complex organizations such as universities can be examined from many different theoretical view-points (section 3.1.1.). The listings of the basic features do not take into account different organizational images, nor try to explify the underlying implicit frames of reference. Most of the descriptions of basic features of universities to which reference has been made seem to be in line with the political image and the ambiguity (organized anarchy) models. The former assumes that the university is fragmented into diverse interest groups and that its organization is too loose and complex to be administered as a bureaucratic system; the latter emphasises unpredictability, unclear goals and the irrational nature of decision-making (Middlehurst 1993; Hölttä 1995)[8]. However, such perspectives provide only partial explanations and capture only some aspects of universities. For example, the incidence of routine bureaucratic procedures (in a descriptive, not in a pejorative sense), standard rules and professional collaboration is underestimated (Birnbaum 1989; Middlehurst 1993; Bush 1995; section 3.1.1.). Examples of such features can be found in any university[9] and may be important, since they may hinder or support academic work. In other words, although traces of fragmentation and ambiguity can be found, universities can also be viewed through other, perhaps equally revealing, theoretical lenses.

A similar emphasis on fragmentation can be identified in interpretations of the so-called "loosely coupled" (Weick 1988) nature of universities. This notion is frequently used to emphasize unpredictability of outcomes and lack of connections between different organizational subsystems (e.g. administration and operational units). But according to Orton and Weick (1990), the often misunderstood notion that universities are "loosely coupled systems" does not imply that there are no ties or connections between its elements (which would be to say that the system is *decoupled* or *non-coupled*), nor that these connections are direct, rigid, and strictly deterministic (as in tightly coupled systems; Orton & Weick 1990, 204-205). Instead, the dialectical concept of "loose coupling" attempts to combine the contradictory concepts of connection and autonomy, and emphasizes both coupling and decoupling (Orton & Weick 1990, 216-218):

> When researchers define organizations as monolithic corporate actors, they overemphasize order and underemphasize elements; when researchers define organizations as mere aggregates of individuals, they overemphasize elements and underemphasize order.

However, our cultural heritage and the tendency to think according to dualistic either/or categories easily leads to a one-dimensional interpretation of the concept, according to which loose coupling is seen as the opposite of tight coupling[10]. Walford (1987, 128-129) notes that historically most influential models of management within higher education have stressed rationality and consensus. Perhaps the popular attacks against rationalistic (structural-functionalistic) organization analysis have led many researchers to assume that it is more fruitful to move from one extreme to another and to view complex organizations as decoupled, irrational, ambiguous and fragmented.

Attempts at Synthesis

But it is also possible to occupy the middle ground and to achieve a synthesis between such seemingly opposite views. For example, Birnbaum (1989) tends to emphasize ambiguity, but manages also to take into account other aspects of university organizations.

---

[8] These assumptions seem to be in line with many of the views expressed in the previous section. However, for example 'the political perspective' is multi-voiced and does not always underestimate the existence or the possibility of formalized and bureaucratic decision-making. As Kogan (1987) concludes in his discussion of the political view of higher education:

> The university and other higher education institutions are indeed intensely politically complex units in which lines of authority cross with lines of influence, but which, nonetheless, produce decision-making structures and formalized relationships which then go on, in their turn, to affect interactions.

[9] According to Höltttä (1995, 147), collegial features are most readily visible in small institutions of higher education. In Finland, most of the universities are relatively small (Jolkkonen 1985; section 2.2.) as are the departments I have studied (section 4.6.).

[10] At times Kontkanen (1994) has this tendency, although she speaks for the dialectic interpretation of loose coupling on the basis of Orton and Weick's (1990) work. Most of her examples seem to emphasize ambiguity, insecurity and decoupling in knowledge organizations, while the (loose) connections and interactions between different organizational levels receive

As already mentioned, Birnbaum (1989, 24-25) connects the cultural approach strongly to the cognitive and the ambiguity approaches. Consequently, he shares the views of Cohen and March (1974) in maintaining that university presidents "may have relatively little influence over the outcomes when compared with other forces that affect organizational functioning". Birnbaum (1989, 35-36) is also inclined to adopt a one-dimensional interpretation of a loosely coupled system: or at least he notes that "the coupling between elements in a system can range from tight to loose". The first kind of system is *deterministic*, while the latter is *probabilistic*. Educational institutions are of the latter (loosely coupled) type, since the consequences of decisions can never be predicted with certainty, and things tend not to work in the way the administrators would want them to (Birnbaum 1989, 38-39).

But doesn't this, to a degree, hold true with most (post)modern organizations? At least it is difficult to find an example of a fully deterministic organization, where future states can be predicted with certainty, or where leaders have a total control over decisions about outcomes. Even if the basic tasks of an organization are simple and clear, human interaction and the competitive environment produce some degree of uncertainty. Conversely, the probabilistic or loosely coupled nature of an organization hardly renders it unnecessary to have leaders who make decisions and organize activities.

In fact, Birnbaum (1989) would seem to accept the point, in that he aims at integrating bureaucratic, collegial, political and symbolic views of the university by introducing the concepts of cybernetic institution and leadership. Birnbaum (1989, 27) claims that complex organizations cannot function effectively without leaders who "coordinate their activities, represent them to their various publics, and symbolize the embodiment of institutional purpose". The leaders need to have a high level of technical competence and an understanding of the nature of higher education in general as well as the culture of their institution in particular (Birnbaum 1989, 27). Good leadership in academic settings may call for constant rebuilding, maintaining and self-correcting organizational systems. In other words, academic leaders and administrators must act as a thermostat: for most of the time "their responsibility is to keep the institution in proper balance, and not to 'run' it", although at times of crisis transformational leadership may become possible and even necessary (Birnbaum 1989, 204-205). According to Birnbaum (1989, 204), those who question presidential leadership tend to overlook what does not happen - that is, problems and crises that do not occur because of effective presidential action.

In a similar vein, Enderud (1980), Davies and Morgan (1983), Dearlove (1995a) and Bush (1995) have put forward a model of the decision-making process which attempts to integrate anarchistic, political, collegial and bureaucratic features of higher education institutions[11]. The phases of the decision-making process can be roughly described in the following manner (Bush 1995, 151-153; Dearlove 1995a, 167).

---

considerably less attention. In other words, the term "loose coupling" - as it is used by Kontkanen (1994) on many occasions - actually ends up meaning "de-coupling".

[11] The model does not take well into account the subjective and cultural images of an organization (Bush 1995, 153).

The process starts with an unstructured *anarchy* where problems are unclear and all possible solutions are proposed. This phase may lead to an initial coupling of problems with potential solutions (Bush 1995, 151). Issues are then discussed further in the following *political* phase of the process, which is characterized by bargaining and negotiation between different interest groups, or their representatives in committees. In the third *collegial* phase, less active members are persuaded to accept the compromise which is potentially reached during the political stage. The solutions are tested against criteria of feasibility and acceptability. This process may result in minor changes, but it often leads to agreed policy outcomes and a degree of commitment to the decisions. The final phase is the *bureaucratic* stage, where administrative considerations may affect and modify the policy. The outcome of this phase may be a legitimate and operationally satisfactory policy (Bush 1995, 151-153; Dearlove 1995a, 167).

Consequently, at least in some cases, the ambiguity and unpredictability of the system will decrease as the decision-making proceeds and as/if the agreed policy becomes legitimated and established. However, the model does not imply that the process will always or inevitably lead to a shared legitimate policy: for example, leaders' attempts to proceed too fast or to bypass some of the stages may result in a breakdown of the process and in a 'loopback' to the earlier phases (Bush 1995, 151-153; Dearlove 1995a, 167)[12]. Or, the collegial phase may become political "as participants engage in conflict instead of seeking to achieve consensus" (Bush 1995, 153). However, the process will not inevitably remain in the anarchical or the political phase. In this sense, the model is useful in highlighting the process-oriented nature of organizing and policy-making in educational institutions, and in acknowledging that - to different degrees - distinct images of organization may be relevant in analyzing and describing the phases of the complex processes within higher education institutions.

As Walford (1987, 138-145) has demonstrated, the need for simplification may still remain. Some researchers have put forward controversial views about 'the key elements' of the decision-making process: for example, for Enderud (1980) the underlying state is organized anarchy, while for Walford (1987, 145), politics is the key element. It is understandable that for various reasons researchers may start from a certain perspective and consequently end up stressing the corresponding aspects (section 3.1.1.). In such cases, however, it is good to be explicit about the emphasis of the study. But if we consider decision-making as a process, it is not necessarily fruitful to make a priori assumptions that some of these phases are always more important than others. Instead, the 'key aspects' of the process may vary in time and place: the distinct phases may come to the forefront in different organizations (or their subsystems) during different eras.

---

[12] Given that the free-thinking professionals are relatively independent and powerful, Dearlove (1995a, 167) maintains that good university leaders are modest "learning leaders" who facilitate and organize, but do not dictate the decision-making process.

3.2.2. Level of Analysis

The key issues connected to leadership, such as the interdependence of the elements as well as the ambiguity and complexity of the goals and purposes depend also on the institutional level we are dealing with (although little is said about this in many studies). We may discuss the broad issues of university steering, governance, management and leadership at least at the following levels of authority ranging from national level to basic operating units (Clark 1983, 108-110)[13]:

Superstructure

- National government
- State, provincial, or municipal government
- Multicampus academic administration

Middle structure

- University or college in its entirety

Understructure

- Faculty (school, even a college in U.S.)
- Department

Clark (1983, 31-33) views higher education systems as matrix organizations which are simultaneously composed of disciplines and institutions. On the level of *superstructure* (Clark 1983) or a national system, we may find profound differences in institutional history, size, purpose, sponsorship, tradition, and values (Clark 1983, 81-83;

---

[13] There are other distinctions as well. Becher and Kogan (1992) have put forward a model of the higher education system which concentrates on the levels of central authority, institution, basic unit and individual. Middlehurst and Kennie (1995) have discussed leadership of professionals at national, institutional, departmental and team levels. Mäenpää and Mäkinen (1989, 18) have classified the organizational levels of a Finnish university in the following manner:

Central Level
- University Government
- Rector
- Central Administration
- Administrative Director (Chief Administrative Officer)

Middle Level
- Faculties (Arts, Science, Social Sciences, etc.)
- Deans, Collegial Councils

Under Level
- Departments
- Heads of Departments, Collegial Councils

(Subjects, Divisions)

Birnbaum 1989, 9). According to Birnbaum (1989, 9) this is one of the reasons why it is so difficult to achieve working "joint Statements on Government of Colleges and Universities". Governmental policies and doctrines (chapter 2) may, nevertheless form a unifying influence, especially at the institutional dimension. Some general characteristics of national systems may be identified (Clark 1987b).

Much of the variety and diversity in goals and purposes in universities derives from the fundamental differences in perspectives and approaches of different, relatively autonomous disciplines and specialisms (Clark 1983, 31-32; Becher 1987c, 289; Becher 1989a). At the level of the individual university (middle structure) the disciplinary dimension still provides considerable complexity, while the institutional dimension should provide at least some integrating elements: certain shared events, the same institutional name, often a common geographic location, and a certain administrative unity under which the departments act (Clark 1983; Höltta 1995, 44-47).

The practical leadership environment of academic leaders at the departmental level (understructure) should be, generally speaking, less complicated than for example that of university rectors, who have potentially to take into consideration many different disciplinary perspectives and numerous interest groups. The leadership tasks and expectations are different at these levels, too: while the professors are expected to be involved with, and to comment on, the specific scientific questions of their field, university rectors of necessity concentrate on more general issues of administration and public relations. As Middlehurst (1993, 131) has noted, a basic unit has a greater degree of integrity and cohesion than the whole university:

> The institutional leader looks out to the wider world; the departmental leader looks in, to the internal life and academic operations of the department.

Clark (1983, 23-26) argues that the operational goals and objectives are much clearer at the bottom levels of authority:

> It is fundamental to recognize that constituent factions have their own objectives, which are, in turn, in a cumulative fashion, the operating goals of the larger system... There is less mystery when we start from the operating levels; ambiguity and anarchy become less appropriate definitions. In the department, chair or institute, key actors generally have a well-grounded sense of why they are doing what they are doing. But like anybody else, they scratch their heads and revert to trivial statements when asked to enunciate, in a sentence or two, the meaning and purpose of the entire institution.

There are other aspects which might indicate a potentially broader scope for - or more direct response to - leadership at the level of academic departments. Leaning on Clark's (1983; 1995) work, Höltta (1995, 45) notes that because of the complex dynamics generated by the matrix structure, academic institutions "require very different forms of leadership and governance" from other types of organizations. Institutional aspects tend to produce a top-down hierarchy, while disciplinary expertise creates a bottom-up hierarchy, in which the most powerful members are respected individual scholars (Hölttä 1995, 42; section 2.4.). Teittinen (1994) maintains that the leadership of the administrative aspects of academic work is fundamentally different from leadership of the scientific aspects. According to him, scientific creativity can only be led to a limited extent, whereas administration is based on authority, co-ordination and formal power-positions.

The matrix structure affects leadership also at the departmental level. For example, a head of department may be mainly responsible for departmental administration - s/he is part of a bureaucratic hierarchy and acts as a mediator between staff and central administration - while the professors are accountable for disciplinary-based leadership. But it is also possible that certain individuals have a quite strong position which is supported by both the disciplinary and the institutional dimension[14]. A clear example of this would be a professor who acts as the head of department: s/he is the key figure in his/her own department who wields "a measure of real power as well as (in part consequentially) a pervasive influence" (Moodie & Eustace 1974, 62)[15].

Due to the somewhat clearer goals and purposes of scholars representing the same or closely related specialisms, the scope for leadership and management in a traditional sense (e.g. formulating strategy, goals and priorities) seems to be potentially greater than at other levels of the higher education system. In fact, most researchers who supervise students, or are able to create schools of thought or to win a following are leaders in this sense. Managerial influence may become obvious if an academic leader is dealing with scholars working on topics which are (or are seen to be) best mastered by him/herself. The combination of administrative authority and scientific power may give the professor a considerable influence in defining the goals and in embedding the culture of the department. After all, s/he acts as spokesman for his or her department within university, s/he is the key person in making decisions about the recruitment and assembly of research staff for projects led by him/her. S/he has potentially considerable power in deciding what kind of research will be conducted and rewarded in the groups and the department,

---

[14] Hölttä and Nuotio (1995, 16) write:

> The department heads act simultaneously both at the institutional and disciplinary dimension of the system. The basic advantage in the quite radical concentration of power and responsibility to the department heads at the University of Joensuu has been that they are firmly at the points of intersection between the institution and their disciplines. Only they are able to transform the signals of change coming from the institutional dimension of the organization into the disciplinary activities, and only they are correspondingly able to translate the initiatives from disciplines into the institutional dimension.

[15] As already noted in section 2.4., in minor university departments scientific and administrative leadership are often invested in one person who acts as a full professor and department head. Full professors have traditionally been very powerful at the basic unit level, since the departments of Finnish universities have been built around single chairs (Järvi, Kivinen & Rinne 1990). The original professor can be considered as the founder of the department, and his/her successor(s) may inherit a position of considerable power and influence.

and in determining which kind of theoretical approaches will be stressed or preferred (Moodie & Eustace 1974, 62-64; Kekäle 1995b).

The ideal of academic freedom forms a counter-force to this kind of direct or indirect leadership influence. Indeed, there are different views on whether or not strong individual leadership is desirable in the academic context. It seems reasonable to maintain that considerable freedom of thought and autonomy is essential to the nature of academic work and scientific creativity in most specialisms, especially in those calling for a strong individual contribution and emphasising theoretical thinking (Becher & Kogan 1992, 188; Becher 1989a, 169; Kekäle 1994b; see also footnote 3 in this chapter; chapter 7). However, the essential point is that at the departmental level some actors are potentially more powerful than others in determining the degree and the manner in which academic freedom is practised and supported.

3.2.3. The Complexity of the Academic Context

While it is legitimate to discuss universities and academic leadership at a general level, what are identified as the 'basic features' of academic organizations inevitably remain partial simplifications[16]. In this chapter, I have discussed several issues which complicate the picture of suitable leadership in an academic context. The application of different frames of reference highlights distinct features of complex academic organizations, and thus makes them less absolute. Different interest groups have distinct normative views about university and academic leadership. Balderston's (1974) notion that the (American) university has become a mixture of institution, enterprise and agency is revealing: according to him, this mixed nature is partly due to the large and confusing range of activities in a university, and happens partly because the major interested parties tend to view universities in different ways. As Becher and Kogan (1992, 177) put it:

> There is a quadrilateral of interests, each emphasising their own value positions, with which higher education must negotiate, and within which it must find its own path. One group of values is professional and derives from academic norms and aspirations. Another is governmental and is concerned with the demands of the state, which can range in different times from those of theocracy to those of the economy. A third is that of the market as it seeks particular skills in its workforce and particular forms of knowledge for conversion into wealth production. And, finally, there is that of public and social utility at large, whose interests may lie both in increased educational opportunities and in the maintenance and enhancement of a civilised society... Such forces, pushing and pulling as they do in most forms of public policy, are further elaborated by changes in the very content of higher education.

---

[16] Of course, all models of organizations and leadership are simplifications in so far as they aid understanding by clarifying highly complex social interactions (Walford 1987, 138-143).

The pressures and the relative weight of the value positions identified by Becher and Kogan co-exist "in different mixes in different institutions and for different functions" and these mixes change over time (Becher & Kogan 1992, 189). By way of illustration, the recent development plans of Finnish higher education have emphasised more and more explicitly the importance of increasing efficiency and effectiveness in academic institutions (chapter 2). But separate interest groups, such as scholars from different fields and institutions, view this development in various ways depending on how the new doctrine serves their interests or matches their values: for example, representatives of large and successful units - often from hard disciplinary areas - tend to view the university as an enterprise and to stress competition, while some other groups - particularly in humanities and social sciences - would rather keep regional and social equality as the basis of allocation of future resources (Kivinen et al. 1993, 222-227; chapter 2). Even if the general policy affects the work of all academics, the diverse interest groups are likely to place different expectations and pressures on academic leadership at the departmental level.

There are other points which indicate that the leadership environment is not necessarily similar for all academic leaders, although they all work within university settings. First, academic leaders at different levels of the institution face somewhat dissimilar leadership environments and tasks. I have argued that, generally speaking, the potential grounds for leadership (formulating strategy, goals and priorities) are clearer at the departmental level (although this also depends on circumstances, e.g. turbulent external environment). Second, there are significant differences in academic fields and specialisms, which make generalizations about suitable leadership problematic. The following examples may clarify the point: in broad outline, scholars in soft and divergent disciplines (Becher 1989a; e.g. some areas of social sciences and arts) operate in less predictable and clear symbolic and epistemological settings than scholars in hard and convergent natural sciences (Clark 1983, 80-81; Becher 1989a). Consequently, the clarity of the guidelines for action provided by the disciplines differ, leaving more or less room for diverse individual interpretation. Again, the working patterns in high-energy physics lean on group work (Traweek 1988), while research in some arts and social science disciplines is more individualistic in nature (Becher & Kogan 1992, 116; Becher 1989a). "Teamwork naturally implies conformity to group norms and a readiness to accept the sovereignty of the team leader" (Becher 1987c, 283)[17].

Thus, Bennett and Figuli's (1993, xvi) notion that the task of the head of department is often "not unlike the job of herding a bunch of frogs", since individualistic researchers tend to follow their own paths, may apply better to some disciplines than to others. Furthermore, while theoretical work in physics and in other disciplines requires academic freedom, when researchers are carrying out routine experiments this demand is less evident. To further complicate matters, the distribution of age, rank and experience will vary within departments (Hearn & Anderson 1996), and the expectations of junior and senior researchers concerning academic leadership are likely to be considerably different.

---

[17] There may be differences between formal and informal leadership, and the leadership roles/functions of scholars in different teams.

Indeed, although some general features, trends and pressures can be identified, academic departments and institutions vary in history, size, personnel, tasks, disciplinary base and orientation. Such differentiation may, as has been suggested (section 3.2.), make management (in the traditional, hierarchical sense) problematic at the institutional level. But at the same time, these kind of major difference also makes it difficult to generalize about 'suitable' academic leadership at the basic operational level, or across other levels of the academic system.

In managerial and leadership research it is often concluded that managerial criteria can never be universally valid, in that they are inevitably connected to the situation and culture within which they have been produced (Juuti 1989, 196; Lahti-Kotilainen 1992, 29). While some highly general features of academic institutions or leadership can perhaps be identified, it is unlikely that we can find one best way of leadership which can be applied with equal outcomes everywhere within academia. Instead, there may be diverse (functioning, formal and informal) leadership patterns and cultures in different disciplines and departments, some of which are possibly unique or non-traditional and others perhaps closer to traditional leadership models (Kekäle 1995a; 1995b).

Since the context of academic leadership seems complex and multi-layered in nature, we are likely to be able to grasp only limited aspects of it. In a cumulative fashion, this complexity increases as the number of subsystems and loosely coupled components we are dealing with expands. The more general our discussion, the more ideal-typical our findings; as the spectrum of variation within the sample increases, the more simplifying our assumptions tend to become[18]. For example, we can more fully and precisely describe the cultural practices of a minor department than the cultural features of an institution or an entire higher education system. On the other hand, an overview cannot be reached through a concentration on local and particular issues alone. As Becher (1987c, 271) puts it:

> To see the whole is to see it in breath, but without access to the particular; to see the part is to see it in depth, but without a general overview.

This brings us back to the question of choice of a frame of reference and level of analysis (Becher 1987c, 272-273). In this study, I have chosen to focus on academic leadership and cultures especially at the level of departments (or operating basic units; Clark 1983; Becher & Kogan 1992), and (to a lesser degree) teams (Middlehurst &

---

[18] In effect, the more levels we are trying to deal with in a single empirical study, the more superficial the discussion is likely to become. Välimaa (1995, 75) has suggested that we should take into account national and institutional traditions, missions, sagas and cultures together with international disciplinary-based cultures and professional traditions and values. In practice it would be difficult to study the complex cultural influences from all these levels in a single enquiry. Even if carried out by a large research team, such a broad project is bound to lead to numerous oversimplifying assumptions at different levels of analysis. Moreover, when analyzing the national, institutional, professional and disciplinary traditions, a researcher has to make some kind of assumptions or claims about the degree of integration or fragmentation of these cultural

Kennie 1995). I have approached these complex issues by means of empirical research, by studying leadership cultures in different departmental and disciplinary contexts, and by trying to capture the respondents' views of leadership features and influences which seem to be particularly relevant for them.

Academic departments are the cells of the higher education matrix, where institutional and disciplinary dimensions meet and intertwine (Clark 1983; Höltta 1995; section 3.2.2.). The disciplinary dimension brings in some international (epistemological and social) influences which may affect departmental leadership (these will be discussed in chapter 5). At the same time, such disciplinary influences mix with local and institutional aspects affecting leadership, which I shall discuss from a cultural perspective at the departmental level in chapter 6.

Departments are the operative units, where the basic tasks such as research and instruction are carried out. Consequently, we may assume that departmental leadership will have practical significance, which becomes evident in well functioning and problematic cases. Our understanding of leadership issues at that particular level is likely to be enhanced during the times when heads of departments are expected to take the final responsibility for the allocation of resources and productivity (chapter 2).

Such knowledge might have a broader significance as well. The leadership of knowledge-intensive expert organizations will become more important as the number of such organizations grows, and as traditional organizations increasingly move in the same direction (Svejby & Risling 1987; Blackler et al. 1993).

3.3. FINNISH STUDIES ON ACADEMIC LEADERSHIP

I have argued that at the departmental level leadership forms a distinct problem-area of academic leadership. Practical guidelines for departmental heads have been provided, for example, by Moses and Roe (1990), Bennett and Figuli (1993) and Tucker (1993). I have referred to the work dealing with leadership in university settings by Richman and Farmer (1974), Walford (1987), Birnbaum (1989), Becher and Kogan (1992), Middlehurst (1993) and Clark (1995), among others[19]. But although the topic is currently important, it has not been much studied in Finland, where research on higher education has been in general rather limited in scope (Järvi et al. 1990, 15)[20]. The few studies

---

dimensions. However, Välimaa (1995, 53) suggests that the issues of integration and fragmentation are not important in the study of academic cultures.

[19] The 1995 issues (numbers 1 and 2, volume 1) of Tertiary Education and Management (TEAM) published by EAIR include papers dealing exclusively with the topic of academic leadership.

[20] I have already discussed studies dealing with the general trends in the higher education system and its steering mechanisms (chapter 2). In addition to this line of research, many Finnish studies have used students as respondents. To mention a few of these: Ruoppila (1967) studied attitudes of young and advanced students in different types of educational institutions. Educational climates and environments as experienced by students in Finnish faculties and departments have been studied by Häyrynen (1970), Marin (1970), Perho (1978), Aittola and Aittola (1985; 1990),

dealing with leadership issues in universities have been conducted by Marttinen (1988), Mäenpää and Mäkinen (1989), Pekkala and Rönkkömäki (1991), and by Hölttä and Nuotio (1995), among others.

Marttinen (1988) interviewed the rectors and chief administrative officers of eight Finnish universities. Since the study did not deal with leadership at the level of basic units, I will not discuss it further here.

Stolte-Heiskanen and Alestalo (1978) dealt with academic leadership (as a subsidiary theme) in their comparative study on efficiency of research groups in different countries (Finland, Belgium, Austria, Poland, Sweden, Hungary). Surveys and interviews were used as research methods. Their Finnish sample included 219 research groups in nine disciplines representing pure and applied natural and technical sciences. The groups were employed by universities, national organizations (such as the Finnish Academy), private research institutes, and by industrial enterprises (Stolte-Heiskanen & Alestalo 1978, 74). The study revealed differences in the leadership of research groups according to the type of institution: at universities, the flow of information was generally considered as unproblematic and researchers participated in decision-making, although power was mainly in the hands of the leaders of the research projects. In other types of institutions decision-making and planning was more leader-centred. No major differences in leadership patterns according to discipline were found (Stolte-Heiskanen & Alestalo 1978, 221-225). This may be due to the relatively homogeneous disciplinary background of the research groups studied.

Hölttä and Nuotio's (1995) study was based on a survey which included some universities in four European countries (Sweden, Norway, the Netherlands, the United Kingdom) in addition to Finland. The idea was to compare decision-making models and leadership responsibilities applied at different administrative levels of the studied universities. They noted that department heads are typically involved in organizing research and teaching. At the university of Joensuu, their duties have a strong emphasis on resource management. In most universities studied, the department heads and deans are appointed by the University Council or the corresponding collegial body (see Hölttä & Nuotio 1995; section 2.4.).

Both the studies by Mäenpää and Mäkinen (1989) and Pekkala and Rönkkömäki (1991) dealt with departmental leadership, and were based on questionnaires. In Mäenpää and Mäkinen's (1989) study, altogether 49 departmental heads or deans in five Finnish institutions of higher education answered the questionnaire focusing, among other things, on their views concerning management duties and effective leadership. The authors considered their study as tentative and preliminary because of their relatively small sample, which included only the heads - not the researchers of the departments studied. Consequently, they were unable to draw conclusions about "the invisible side of organizational cultures in higher education" (Mäenpää & Mäkinen 1989, 106).

There was considerable variety in the respondents' views about effective management/leadership. This variety in views and definitions supports the assumption

Kuittinen (1992) and Häyrynen et al. (1992a and 1992b). Student cultures have been studied by Kekäle (1991) and Aittola (1992), among others (see also Mäkinen & Määttä 1989).

that it is "quite impossible" to find an "unambiguous frame" for "efficiency or 'effective' leadership" in higher education (Mäenpää & Mäkinen 1989, 72). The deans stressed the need for better organization, less bureaucracy and fewer meetings as a means of improving efficiency, while departmental heads placed more emphasis on human relations and leadership aspects and the need for more resources (Mäenpää & Mäkinen 1989, 70-73).

The research did not bring out many systematic or measurable differences between distinct institutions, or distinctions in relation to their age or size. However, respondents in arts subjects tended to view the current situation and leaders' possibilities in an apparently "idealistic and naive" way, perhaps displaying a "humanistic trust" of people. Scholars in science tended to emphasize straightforward, linear thinking and measurability, as well as accepting sanctions as management tools; they would also give more power to leaders. Social scientists tended to be more "cynical" and less optimistic than other respondents when possibilities of development were considered (Mäenpää & Mäkinen 1989, 105-106). In their conclusions, Mäenpää and Mäkinen (1989) stress the tensions between administrative and scientific/expert tasks. The respondents generally viewed the administrative tasks as less important than the basic tasks of research and instruction.

In their master's thesis, Pekkala and Rönkkömaki (1991) studied the opinions of heads of departments on the applicability of Management by Objectives (MBO) in university settings. Semi-structured questionnaires were sent to departmental heads at the university of Oulu. Most of the respondents viewed efficiency as an intentional and processual way of acting and thinking. The majority of the respondents considered that MBO could be applied in academic settings, although the application of over-mechanistic or external criteria of assessment was often feared. The heads of departments of the faculties of technical sciences and arts were in favour of MBO. Most of the respondents held that direct management is not suited to an academic context. However, most heads also considered it essential to develop academic leadership. The study did not take into account researchers' views on leadership issues, since only the heads of departments were included in the sample.

Aittola (1983; 1984) studied administrative processes and decision-making in the departments of the university of Jyväskylä. Both his studies aimed at monitoring the changes in departmental administration at the university after the administrative reform process which gave rise to a new governmental act relating to the university of Jyväskylä in 1981. At the departmental level, the intention of the reform was to broaden the collegial basis of decision-making and to make it more democratic, since departmental administration and decision-making had previously been professor-centred (Aittola 1983, 15; section 2.3.1.).

Altogether 182 members of staff at all levels of the departmental hierarchy answered the questionnaire. The results suggested that the reform had succeeded in increasing democracy, but it had also increased administrative bureaucracy in decision-making (Aittola 1983; Aittola (1987, 101-103, 135) has concluded later that the reform resulted in practices which only seemed to be democratic, but which were actually based on administrative bureaucracy; section 2.3.1.). In the departments with only one subject and chair, administration was carried out largely in collegial councils after the reform. In the departments which consisted of two or more subject areas, the actual decision-making was mainly carried out within each subject field. In minor departments, the practices within collegial councils still depended considerably on the leadership style of the professor (Aittola 1984).

My licentiate dissertation (Kekäle 1993) was based on a case study dealing with the differing organizational cultures of a small university department[21]. The department in question has two separate subjects or main lines of study, here described as courses a and b. The study was based on interviews with teachers and students and on discussions with a key informant (see Kekäle 1995b). Additional data were derived from participant observation during group discussions and the examination of written documents and annual reports of the department. Two teachers commented on the final analysis of the material.

On the basis of the data, I formed an interpretation of the organizational cultures of the department during the late eighties. The cultural differences of the courses seemed to be connected to their different leadership styles. The culture of course a was individualistic. Teachers were not much motivated to supervise students. The students of course a pointed out that they were expected to work on their master's thesis on their own, a claim confirmed by some of the supervising teachers. The professor devoted himself largely to tasks outside the department. This was not particularly deviant behaviour: historically, it has been quite common in Finnish academic culture to stress the importance of academic independence in the fostering of an individual's own work and talents (Häyrynen et al. 1992, 17-18).

In contrast to the teachers of course a, the teachers of course b took their teaching tasks more seriously and stressed the importance of social support and supervision. The teachers of the course valued both the teaching and the research tasks of the department. They tended to have much closer interaction with each other and with the students than the teachers of course a. About fifteen years ago, course b acquired a new leader who criticized the traditionally individualistic nature of academic studies and stressed the importance of effective supervision of both master's theses and advanced postgraduate studies. Since then, the students in course b have been encouraged to consult their teachers at any time during the day with their problems. These changes proved success-ful. According to the teachers, the more effective supervision has contributed remarkably to the growth of the numbers of the students annually graduated. According to statistics, course b produced annually 1,5 - 4 times more graduates than course a over a period of several years. There have subsequently been changes in key personnel and the situation is likely to change.

During 1995, the Finnish Ministry of Education funded two additional research projects on leadership in the university context. The first of them (Pirttilä 1995) concentrates on budget negotiations between university rectors and departmental heads. These negotiations are connected to the practices of Management by Objectives or

---

[21] For another case-study of organizational culture of a university department see Alvesson (1995, 95-109).

Management by Contracts, and concern desired goals and the allocation of economic resources (see Rekilä 1995). The second research is a comparative case-study (Summa & Virtanen 1995) which deals with researchers' views and metaphors on MBO, departmental leadership and prerequisites of personal qualification. The study involves departments from different subject fields. Both projects are expected to publish reports by the end of the year 1996.

Some Finnish writers have dealt with the practical issues of the leadership and management of expert organizations at a general level (Sipilä 1991; Eklund 1992). There is also Hölttä's (1995) detailed study on the steering mechanisms and self-regulating processes of a university institution. To my knowledge, however, no qualitative case studies dealing with academic leadership in the contexts of different disciplinary or departmental cultures have been undertaken in Finland. This kind of study would need to take into account the informal and contextual aspects of leadership and the loosely-coupled nature of the organization (Orton & Weick 1990) as well as the opinions of researchers. Consequently, it would seem important to deepen our understanding of academic leadership in its departmental and disciplinary settings. This is the task to which I shall turn in the following chapters.

Chapter 4

METHODOLOGY AND DATA

4.1. Paradigms and Assumptions

Scientific action and schools of thought are often seen to be based on some sorts of presuppositions or background assumptions (e.g. McGregor 1961; Kuhn 1970, Hanson 1979; Burrell and Morgan 1985; Trigg 1993; Guba and Lincoln 1994). The notion that researchers should reflect their own ontological, epistemological and methodological assumptions has been widely shared among the scholars studying organizational cultures (e.g. Smircich 1983, 355; Frost et al. 1991, 168)[1]. In the previous chapter, some of the underlying assumptions of different theoretical perspectives to leadership were discussed. In this chapter, I shall start my methodological discussion by reflecting briefly on my own assumptions concerning epistemological, ontological and methodological matters on the basis of Guba and Lincoln's (1994) model.

The aim of the speculation is to provide background information and a point of reference for the reader; I do not intend to offer a definitive answer to these issues, some of which can be considered as the most central of all metaphysical questions (Trigg 1993, 38). Through this short discussion, I hope to be able to clarify and support my views on some of the underlying themes already apparent in the previous chapter (e.g. local vs. universal 'truths'; realism vs. relativism), and on which the argumentation in the next chapters will also be based. After this, I will move on to concrete questions concerning the methods and data in my study. In order to give the reader the means to assess the

---

[1] Some postmodern researchers have preferred to remain 'nomads', on the move, as far as their philosophical positions are concerned. Czarniawska-Joerges (1992, 7), who does not perhaps share the postmodern outlook, notes:

> Self-labelling is, of course, a risky enterprise. It gives an appearance of a static picture to something that is basically an ongoing process. I am all the things mentioned above [a symbolic realist, both determinist and voluntarist with an emphasis on the latter - J.K.] when writing this book, but I used to be a functionalist positivist, and do not know who I shall become by the time this book is in print. The only safe position, then, is that of a methodological pluralist who tries to be tolerant toward all traditions, knowing that one might need this tolerance oneself.

grounds of my interpretations, I will give a description of the process of study, as well as the nature of the data and methods in this research (Altheide & Johnson 1994, 489).

Guba and Lincoln (1994) have recently discussed - at a general level - competing paradigms of qualitative research and their underlying assumptions[2]. The paradigms are, from early to more recent origin, the following: *positivism*, *postpositivism*, *critical theories* and *constructivism*. According to Guba and Lincoln (1994) paradigms are basic belief systems which are based on ontological, epistemological and methodological assumptions. They start with Kuhnian notion that such beliefs

> are basic in the sense that they must be accepted simply on faith (however well argued); there is no way to establish their ultimate truthfulness. If there were, the philosophical debates reflected in these pages would have been resolved millennia ago (Guba & Lincoln 1994, 107).

Consequently, Guba and Lincoln (1994) maintain that advocates of any particular paradigm must rely on persuasiveness and utility rather than proof in arguing their position[3]. In any case, they hold that researchers should be clear about what paradigms inform and guide their approach.

In the model put forward by Guba and Lincoln (1994), the ontological, epistemological and methodological assumptions of different paradigms vary in the following manner (Guba & Lincoln 1994, 111-112):

---

[2] Guba and Lincoln (1994, 106-107) also discuss the problems associated with quantitative studies in social sciences.

[3] In defending a realist outlook, Trigg (1993, 216) argues that even physical science must be rooted in metaphysics. The demand for the justification of science will never end, for "every grounding will have to be grounded in something else" and "any reason that can be provided can always be challenged":

> Science is in fact powerless to explain the apparent regularities it discovers. They are the foundations it has to take for granted as the basis for all explanations. Even theories which try to re-establish randomness and change can only do so by being built on a science which has already assumed regularity... Science needs the notion of a continuing order, a cosmos, but it also assumes that this is something it has to look for. It cannot be established by reason alone. The world is contingent, and does not have to be as it is. Only the assumption of a contingent order can give empirical science the scope it needs, whilst giving it assurance that there is an underlying rationality waiting to be uncovered. Contingency demands an empirical method. We actually have to observe and experiment to see the way in which physical is constituted. The concept of contingent order saves science from the necessity of mathematics on the one hand and the chaos of total arbitrariness on the other (Trigg 1993, 235-236).

"We must trust, believe, before we can know", but the balance between reason and faith is difficult to accept in a secular time like ours (Scott 1994, 34-35).

Ontology

Guba and Lincoln (1994, 111) note the move from:

> 1. Positivism's position of naive realism, assuming an objective external reality upon which inquiry can converge; to
>
> 2. postpositivism's critical realism, which still assumes an objective reality but grants that it can be apprehended only imperfectly and probabilistically; to
>
> 3. critical theory's historical realism, assuming an apprehendable reality consisting of historically situated structures that are, in the absence of insight, as limiting and confining as if they were real; to
>
> 4. constructivism's relativism, which assumes multiple, apprehendable, and sometimes conflicting social realities that are the products of human intellects, but that may change as their constructors become more informed and sophisticated.

Epistemology

Guba and Lincoln (1994, 111) note the move from:

> 1. Positivism's dualist, objectivist assumption that enables the investigator to determine "how things really are" or "how things really work"; to
>
> 2. postpositivism's modified dualist/objectivist assumption that it is possible to approximate to (but never fully know) reality; to
>
> 3. critical theory's transactional/subjectivist assumption that knowledge is value mediated and value dependent; to
>
> 4. constructivism's somewhat similar but broader transactional/subjectivist assumption that sees knowledge as created in interaction among investigator and respondents.

Methodology

Guba and Lincoln (1994, 111-112) note the move from:

> 1. Positivism's experimental/manipulative methodology that focuses on verification of hypotheses; to
>
> 2. postpositivism's modified experimental/manipulative methodology invested in critical multiplism focusing on falsification of hypotheses; to

3. critical theory's *dialogic/dialectical* methodology aimed at the reconstruction of previously held constructions; to

4. constructivism's hermeneutic/dialectic methodology aimed at the reconstruction of previously held constructions.

Caldwell (1982, 89-90) notes that positivism as the general epistemological-methodological foundation for philosophy of science has been in decline, even in eclipse:

> In their haste to eradicate the flights of metaphysical fantasy, which they felt characterized the system built by idealist philosophers, positivists became dogmatic in their refusal to allow any subjective, qualitative elements to enter into their rational reconstructions of science. That refusal artificially limited their analyses, and created gaps in their description of science... They believed that theories and explanation in science were uniform, and always (if legitimate) translatable into a specified axiomatic form - and missed the rich and complex diversity of patterns of explanation and theorizing in science... they failed to see that the most important decisions made in science... are in final analysis made by men who should be aware of their fallibility, but who hopefully attempt to be rational anyway.

Critical theory and constructivism differ mainly from the other two paradigms in relation to their epistemological positions (Guba & Lincoln 1994, 111). The relativist ontological position differentiates constructivism from the other paradigms. In the cases of critical theory and constructivism, the conventional distinction between ontology and epistemology disappears.

The move from positivism towards constructivism can also be seen in the historical development of leadership theories discussed in the previous chapter. Broadly speaking, the trait and behavioral theories were based on positivistic assumptions, and power and influence theories are often connected to a critical outlook. More recent cultural and symbolic theories are inclined to lean on the assumptions similar to those of constructivism (Bensimon et al. 1989; Middlehurst 1993, 37). Also the application of multiple perspectives in leadership studies, as discussed in the section 3.1.1., demonstrates a leaning towards constructivism, since the approach acknowledges the coexistence of numerous 'knowledges' about the organization in question. It also highlights the significance of the interpreter's frame of reference or stand-point in the outcomes of an inquiry. On the other hand, many of the previously discussed analyses of the basic features of university institutions (section 3.2.) essentially seem to start from the ontological and epistemological stand-points of realism and objectivism (positivism, postpositivism), since they aim at identifying general and context-free features of higher education institutions.

4.1.1. Problematic Extreme Positions

Guba and Lincoln (1994) view the different paradigms basically as alternatives (some of which are still in their formative stages). Although there seems to be considerable paradigmatic variation between individual studies, the ideal would be that a researcher identifies the paradigm that guides his or her research and then sticks to it throughout the study[4]. But this is not an easy task, as the contradictions in Guba and Lincoln's (1994) own position would suggest.

Guba and Lincoln (1994) commit themselves explicitly to constructivism and relativism. Yet, as Trigg (1993, 220) notes: "Any scientific theory is put forward on the tacit assumption that its proponents can recognize what is true, or at least what seems to be so". Even the extreme relativist notion that 'there is no truth to be found' is itself a metaphysical truth claim. That being the case, the problem of course is: how can, or why should we believe in the truthfulness of such a claim (Trigg 1993, 171).

Consequently, although Guba and Lincoln (1994) hold that their model is their construction, they also (must) discuss the different paradigms and their proponents as if they were true, objective and real, and as if they knew "how things really are". For example, they maintain that "Postpositivists... tend to control publication outlets, funding sources, promotion and tenure mechanisms, dissertation committees, and other sources of power and influence" (Guba and Lincoln 1994, 116). Moreover, they recognize that the criteria of quality and 'goodness' of research in constructivism have considerable similarities with positivist criteria, "which makes them suspect" (Guba & Lincoln 1994, 114).

Puuronen (1995) found that authors of Finnish youth studies have frequently leaned on assumptions derived from multiple and competing paradigms identified by Guba and Lincoln (1994). At the end of his study, Puuronen (1994) finds that he has not been able to stick strictly to the assumptions of constructivism either. He concludes that a researcher should reflect his/her assumptions, but s/he should also be critical towards the different paradigms and schools of thought (Puuronen 1995, 147).

Buchanan et al. (1988, 53-54) maintain that doing research is a different kind of enterprise from thinking and writing about research: the fieldwork

> is permeated with the conflict between what is theoretically desirable on the one hand and what is practically possible on the other... whatever carefully constructed views the researcher has of the nature of social research, of the process of theory development, of data collecting methods, or of the status of different types of data, those views are constantly

---

[4] Guba and Lincoln (1993, 116) note that their presentation of the "paradigm wars" is perhaps more confrontational than necessary. They maintain:

> A resolution of paradigm differences... is most likely to occur if and when proponents of these several points of view come together to discuss their differences, not to argue the sanctity of their views.

compromised by the practical realities, opportunities, and constraints presented by organizational research (Buchanan et al. 1988, 53-54).

But should we view 'reality' as monolithic, i.e. as *either* socially constructed *or* as an objective entity? Is it fruitful to assume that the same epistemological and ontological assumptions are valid in relation to all kinds of data, or in relation to all aspects or layers of 'reality'? Kosko (1994) claims that the classic Aristotelian binary logic leads to intellectual dead-ends when it is applied to fuzzy and imprecise symbols and phenomena. He defends the in-between positions (different shades of grey) as against exhaustive binary opposites (black or white)[5].

Consider the following example: during the history of mankind, there have been different conceptions about the shape of the world (i.e. whether it is flat or round). We may, first, discuss these different and historically changed conceptions about the shape of world and their consequences to human life. Such 'sociological' inquiry would probably produce relevant information about the social sphere of life and its socially constructed nature (e.g. how our beliefs guide our actions and our life). In this context, the constructivistic frame of reference would highlight important aspects of culture and social world (yet, at the same time, it would be forced to make some kind of truth-claims about this world). But we might as well discuss the evidence provided by the natural sciences about the fact that the world is indeed round. In this context, a realistic approach has opened new possibilities for us. From this perspective, many would claim that what makes the notion of the round world knowledge "is its relationship with the world and not its role in society" even if social forces may obstruct or facilitate the production of such scientific knowledge (Trigg 1993, 157). Becher (1989a, 4-5) makes a good point when he notes:

> If questions of truth and falsity owe nothing to phenomena outside the socially constructed interpretations of members of contemporary society, it

---

[5] A good example of black and white thinking can be found in Välimaa's (1995) dissertation. He discusses cultural approach in higher education from the perspectives of rationalist and humanist traditions. The first tradition concentrates on general principles and laws, while the second focuses on particular local understandings and practices. By identifying the roots of a certain approach or an author as being at the opposite poles of this sharp dichotomy, Välimaa (1995) then tries to inspect if the author in question really sticks to the tradition s/he seems to belong to according to his analysis. No in-betweens are allowed. However, in his analysis Välimaa (1995) leans on classic bipolar logic which belongs closely to the realm of the rationalist tradition, while he explicitly identifies himself with the humanistic tradition. Indeed, his central intellectual tool, the sharp either/or dichotomy between general knowledge and local understandings, is a problematic oversimplification. Altheide and Johnson (1994, 490) note that many of most famous ethnographers "have decidedly straddled the fence on this issue, wanting to have both substantive particularity and processual abstraction, and usually concluding with neither". Alvesson (1995) discusses ten different metaphors of culture in organizational analysis, "which in no way exhaust the ways in which culture is used in organization research" (Alvesson 1995, 24-35). He notes that some of the metaphors he discusses seem to represent the opposite poles of such dimensions as objectivism vs. subjectivism or functionalism vs. non-functionalism, while others fall in between the opposite poles.

would seem no more than a matter of arbitrary consensus that Newton's laws of motion were held to be valid, or that the atomic bombing of Hiroshima foreshadowed the end of the Second World War.

Extreme 'postmodern' constructivism may lead to an assumption that we can get rid of all our problems - say, for example, a hole in the ozone layer - if we just stop constructing such problems by discussing them. With good reasons, Allardt (1995, 11) asks whether the recent emphasis on language games and social meanings has gone too far: severe problems in society are ignored, as the relativistic assumption that 'anything goes' seems to became increasingly accepted.

4.1.2. A Pluralistic Perspective

I believe that both realism and constructivism are fruitful and valid approaches in certain contexts, and that both of them highlight relevant and intertwined aspects of the world. Schwandt (1994, 126) maintains that:

> One need not to be antirealist to be a constructivist. One can reasonably hold that concepts and ideas are invented (rather than discovered) yet maintain that these inventions correspond to something in the real world.

In this study, I start from the assumption that the local leadership practices of the departments - which I will concentrate on - are socially constructed, but that this construction inevitably happens *within* a broader physical, biological, and social framework. Our conceptions of these kinds of 'external' factors are important, and they may indeed vary. We can, for example, have different views about which aspects of them are the most important. But in any case, it would be difficult to arrange work in an academic department without taking into account the existing laws, economic resources, or biological and physical facts. Ignoring them on the basis of an extreme 'anything goes' relativism and constructivism - as if they were mere products of our interpretation or imagination - would lead to a potential disaster. Without economic resources, the whole existence of the department in its current form would come to an end, but of course different persons might still adopt different attitudes towards the matter. The same holds true with the broad ecological issues: we can have diverse attitudes towards them - at least as long as they do not directly affect our life and survival.

To take still another example, which concerns our ability to change social realities: a critical researcher who adopts the assumptions identified by Guba and Lincoln (1994) might want to change the existing laws or the basis of allocation of (inevitably) limited economic resources. Whether or not this attempt is seen as worthwhile is a matter of the researcher's values and priorities. But whatever the values or conceptions of an individual researcher, such large change-projects - if taken seriously - will require time and energy, which could otherwise be devoted to other practices. Moreover, the outcome of the researcher's efforts would probably be compromised because of the competing views and efforts of those who are in favour of the current laws or the previous allocation of resources. Because of the complexity of social interactions, the outcomes of such a project might turn out to be quite dissimilar from what was expected: while a single social enquiry may change and affect the phenomena it studies, this potential impact is only one force among other political and social forces, many of which may have a longer history and stronger implications for the actors.

However, this does not have to make all critique unnecessary or hopeless. Instead, my point here is to stress that in a sense people do indeed construct their reality, but that this construction inevitably happens within a field of possibilities loosely framed by some preexisting 'realities'[6]. These are loose in the sense that they may permit multiple, diverse solutions and cultures to function and co-exist, whereas some other patterns would obviously contradict them. Moreover, our conceptions mould, sustain and even construct these 'realities' - and may highlight different *layers* and *spheres* of the complex reality.

Some *layers* of reality may be *fluid* and readily alterable, at least in principle (as our conceptions and opinions sometimes - but not always - are). Other layers of reality may be more *viscous* - that is, difficult to alter in the short run, and less dependent on the will of an individual actor (e.g. laws, deeply valued cultural traditions, assumptions and values, some broad processes in nature and in society such as recession). In contrast, some layers and basic processes of (physical and biological) reality are probably *solid*, constant and unalterable despite of our actual and perhaps changing conceptions of them (e.g. gravitation, laws of nature; see footnote 3).

My ontological premise is that organizational and social 'structures' - such as cultural norms, values, and basic assumptions - as well as the behaviour constructing them belong to the first two categories. Cultural phenomena can be considered as processes, potentially changing and evolving, though some of them (typically characterized by a strong commitment and a taken-for-granted nature) tend to be more enduring than others (Kekäle 1995b). When we concentrate on such aspects, we find 'truths' which may change according to context, but which may nonetheless be relatively stable and relevant for the people in a given culture.

This view does not have to lead to extreme relativism, since such social and cultural features and practices may be, at least to a degree, assessed in relation to the framing aspects or facts of solid layers of reality, and in relation to their 'match' with the viscous aspects of the other (e.g. economic, physical, cultural, ecological) *spheres* of reality. In other words, although the 'truths' connected to fluid and viscous layers of reality may change, this does not mean that 'anything goes'. We are able to make more or less reasonable and well-founded interpretations of the loose field of possibilities within which we live; understand, describe and assess different social practices in relation to their relevant contexts.

In addition to the different layers of reality, we may also pay attention to various (distinct or overlapping) *spheres* of the complex reality as typically highlighted by

---

[6] I will develop the idea of field of possibilities further in a forthcoming article (Kekäle forthcoming).

different disciplines. When we, for example, view the world as an ecological whole, the worry about the state of our environment is well grounded. But when we concentrate on a company's standing within man-made economic systems, the worry about losing the competitive edge may come to the forefront. Both these viewpoints start from a certain distinct value orientation or perspective, and they both concentrate on certain spheres of reality. They both are, paradoxically, grounded on facts. Both seem reasonable when viewed within their own disciplinary frameworks (both of them stress the conditions necessary for 'surviving' within the sphere in question)[7], but not necessarily when viewed from the value-orientation of the other framework.

During unproblematic periods and 'normal times' it is easy to live life by concentrating (mainly or solely) on a certain sphere of reality. However, severe economic crisis such as the one described in chapter 2 is bound to bring economic values into the forefront, whereas at least that kind of ecological crisis which threatens to affect our lives reminds us about the importance of ecological values. While it is always possible to highlight only certain aspects or spheres of reality, gradually changing conditions and surprising events may sometimes change our mind-sets and values.

This kind of multi-layered and multi-dimensional conception of reality is perhaps not without its problems, but it would seem to help us to understand conflicting, but equally 'true' views which pay attention to different aspects of reality. Similarly, when we are trying to understand the multi-layered and multi-dimensional nature of the field within which those who are in charge in academic departments have to work, an insistence on applying opposite ends of dichotomies such as realism/relativism or objectivism/subjectivism seems to me to be problematic and misleading. Schwandt (1994, 132) maintains that such dichotomies "simply are not very useful any more" (see also Leininger 1994, 110-111). Alvesson (1993, 1007) notes:

> I resist a clear-cut objectivist or realist dualism between rhetoric, ideology, symbols and other 'non-real' elements on one hand and the real, the true, substance and other 'non-invented' stuff on the other hand, and resist also a strong rhetorical, relativist, symbolist, postmodernist or subjectivist thesis in which all distinctions between reality and appearance are viewed as fictions. I am not denying that sometimes we can sort out the real from fabricated - the holocaust was not a fiction; it is more likely that a person will survive an operation by a surgeon than by a witch doctor. Most interesting research questions in social science do not, however, fit into such a pattern of thinking. The constructedness of reality and the reality of construction, the realness of symbols and the symbolic character of reality should be borne in mind... especially, perhaps, when KIFs [Knowledge Intensive Firms] are studied.

---

[7] In chapter 5, I shall discuss the spheres of different disciplinary fields insofar as they affect the leadership issues in academic departments.

Yet the classic bipolar logic seems to force us into making the choice between strictly opposite positions. Moreover, the demand that one should be consistent either with the subjectivist or the objectivist stance makes it impossible to overcome this kind of unfruitful dichotomy[8] and forces one to extremes which are problematic (see Alasuutari 1994, 63).

My assumption is that my interview data (at least potentially) reflects the respondent's views, values and interpretations about academic leadership. By discussing key issues with the respondents and by observing their interactions, I supposedly will be able to understand and gain relevant insights into the leadership cultures of their departments, and their views about related considerations, although this understanding is bound to be incomplete and partial. Moreover, this thesis will inevitably be dealing with my interpretations, which are, however, grounded on the respondents' views, and, therefore, correspond to something in the cultural sphere I have studied. In other words, I believe that there is some objectivity intertwined with the subjectivity of my interpretations. Without an ability to understand and interpret each other our social life would be impossible. When discussing my findings and interpretations, I will point out the grounds for my views.

As noted in the previous chapter, data can be interpreted from several theoretical perspectives, and the lessons learned cannot necessarily be directly applied to other contexts (Birnbaum 1989, 209; section 3.1.1.). This position also takes into account the possibility that the opinions of the respondents may be conflicting, changeable, 'fluid' or ambivalent. On the other hand, some values and preferences of the respondents may be - to use the previously presented metaphor - more 'viscous' and constant, thus providing rather stable grounds for comments and notions, which are valid at least in these basic conditions.

Some aspects of the interview data may be more precise (e.g. the age of a respondent, or a description of a concrete behaviour observed by many respondents), while other parts may deal with more fuzzy interpretations or phenomena (e.g. a respondent's ambivalent views of the importance and meaning of leadership). However, I would claim that such fuzzy aspects may be as important as the more precise aspects: those who are in a leading position must live in the cultural realm, and take into account the more or less clear emotional commitments of those they lead. During the course of this study, I will offer interpretations of the significance and the 'degree of solidness' (in the meaning

---

[8] *The law of the excluded middle* states that everything must be *either* true *or* false. Rejection of this principle may indeed lead, as Trigg (1993, 54) suggests, to a weak form of relativism, but not necessarily to the principle that "there is nothing against which different claims can be measured". As the discussion in the previous and present chapter have suggested, it is often possible to find claims, ideas and practices which seem to be valid and hold true in a particular context, but not necessarily in others. Neither do we have to be imprisoned forever in our own context: although our cultural sphere and our theories more or less affect our interpretations, knowledge is not an "exclusively social category" (Trigg 1993, 151). The paradox is that we are grounded in a particular social community, and yet we sometimes,

> somehow have the ability to abstract ourselves from our situation and apprehend at least something of what is true about ourselves and about the world we live in. We are not then just following the rules of our community (Trigg 1993, 223).

described above) of the views of the respondents on the basis of the available material, by using certain theoretical and conceptual tools.

4.2. RESEARCH METHODS

I have chosen to use qualitative research methods, which involves an attempt to "study things in their natural settings" and "to make sense of, or interpret, phenomena in terms of meanings people bring to them" (Denzin & Lincoln 1994, 2; see preface). This basic choice is very much in line with the approach of cultural studies in general (e.g. Schein 1985; Becher 1989a; Kekäle 1991 and 1993a). The main research method in this study was interviewing. There were practical reasons for this choice: it would have been very difficult to arrange long periods of participant observation at the eight departments under study. The researcher's participation could well have changed the nature of the situations to be observed, since the purpose of the study was well known by the participants. Moreover, it would have been unlikely that I could manage to be present in the informal but important circumstances in which many decisions are prepared or made, and where important aspects of leadership are manifested. My assumption was that I would be better able to create (or contribute to the development of) a climate of trust during individual interviews, where each respondent would be on his/her own and free to speak his/her mind without having to guard against possible reactions of other members of the staff. Later on, the views of the individual respondents could be easily compared.

Moreover, as noted already in the introductory chapter, in some departments I have been able to compare my interview data with the picture gained through prior participant observation. In many cases, I have been able to compare the respondents' views with the information and interpretations derived from my previous studies of the same disciplinary tribes (Kekäle 1991; 1993a; Kekäle & Kuittinen 1993)[9]. To some extent, triangulation between the different methods of these studies (participant observation, non-active role-playing, group interviews and individual interviews; see Kekäle 1995b) has been possible.

---

[9] In practice, my contacts with these disciplinary tribes started in the beginning of the 1990s. The first mentioned study (Kekäle 1991) dealt with climates of discussion and student cultures within three different fields of study (including biology), which represent three academic cultures as identified by Snow (1969): The cultures of literary intellectuals (humanities), natural science and the so-called third culture (some areas of social sciences), which contains elements of the two other cultures. The research methods were group interviews and non-active role-playing. The second research (Kekäle 1993a) was a case study dealing with the organizational culture of a university department (section 3.3.). The case-study was based on interviews and participant observation (for short English summary of these works, see Kekäle 1995b). Altogether eight departments participated in the pedagogical development project, in which I worked as a researcher in 1991-1993 (Kekäle & Kuittinen 1993). Three of them are among the disciplines and departments participating in this study. The development project involved frequent meetings with the staff at each department, as well as interviews with the researchers. In all cases, I wrote descriptions of the situations I participated in as soon as possible after the meetings.

Interviews can range from structured to unstructured (Fontana & Frey 1994). The former type aims at capturing precise data and at explaining behaviour within pre-established categories, while the latter is used in an attempt to understand complex behaviour without limiting the field of inquiry by imposing any a priori categorization (Fontana & Frey 1994, 366). During most interviews, the interviewer more or less controls the situation and directs the interaction with his/her questions and nonverbal communication (Puuronen 1995, 67). Consequently, as Silverman (1993, 208) puts it: "all data is mediated by our own reasoning as well as that of participants". In order to give more room for the voices of participants, but to remain within a loose framework chosen by myself, I have used semi-structured interviews. I have not attempted to analyze the non-verbal interactions during interviews, neither the form nor the local character of the interview talk (conversation analysis and discourse analysis; see for example Silverman 1993; Puuronen 1995).

As in Becher's (1989a, 174-175) study, my interviews can be characterized as semi-structured and in-depth. I had a general checklist of points and questions to be raised (appendix 1), but the respondent's interests conditioned the order and form in which points were introduced during the discussions. I also adopted Becher's (1989a) approach in stipulating that not every interview need span the complete agenda, although the main themes were usually discussed with each respondent[10]. In Becher's words: the study can be seen

> as analogous with detective investigation, in which significant clues can be followed up and interesting testimony corroborated with (or contradicted by) other witnesses (Becher 1989a, 174-175).

By adopting this kind of open-ended approach, it was possible to discuss those unanticipated but closely related topics which seemed to be particularly important for the respondent, and which appeared to provide relevant information about the issues under study. I was also able to ask for the respondents' explanations and views about the backgrounds of the phenomena and the practises they were describing.

4.3. THE CHOICE OF THE DEPARTMENTS TO BE STUDIED

The departments to be studied were chosen to represent different disciplinary cultures on the basis of Becher's (1989a) study 'Academic Tribes and Territories' (I will discuss his frame in more detail in the next chapter). Because I wished to take into account this disciplinary context, it was my deliberate intention to study academic leadership in sufficiently different disciplinary settings (see Kekäle 1994b). So I chose the departments of **physics**, **biology**, **history** and **sociology** at two Finnish universities. The basic

---

[10] As will be seen later, there is one partial exception to this rule: I did not discuss all the general features of the discipline with sociologists as thoroughly as with the respondents in the other fields, since I studied sociology for my second master's degree.

disciplines were studied in two universities, so that also comparisons between departments representing the same discipline could be made. In other words, this enabled me to make useful comparisons between disciplinary perspectives on one hand (chapter 5), and departmental cultures on the other (chapter 6). Because I aimed at qualitative case studies, my approach inevitably limited the number of departments to be studied. It would have been impossible for me to study comparative departments at three universities, and still be able to complete the study in three years.

The choice of the disciplines was also guided by the following practical considerations. First, I wanted to use my previous studies (Kekäle 1991; 1993a; Kekäle & Kuittinen 1993) as points of reference, and to study disciplines of which I already had some previous experience, based on research and consultancy. Second, some disciplines studied by Becher (1989a) are not represented at the universities which I planned to study[11], which ruled them out from the research: but the ones I chose are, giving a further context. The third point concerns my personal interest in these particular disciplines, which I thought would help to maintain motivation and concentration during a long and extensive study.

I was aware of a dilemma inherent in this kind of research: namely that the researcher should provide enough information about the organizations under study, and yet at the same time protect the identity of the subjects[12]. It seems very difficult to solve this problem completely. As Kaukonen (1990, 40) notes:

> I have also experienced - while studying the interviews of Finnish social scientists - that it is often most difficult to draw a substantiated line between what is a personal matter and should not be made public and what is of more general interest.

My solution to these problems is the following:

1. I have sought to study departments which appear to work well. Consequently, I initially picked departments whose production of basic and doctoral degrees is (according to the statistics) above average among the departments within their faculty[13]. Arguably,

---

[11] There were practical reasons for the choice of universities, such as my previous knowledge of them, and some useful personal contacts which helped me to get started with the empirical study. The relatively small size of the departments helped me to achieve a better picture of the leadership cultures during the study.

[12] For example, Fontana and Frey (1994, 372) stress the following ethical aspects which should be taken into consideration in qualitative research: informed consent (received from the subject after he/she has been carefully and truthfully informed about the research); right to privacy (protecting the identity of the subject); protection from harm (physical, emotional, or any other kind).

[13] This criterion was used especially in the university A, which was first thought to be the major university to be studied (Kekäle 1993c). In the year 1995, however, also the departments of university B were studied in an equally thorough manner, so that valid comparisons between two departments representing the same basic discipline could be made (Becher 1989a). Roughly, the studied departments of university B gave an impression of or unproblematic functioning and

this can be taken at least as a rough indicator of the reasonably unproblematic functioning of the departments. Studying basic units which are facing severe problems in terms of productivity or leadership would have been difficult in this respect: publication of my findings might cause additional harm for departments already in crisis.

2. As far as possible, the universities to which the studied departments belong will not be explicitly identified. Instead, I will refer to them as **University A** and **B**. It nonetheless seems impossible to disguise my cases completely, since I will have to provide some background information concerning them.

3. Partly because of this, the analysis was discussed with the respective staffs before the publication of the dissertation. This was done by sending the preliminary empirical analyses to the departments, including both a preliminary version of my first article based on data gathered in 1994 (Kekäle 1994b), and the preliminary versions of the empirical parts of chapter 5 and 6 dealing with the department in question[14]. In this way the subjects, or their representatives, were able to comment on interpretations that might seem harmful, or which did not, in their opinion, capture their views or practices.

4.4. ACCESS

I started to negotiate the access to departments by contacting (by telephone) the heads of the departments. During this introductory call, I gave a short description of the purpose and the background of the study. This short introduction included the following aspects:

1. The research is a doctoral dissertation dealing with leadership issues in different disciplines and departments.

2. The study will take three years to complete; it is funded by the Ministry of Education.

3. It has been prompted in part by changes in the legal authority and position of the head of departments, the decline in economic resources and the increased emphasis on efficiency.

---

increasing productivity on the basis of statistics concerning the numbers of basic and postgraduate degrees produced. This impression was reinforced on the basis of the interviews.

[14] I sent the preliminary versions to one or two key figures in each department. In the covering letter, I asked them to copy or to give the analysis to everyone willing to comment. In 1994, one physicist commented my analysis; in 1996, altogether two respondents (a historian and a sociologist) expressed their views on the preliminary text. All these commentators basically agreed with the general line of my interpretations, but suggested some minor corrections, or aspects to be pointed out which were not previously brought up. I have placed the comments in footnotes in the passages where the issues are discussed.

4. In terms of possible issues to be raised, I am interested in hearing researchers' views of leadership in their departments and disciplines, in the context of the recent changes. For example:

- what kind of leadership practices can be found in the different departments?
- what kind of opinions about good leadership do the department's researchers have?
- what kind of tasks and practical issues are connected to the leadership at the level of academic departments?
- what is the meaning and significance of the academic leadership in different departments?

5. I am especially interested in each respondent's own opinions and experiences.

6. Each interview is expected to last between one and two hours.

7. The interviews are confidential and the identity of the individual respondents will be disguised as far as possible.

8. The staff will be given a chance to comment on the interpretations and the findings of the study before the publishing of the thesis.

After this introduction, I asked each head of department if he and the staff of the department in question would be willing to participate in the research. I also suggested that I might visit the department in order to inform the researchers about the project, if and when this would be suitable (see chapter 1). At university A, this procedure was followed. During the short meetings with the faculty in each department, I communicated basically the same information as described above. If the staff agreed to participate, I usually contacted each would-be respondent later by telephone in order to arrange the personal interviews at a suitable time in his/her office. At university B, I introduced the project for each potential interviewee along the same lines when I contacted them by telephone. After that, I asked about their willingness to participate.

Seven departments out of eight immediately volunteered to participate in the study. In one of the departments of sociology, suspicions about the purpose and the potential uses of the study were expressed. However, after a period of consideration and negotiations, most of the faculty members finally decided to participate. In general, women respondents seemed to express more hesitation than men when they considered their participation in the study. The negotiations with women tended to be longer, too, since they often requested more information about the study and more justification for their participation than their male fellow researchers did. All in all, three women as opposed to two men refused to participate, while the overall ratio of men to women was forty three to thirteen in my sample.

4.5. THE PHASES OF THE STUDY

The research process can be loosely divided into two phases. The first, preliminary phase of the study, carried out in 1994, was based on thirty interviews conducted in the spring of 1994. In this phase the frame of reference was leadership in the context of disciplinary and departmental cultures. In the preliminary phase, the study was connected to a project developing academic leadership at the University of Joensuu (Hölttä & Pulliainen 1992; Hölttä & Halonen 1994). Consequently, the practical aim of the phase was to identify leadership cultures that worked well and were considered as good and valid by the researchers of the given department (for a report on this phase of study, see Kekäle 1994b; 1995a).

In the second phase of the study (1995 and 1996), academic leadership was analyzed from other theoretical frames of reference (Kekäle 1995d). However, the main focus of the research remained on the relationship between leadership and the cultures of the different departments. I carried out twenty-six additional interviews during the spring of 1995. In 1996, I moved to England (University of Sussex) for a year, where I finished the dissertation under the supervision of Professor Tony Becher.

4.6. THE INTERVIEWS AND THE RESPONDENTS

The interactive interviews were organized on the basis of Schein's (1985), Becher's (1989a) and Tierney's (1988) theoretical frameworks (appendix 1). This highlights the fact that my starting point was organizational and disciplinary culture research (Kekäle 1993a; 1994b; 1995b). Maassen (1996) sees these as the basic approaches to studying culture in higher education; my idea has been to combine them in this study of academic leadership in its cultural contexts. Starting from such a perspective, I was interested in leadership issues as well as the related cultural practices, values and assumptions of different departmental and disciplinary communities.

Rather than studying organizations as such, the organizational culture approach sees them as open systems and takes to some degree into account the dynamics of an organization with its environment (Schein 1985) - although the main emphasis is usually on internal culture of an organization. Since Finnish higher education was facing the worst economic recession on record during the time when the interviews were carried out (chapter 2), I assumed that this approach might be particularly fruitful. I also took the view that the disciplinary context might affect leadership.

Before the actual interviews, I discussed the basic checklist of interview questions with several colleagues. The questions used were formed after these discussions. After the first interview cycle, I made some minor alterations to the basic checklist by adding or removing a few questions for the interviews made in 1995 (see appendix 1).

During the spring of 1994 and 1995, as already noted, I interviewed altogether fifty six (56) researchers in eight departments representing the disciplines of history, sociology, biology and physics at two Finnish universities. In each department, the respondents represented all the levels or groups within the administrative and scientific hierarchy: The heads of departments, members of professorial staff (full and associate professors), representatives of research assistants and lecturers. Four to ten members of staff were interviewed in each department, the number of permanent posts varying from five to twenty six in the departments in question (Table 1).

The respondents were chosen on the basis of their availability, by contacting, in random order, the researchers listed in the telephone books of the universities in question. In other words, I phoned a certain researcher; if I could not get in touch with him or her, I phoned another potential respondent. I repeated this practice until enough interviews with respondents representing the professional groups and departments were arranged. I interviewed mainly those members of academic staff who had at least a master's degree in the subject and who participated in the daily tasks of their department (research, teaching and administration) on a regular basis. Part-time lecturers and researchers (who, for example, visit the departments only during short periods of lecturing) were excluded from the sample, because of their (assumed) lack of involvement with the day-to-day leadership practices. I did, however, interview some younger researchers working as assistants on the research projects of the departments, because in some cases they were the only female members of the staff.

During the first interview cycle in the spring of 1994, all respondents but one were men. All the interviewed department heads were men as well. Consequently, this phase of the study could not take adequate account of the experiences of female academic leaders. As said, the purpose of the study was to focus on leadership issues in different departmental and disciplinary cultures; to compare the relevant differences in terms of gender was not the main objective. However, during the second interview cycle in 1995, I tried to overcome the imbalance in the sample by interviewing more women. I interviewed two female professors and ten female researchers. There still remains an evident imbalance in absolute terms, but not in relation to the basic population of the researchers in the departments to be studied: the ratio of interviewed men to women was approximately 3:1, while the overall ratio of men to women was approximately 4:1 among the holders of permanent research/teaching posts at the studied departments[15].

The interviews took place at the offices of the respondents. No others were present during interviews, all of which were recorded. Each interview lasted between 1/2 - 2 1/2 hours. The variation in length depended on factors such as the time set aside by the respondent and the length of his/her answers. By the end of the second interview cycle, the same themes had been discussed several times with different respondents, so that saturation had been reached. The following table summarizes the interviews carried out at the studied departments (Table 1).

---

[15] This kind of gender gap in higher education has been widely reported in different countries (Lie et al. 1994). My female respondents generally maintained that they have been treated on a fair and an equal basis (when compared to their male counterparts) in their departments. When my data gives grounds to it, I shall point out some differences in views according to gender in my case-studies (chapter 6).

Table 1. Data base

Department	Approx. number of permanent posts for teaching/research staff	(Male/ female)	Number of interviews	(Male/ female)
University A				
Physics	15	(12/3)	10 (+8)	(8/2)
Biology	20	(14/6)	10	(7/3)
Sociology	5	(4/1)	4	(3/1)
History	8	(7/1)	6	(5/1)
University B				
Physics	26	(24/2)	9	(7/2)
Biology	20	(15/5)	6	(5/1)
Sociology	7	(6/1)	5	(4/1)
History	11	(8/3)	6	(4/2)
	112	(90/22)	56 (+8)	(43/13)

In the department of physics in university A, an action research and development project concerning academic leadership was carried out during 1995. This separate project involved three sessions and discussions with the head of department as well as about 5 additional interviews with the staff (eight additional interviews indicated in the table 1). The project-work was connected to a course on organizational consultancy in which I participated during 1994-1995.

All the studied departments or research communities are now over twenty years old. The departments can be classified as "pure" as opposed to "mixed", since the faculty members are trained, teach, and have common backgrounds in the same basic discipline (Tucker 1993, 15). The departments are generally established around single chair. In two cases the original professor still works at the department; in most cases s/he retired only some years ago. As already stressed, this is likely to underline the original professor's impact on the leadership cultures.

As noted earlier, a number of interviews prior to 1994 were carried out in university A during my previous research projects. They comprised three interviews with physicists, four interviews with biologists and five interviews with historians. In addition to these individual interviews, group interviews for students were arranged and the staff and the students of the three departments concerned were encountered during many meetings and seminars. The resulting data were not directly re-analyzed during this study, but my previous interpretations and analyses have provided background information for this research.

4.7. CODING AND ANALYSIS

Qualitative research is commonly guided by a concern to remain true or loyal to the studied phenomena, rather than to any particular set of methodological techniques or principles (Altheide & Johnson 1994, 488). Patton (1990, 372) notes that in qualitative data analysis,

> there are no absolute rules except to do the very best with your full intellect to fairly represent the data and communicate what the data reveal given the purpose of the study... However analysis is done, *analysts have an obligation to monitor and report their own analytical procedure and processes as fully and truthfully as possible.*

When assembling and analyzing the data in this study, I adopted the following procedure: the 56 main interviews conducted during 1994-1995 were recorded on audiotape. Recorded interviews were then typed (verbatim) by two professional typists in WordPerfect form. When typed, the interviews totalled over 900 pages of written text.

Then I coded the data by using WP-index program, which can be used for finding selected themes or fragments in the data so that they can be analyzed and interpreted separately. The codes dealt with themes and subjects which were central in this study. In order to take into account closely related issues and contextual factors, I chose to use broad rather than narrowly defined categories as the basis of coding. The codes referred to the following themes (see appendix 1):

- notions of social atmosphere, social relations and support
- culture, traditions and patterns of action in the department
- comparisons with the cultural practices of other departments
- leadership history, patterns and practices
- critical comments & proposals for change
- notions of well-functioning and effective leadership
- values and philosophies of leaders and respondents
- valuation of leadership tasks
- tasks and functions of leadership; power issues
- comparisons with leadership practices of other departments
- professional background of the respondents
- the primary professional reference-group of the respondents

- conceptions of good and ideal leadership
- the working environment of the department; co-operation with external bodies and quarters
- descriptions relating to the personnel (professional history, changes in personnel)
- opinions about management by objectives (MBO) and its applicability in university settings
- reward structures and values of academic culture
- features and perspectives of the discipline
- strategies of survival of the department
- comments on powerful persons in the department
- scope of academic freedom left for researchers
- gender issues; experienced differences in treatment, etc.
- initiation into work

Each fragment was usually marked with numerous codes. In principle, I started with a case-analysis of each departmental or disciplinary unit, and then continued with cross-case analyses of their differences (Patton 1990, 376). In practice, however, the two phases had considerable overlaps: while going through a particular case, its characteristics usually became visible because of their differences in relation to other cases (Heiskala 1990, 248-249).

All in all, I basically went through the data several times:

1. Preliminary understanding was reached during interviewing.

2. I read through all the interviews and coded the fragments.

3. I read through the data theme by theme, classified it, compared the views of the respondents, made summaries (in Finnish or in English) as well as initial interpretations, which I also checked.

4. Since the fragments of interview were usually marked with various codes, I read most of them several times by concentrating on different aspects. When I was reading through themes, I was often able to gain fresh insights and ideas about the interaction and connections between theme-areas, and sometimes found new or conflicting aspects.

5. After these phases I wrote the preliminary English descriptions, sometimes after the phase 3., sometimes simultaneously with it.

6. When I compared different cases, new interpretations and insights emerged.

7. The preliminary descriptions were sent to the key persons in the departments (section 4.3.). Also my English supervisor read and commented on the preliminary versions (as well as the final chapters).

8. I frequently returned to the original summaries and interview texts when I was going through the preliminary versions of the chapters 5 and 6. At this phase, I also added some illustrative fragments from the original interview data, translating the fragments to English.

Thus, in this study the WP-index -program was mainly used as a tool for cutting and pasting the data. The WP-index -program can be also used to pick up fragments which include a certain word or term. Because of this, it was easy to find and analyze fragments on the basis of inserted codes and on the basis of certain terms or words. In order to be able to check my analysis and interpretations, I saved all the versions of the text (original and coded interviews, the summaries including original fragments) and returned to them when needed. Used this way, the program leaves considerable manual work for the researcher. According to Patton (1990, 423):

> Interpretation means attaching significance to what was found, offering explanations, drawing conclusions, extrapolating lessons, making inferences, building linkages, attaching meanings, imposing order, and dealing with rival explanations, disconfirming cases, and data irregularities as part of testing the viability of an interpretation.

Interpretations largely depend on intuition, insights and sociological imagination of the researcher; no machine or program can do such creative work as s/he can (Patton 1990, 372; Bryman and Burgess 1994, 221).

4.8. A NOTE ON CREDIBILITY OF INTERPRETATIONS

In qualitative studies, the issues of accuracy, validity and generalizability are complex, problematic, controversial and paradigm specific (Altheide and Johnson 1994; Denzin 1994). Much of this seems to be connected to the "embarrassment of choices" which now characterize the field of qualitative research: "there have never been so many paradigms, strategies of inquiry, or methods of analysis to draw upon and utilize", and new ways of interpreting, arguing and writing are still being discovered and debated (Denzin & Lincoln 1994, 11).

Although the criteria are diverse and often ambiguous, most paradigms of qualitative research seem to call for some justification of their validity and credibility (Denzin & Lincoln 1994, 13). However, there are exceptions. In postmodern, poststructural and feminist texts such justifications are not apparently considered necessary (Denzin 1994, 511; see footnote 11 in chapter 5). In critical cultural studies the starting point is often to question the existing patterns of thought rather than to verify one's own hypotheses. From such a perspective, the questions of generalizability and validity are not interesting or important - raising such problems may even imply that the researcher has misunderstood his/her emancipatory task (Alasuutari 1994, 206-207; see Altheide and Johnson 1994, 488). Gergen (1989, 476) describes this emancipatory function (of social constructionists) in the following manner:

> as the investigator demonstrates variations in perspectives, the effect is to break the hold of common sense realities of contemporary culture. It is to deconstruct local ontologies, and thereby free the individual from the constraints of existing conventions.

I have tried to leave room for this kind of emancipation from existing conventions. However, it is questionable if such emancipation does automatically or in every case lead to a 'better' situation from the viewpoint of an individual. Since such views are often expressed by researchers supporting extreme relativism and subjectivism, the problem arises: why should anybody change their subjective beliefs in favour of the researcher's subjective values (section 4.1.1.)? Moreover, as I have highlighted in this chapter, research is only one force which contributes to the construction, maintenance or change of local "common sense realities". There are many other factors deriving from different 'spheres', which may have a longer history and stronger implications for the actors (see section 4.1.2.). In many cases research reports do not even reach a sufficiently wide or deep readership (although classics such as Freud and Marx have indeed broadly affected our cultural sphere). For these reasons, the positions described above seem to reflect a somewhat optimistic faith in the power and impact of research texts aiming at the deconstruction of local realities. When deeply rooted values and assumptions are in question, the viewpoint stressed by Carr and Kemmis (1986, 97) may often be closer to reality:

> It is precisely because an individual's identity is so closely related to values, beliefs and attitudes inherent in the style of thought of the social group to which he or she belongs that any alternative interpretation of what he or she is doing will be invariably resisted. Far from changing individuals' conceptions of themselves or others, any new interpretations will be perceived as an emotional threat to the individual's self-concept and discarded as 'unrealistic', 'ridiculous' or 'irrelevant'.

On the basis of their longitudinal study, Häyrynen et al. (1992b, 100) note that educational climates have not changed much in Finnish universities during the past 15-20 years. They conclude that such aspects are determined by relatively stable factors connected to educational traditions and disciplinary cultures. In this study, I have sought to describe and understand established core value-orientations and cultural patterns. I believe that such 'viscous' aspects may change over time, or when the conditions are right[16], but the postmodern criteria of unclarity and continuous change seem to apply better to 'fluid' aspects of reality (section 4.1.2.).

Since I have expressed a belief that there is some objectivity intertwined with the subjectivity[17] of my descriptions and interpretations, and because I have leaned on the assumption that my interview data (at least potentially) reflect the respondents' views, values and interpretations about academic leadership (section 4.1.2), I feel obliged briefly to address the issue of credibility and validity of the interpretations in my study. Since my data are rather substantial (section 4.6.), I cannot go into details here[18]. Instead, I shall discuss some points at a general level, which will, I hope, shed some light on the grounds of my interpretations. The following points will concern especially the analysis of my empirical data. The credibility of my views on changes in legislation and economic situation in society can be checked from various other sources, some of which were mentioned in chapter 2.

One of the main strategies for establishing and enhancing validity is triangulation, which involves "seeking information from multiple data sources, multiple methods, and multiple prior theories or interpretations, and assessing convergence" (Stiles 1992, 11; section 4.7.). Schein (1985, 135) considers triangulation of data and information and discussions with insiders as the most reliable approach when culture is studied. Patton (1990, 464) distinguishes four kinds of triangulation that contribute to the validation of qualitative analysis. These are 1) checking out the consistency of findings from different data-collection methods (methods triangulation), 2) triangulation between different data sources within the same method (triangulation of sources), 3) using multiple analysts to review findings (analyst triangulation), and 4) using multiple perspectives or theories to interpret the data (theory/perspective triangulation).

At university A, I have been able to receive insights from previous participant observations and interviews, but at university B my analysis has depended on the interviews alone (section 4.2.). Especially in relation to the characteristics of disciplines and specialisms (chapter 5), written material such as studies by other researchers have provided useful points of reference. This is obvious particularly in the case of sociology, where the numbers of responses to certain questions were low, but where my years of experience in studying the area provided me with the most substantial background among the disciplines studied.

---

[16] Fundamental and deep changes of such core aspects would seem to require personal commitment and psychical work - a construction of a new direction and identity (see Kuittinen & Kekäle 1995). This psychical work can be helped by outsiders if there is motivation to receive such help, but in any case, the actual work must be done by the individuals concerned. In this sense, a research may often change *its author* most, if only s/he is willing to reflect his/her own values and assumptions.

[17] My interpretations are inevitably based on certain perspectives and assumptions, but they may still be grounded on reasonable insights into empirical data and on diverse contextual factors (section 4.1.2.): while it would be impossible to highlight all the aspects of the complex issues under discussion, the points I shall raise in the forthcoming chapters seem nonetheless relevant.

[18] I have sought to point out the grounds for my interpretations in each relevant section of the text. I have discussed my methodology and assumptions in this chapter, and theoretical perspectives in chapters 3, 5, 6 and 7 (see Patton 1990, 461).

In all cases I have used triangulation of sources by comparing the views of different respondents in relation to each theme discussed during the interviews; this means not only the consistency of the views by different persons, but also the consistency of the views expressed by the same respondent (section 4.7.). However, it should be noted that I shall mainly discuss the leadership issues at the departmental level in an idealtypical sense: while I shall point out relevant differences between the respondents' views, it would have been impossible (and, given the level of analysis, beside the point) to try to bring out all the subtle differences between the individual ways of expressing things. I have also compared the views inspired by different cultural perspectives (chapter 5 and 6) and by other theoretical perspectives as well (chapter 3). Analyst triangulation or peer debriefing (Stiles 1992, 13) have not been carried out as such, but my numerous colleagues and the referees of my papers have commented on my analyses and the coherence of my interpretations (see preface).

Since the interviews were carried out in two different cycles, and since I carried out several interviews in each department, I have been able to check and discuss my preliminary interpretations with many respondents. (As pointed out in section 4.3., I also sent my preliminary empirical analyses to the departments and asked the respondents to comment them.) Sometimes the comments led me to rethink my interpretations, but usually the support provided by respondents' comments seemed to add to what has been called representional validity, credibility, or testimonial validity (Stiles 1992, 12). However, this may not be sole criterion of validity, since the "participant may not understand himself or herself, or the interpretation may be targeting a self-deception" (Stiles 1992).

In his discussion of external validity[19] in case studies, Yin (1989, 43-44) maintains that survey research relies on statistical generalization, whereas case studies rely on analytical generalization, in which the researcher is striving to "generalize a particular set of results to some broader theory". In chapters 5 and 6, I have attempted to do that in relation to Becher's (1989a) frame, and in relation to the theoretical framework presented in section 6.2.

---

[19] Yin (1989, 40-45) discusses four types of validity in relation to case-studies: construct validity, internal validity, external validity and reliability. Construct validity is partly connected to the triangulation of sources and methods. It also involves the establishment of a chain of evidence and key informants to review draft case study reports. As noted, I have tried to make the grounds for my interpretations explicit in each segment, and I have sent draft versions to key informants (section 4.3.). Internal validity means checking my inferences, which I have tried to do in each case. However, as Yin (1989, 43) observes, the specific tactics for this are especially difficult to identify in case studies. Reliability means that another researcher who replicated the same case studies would arrive at the same findings and conclusions (Yin 1989, 45). This criterion has some positivistic overtones which seem problematic for several reasons: interpretations largely depend on the intuition, insights and sociological imagination of the researcher and may thus vary according to the observer; it is always possible to pay attention to other relevant, revealing aspects in the studied cases; and some aspects of the field being studied may change. However, I believe that the basic cultural patterns and the major contextual pressures for leadership would have been identified by any qualitative researcher studying the same cases.

On the basis of the data and research literature, I have made interpretations about academic leadership in its disciplinary and departmental context, and have sought to describe, interpret and understand the background of current leadership cultures of the departments, as well as the head's position within this context. This analysis will be presented in the following chapters.

Chapter 5

DISCIPLINARY CULTURES AND ACADEMIC LEADERSHIP

Within academic disciplines and specialisms, relatively stable patterns and unifying aspects as well as forces of fragmentation can be identified (Becher 1987c; Becher & Huber 1990). Overlaps between disciplinary borders (e.g. biochemistry), migration, changes in orientation and the increasing number of subspecialisms all contribute to the impression of complexity and a "constantly changing kaleidoscope of smaller components" (Becher 1990a, 333).

At the same time established disciplines and specialisms - in broad outline - seem to contain and favour some inherent and distinct features, values and perspectives, which highlight different spheres or aspects of the world. For example, a biologist and an economist would probably highlight different relevant viewpoints of global industrialization (section 4.1.2.); the psychological, juridical and economic consequences of an accident may be completely different (see also Becher 1994, 59). In a similar manner, expectations concerning good leadership may be different in distinctive disciplinary communities.

In this chapter, I will concentrate on those social and cognitive aspects of the disciplines and specialisms under study which apparently have an impact on academic leadership. One of my points of departure is Becher's (1987c; 1990a, 334) notion that - depending on our purpose at the time - we may legitimately discuss knowledge fields at different (e.g. sub-disciplinary, disciplinary, or more general) levels. In this chapter, I adopt a perspective of disciplinary culture study (Becher 1987a; 1989a; see Maassen 1996) and use the term disciplinary feature to refer to those ideal-typical value-orientations and aspects which seem to be 'inherent' and relevant to the discipline or specialism in question (given its perspectives or tasks).

I follow in Becher's (1989a, 4) footsteps in that I adopt an internalist rather than externalist standpoint in this chapter; that is, I concentrate on disciplinary features instead of paying attention to the broader political or economic structures in which human inquiry takes place (the latter viewpoint is often stressed by sociologists of knowledge (e.g. Huber 1990; for broad contextual factors, see chapter 2). Since I have studied

Finnish universities I will not systematically stress the differences between disciplinary communities in different countries as demonstrated, for example, by Becher (1987a, 182-183). In other words, although I speak about disciplinary features, I do not claim that all the aspects I discuss will necessarily apply to other distinct sub-disciplinary, national or social contexts. My sample is too small to allow broad generalizations. But when findings are compared to international studies like that of Becher's (1989a), some features which seem to be typical to the discipline or specialism can be pointed out. In this sense, we can also speak about preferred disciplinary leadership patterns: that is, idealtypical styles of leadership which seem to be connected to the international disciplinary cultures. The actual departmental leadership patterns may vary somewhat depending on local aspects and social processes in departments, but the disciplinary basis nonetheless affects leadership.

In what follows, I shall discuss those features and perspectives of the studied disciplines and specialisms which show up in comparison with other fields under study, which are relevant on the basis of research literature, and which are identified and stressed by the respondents. Such aspects are not necessarily shared by all the respondents, but the features in question seem nonetheless relevant and dominant enough to sustain and favour certain leadership patterns within the disciplinary community in question. As the need arises, I will make further distinctions between different specialisms. Before discussing my interpretations and empirical findings, I will review Becher's (1989a) frame, which formed a basic theoretical framework for this chapter and study.

5.1. BECHER'S (1989A) FRAME

As pointed out in the previous chapter, I have chosen to study academic leadership in distinctive disciplinary and departmental settings. The departments studied were chosen to represent different disciplinary cultures on the basis of Becher's (1989a) study 'Academic Tribes and Territories': the departments of **physics, biology, history** and **sociology** at two Finnish universities. These departments also represent the three broader academic cultures identified by Snow (1969), namely the cultures of humanities (literary intellectuals), science and the so called third culture, which contains elements of the two other broad cultures[1]. This third culture represents disciplines such as sociology, psychology, medicine and architecture.

Becher (1989a) divides disciplines into different categories by separating the cognitive and social dimensions of the discipline (Becher & Huber 1990, 235). These dimensions represent the epistemological aspects of the discipline (the intellectual content or 'territory') as well as social features of academic communities or 'tribes'.

---

[1] Snow's (1969) study was a starting point also for Becher (1989a, xi), who considered that it offered "a superficial and conceptually flawed polarization between the worlds of the sciences and humanities".

The **cognitive dimension** includes a continuum from hard to soft sciences as well as a continuum from pure to applied sciences[2]. *Hard* fields tend to have a well-developed theoretical structure embracing universal laws, causal propositions and generalizable findings. The knowledge is cumulative. Hard sciences lean on quantitative issues and measurements - for example the language of physics is mathematics. *Soft* knowledge, on the other hand, has unclear boundaries and a relatively unspecific theoretical structure. It focuses on qualitative and particular issues and broad and loosely defined problems. In hard fields the methods tend to determine the research problems, whereas in soft fields the opposite pattern seems to be typical. Although the distinction is not always extremely sharp, *pure* knowledge is essentially self-regulating whereas *applied* knowledge areas are basically open to external influence (Becher 1989a, 150-154)[3].

By their **social dimension**, disciplines can be divided into convergent or divergent and urban or rural fields of inquiry. *Convergent* fields maintain a relatively stable elite and reasonably uniform standards and procedures. *Divergent* fields (in the opposite end of the continuum) lack these features; researchers in these disciplines tolerate "a greater measure of intellectual deviance", in some cases "degenerating into self-destructive disputation" (Becher 1989a, 154).

Urban researchers occupy a narrow section of intellectual territory. Their pattern of communication is intense and their 'people-to-problem ratio' is high: the number of issues being pursued is relatively small, though the number of researchers working on them may be quite substantial (Becher 1989a, 77-78). Problems are likely to have short-term solutions. *Rural* researchers span a broader territory, which is not sharply distinguished. The 'people-to-problem ratio' tends to be low. Articulating solutions to research problems takes considerably more time (Becher 1989a, 154).

All the chosen disciplines represent mainly pure fields of enquiry, although the department of physics of university A has been recently moving towards applied research. (Because of the dramatic budget cuts (chapter 2), there is a growing pressure to acquire external funding from all possible sources.) However, the studied disciplines are quite different in relation to the other continua: **Physics** represents a hard and mostly pure science, which is convergent and urban in its social aspect. **History** is a soft and pure discipline, relatively convergent and rural. **Sociology** is a soft, divergent, rural, and pure discipline, whereas **biology** is a pure, mostly rural science, which is also a mixture of soft and hard elements. It may be located somewhere between the ends of the convergent vs. divergent dimension. It should be noted that these properties are relative rather than absolute and their attributions may change in time and place (Becher 1989a, 150-158). Figure 1 shows the locations of the chosen disciplines in relation to Becher's (1989a) framework.

---

[2] These continua were also used by Biglan (1973; quoted in Becher 1989a, 11).
[3] Becher (1989a) views these cognitive dimensions as interrelated. Since my cases are predominantly pure, I shall concentrate in this study mainly on hard/pure and soft/pure knowledge areas.

Figure 1. The Disciplines of Physics, Biology, History and Sociology in Becher's (1989a)
Taxonomy of Disciplinary Cultures

Cognitive Dimension

Hard	Physics	Biology	History	**Soft**
			Sociology	

	Biology	
Pure	Physics	**Applied**
	History	
	Sociology	

Social Dimension

Convergent Physics History   Biology Sociology **Divergent**

Urban Physics   Biology History **Rural**
                                                   Sociology

5.2. INTERPRETATIONS OF DISCIPLINARY PERSPECTIVES AND VALUES

The following analysis dealing with disciplinary differences is based on about 240 pages of text, which represents over one fourth part of my whole interview data. This is the part of my interviews which was based on themes for discussion inspired by Becher's (1989a) study (appendix 1). I shall discuss here those issues which seem to contribute to leadership within the specialism in question. The rest of my interview data deals with more specific questions connected to departmental (leadership) features, and is to be discussed in the next chapter[4].

If I had to mention just one feature, perspective or value-orientation that seems to be typical of each specialism under study on the basis of my data, I would choose the following: valuation of hard and exact knowledge in physics, emphasis on democracy and emancipation in (critical) sociology, the individualistic tradition of history and the green values and concern for environmental issues in biology (ecology). Such values may of course be held by persons with different backgrounds: a historian, for example, may worry about the state of environment as much as a biologist. The perspectives mentioned are not necessarily universal or shared by all scholars of the field, either. Indeed, there seems to be variation in relation to different individuals and subgroups. However, these

---

[4] The main focus of the interviews was usually on the features of the given department (appendix 1). In many cases disciplinary differences can be analyzed also in relation to such questions, since the studied departments were chosen on the basis of disciplinary differences, and since two separate departments were always chosen to represent each field of study. The relevant departmental data were tested against the material discussed in this chapter.

features were frequently brought out as inherent and typical for the discipline or specialism in question; the variation between specialisms is much greater than it is within a specialism, where such issues are concerned.

Thus, when we speak about different emphases, priorities, and degrees of commitment to certain values, the connections mentioned between the studied disciplines, specialisms and different perspectives or values seem to arise on the basis of the data. Next, I will discuss these distinctive, idealtypical perspectives and values in more detail, relating them to Becher's (1989a) frame and to the social and leadership features of the studied departments. This will be followed by discussion about the respondents' views on the existence of schools of thought and on mobility between specialisms.

5.2.1. The Individualistic Tradition of History

The individualistic nature of research work in history (and humanities) was stressed by all respondents in the discipline. This was explicitly considered as a central feature of the discipline; "history has no tradition of team work" (Becher 1987c, 289; Becher, 1989b, 271). Two researchers mentioned that nowadays there is a tendency towards project work, but the individualistic tradition seems to change slowly. The respondents in both departments mentioned that researchers work largely on their own even in the context of projects. The following quotation[5] describes this:

> [Our research] has been traditionally quite individualistic, no uniting themes.. it has been a tradition: 'may thousands of flowers blossom'... Recently we have organized students around some kind of themes... at the moment it seems that a certain kind of project might be a certain century... but even this has been quite unusual...

In part the knowledge of soft and rural discipline seems to lead to individualistic manners of work, despite the intellectual kinship of a convergent science (Becher 1989a, 156; Becher 1987c, 289). Since the source material is mainly in written form, the division of work becomes the issue. Some respondents stressed that it is difficult to divide loose research problems with unclear boundaries into meaningful, closely related, but not too much overlapping sub-problems, which would then be studied in groups by two or more researchers. Instead, researchers or students simply choose their own problems or themes and end up working on their own; there are plenty of topics to choose from, so there is no point in choosing the same topic as someone else (Becher 1989a, 79).

---

[5] Quotations were translated by the author. When compared to the Finnish originals, the passages are not always full in length, but the missing sections are marked with three dots (...). Questions in *italics* were made by the author. In all cases, I have tried the keep the information content of the translated fragments as close to the original as possible. In some cases I have added clarifications within square brackets.

But the values of the researchers seem to be involved, too. Some historians seemed to value and emphasize originality and the contribution of an individual (Becher 1989b, 271). One professor of history, for example, argued that the academic freedom and trust of the individual are the best features of academic life; too collective a mode of study would only hinder the researchers from being creative and from doing their work. In the other department, a lecturer had tried to get students to work together on their master's thesis. A couple of years later he gave up, since the students were obviously unwilling to work in pairs. According to him, a similar preference for personal work is typical of the department and discipline, too. It is expected that everyone should carve their own niche:

> [The pattern of work is...] strongly individualistic. There have been some projects.. if you can call them projects; researchers work on similar themes, but there are no common, regular meetings and the 'project' has no leader...
>
> *So everyone works on their own?*
>
> Yes. This is the typical pattern, at least in our department, and I think it is typical for history in general... few years ago I tried to get the students to work in groups, but the results were not promising... they wanted to work on their own... it may depend also on supervision, but I gave up...

The individualistic pattern of history was not always seen in an entirely positive light. In department A, for example, some researchers felt that their department lacks a clear strategy, since everyone is just minding their own businesses. Especially young researchers with only temporary appointments stressed that some kind of common strategy would be essential because of the dramatic budget cuts, whose first effect will be to shorten the tenure of young scholars (Kekäle 1995c; section 2.3.2.).

The head of the department A pointed out that the head's possibilities of defining priorities and strategies are limited, since researchers ought to have the right to define the research problems by themselves[6]. Because of the nature and tradition of research work, it is not easy to find common topics. The head of department thought that the professors of general history and Finnish history might have more power concerning research issues. But the professors interviewed seemed to be reluctant to use their power on issues such as teaching and research, which were seen to belong to the realm of academic freedom (see Ylikangas 1990, 27). Such a culture fundamentally affects departmental leadership, since a major part of decisions concerning basic tasks such as research and instruction are left to individual researchers. The problem seems to be that the individualistic tradition and

---

[6] A similar emphasis concerns the relations of students and supervisors in history: "In direct contrast with some scientific disciplines, it is students rather than supervisors who are called upon to choose their research topics" (Becher 1989b, 271), although supervisors in history may also prefer to work on their own special field. According to my previous study (Kekäle 1993a) two professors of history had demonstrated different leadership styles and philosophies in that regard (section 3.3.).

emphasis on academic freedom is in contradiction with some recent trends in academia, such as the decline of resources, the pressure to concentrate on certain strong areas of study and the emphasis on project work in research (chapter 2; Becher 1994, 62-63).

In line with the individualistic tradition of history, leadership styles in the departments studied have been quite personal. When compared to other fields and departments, there seems to be far more variation according to person: no clear departmental traditions have emerged, but the leaders have had their own preferences. According to Becher's (1989a, 156) study, however, integrating features among historians can be found, such as

> 'a sense of inhabiting a particular and definable world', a sharing of 'common assumptions and styles of thought' and a strong tradition of intellectual kinship.

The individualistic pattern discussed above seems to deal mostly with the content and patterns of academic work; the studied departments are rather small and the members of the staff see each other frequently during coffee breaks. Because of this, even some scholars from other fields considered historians as a social and a coherent group. But this may also be a local feature, since some respondents maintained that in larger Finnish universities historians prefer to work at home whenever possible. In any case, it seems that soft, rural and divergent fields are more prone to individualism in research - or at least these fields have less integrating disciplinary elements to build on. An example of a such field is sociology, which can be classified as divergent, as opposed to convergent history (Becher 1989a).

5.2.2. Critical Sociology: Emancipation and Democracy

Kleinman (1983) has studied a department of sociology at a Canadian university. She argues that students of sociology learn that "individuation is important" (Kleinman 1983, 207-210). In this case, the emphasis led to an ideology of individual work and represented the choice of special area as an individual problem which is to be solved alone. On the basis of my data, the situation seems somewhat different in those departments of sociology which I studied. I did not study culture among graduate students, as Kleinman (1983) did, but it seems to me that the cultures of the studied departments of sociology have stressed collectivism rather than individualism, as far as the issues of leadership and decision-making are concerned[7].

---

[7] Research and basic studies are not strictly individualistic either. Research is conducted both in groups and on an individual basis; the main emphasis has been on the work of sole researchers, but the trend is increasingly towards project work. In both studied departments, students often discuss the problems concerning their master's thesis in groups. Sometimes the whole staff participates in these discussions.

Possible differences in departmental cultures may be connected to the soft, fragmented and diverse nature of sociology as a discipline (Becher 1989a, 157), which allows plenty of room for variation between teams and individuals. The departments which I have studied are small and the researchers do not represent the whole spectrum of sociology. Instead, their special areas are often relatively closely related and many researchers of these departments shared a strong Marxian[8] background, which was quite common particularly among young social scientists in Finland and other countries during 60's and 70's[9]. As is well known, the Marxian approach stressed collectivism (as opposed to individualism), conflicting interests of dominant and submissive classes as well as political struggle in overcoming such antagonisms. The radical movement attempted to democratize society and universities by raising the status of the 'oppressed' (Eskola 1973, 311-313; chapter 2).

A professor of sociology connected himself to the "generation of the sixties, which tried to democratize the universities", and linked this background to their preferences concerning leadership (see section 2.3.1.). One sociologist interviewed described his own generation as "children of Marx and Freud". In broad outline, both Freud and Marx shared the emancipatory interest of knowledge (Habermas 1978; Kangas 1989): they stressed critical reflection as a means of liberation from current misery, such as

---

[8] A respondent who commented on the preliminary version of the chapter proposed that I should change the term Marxism to critical approach. He stressed that the broad "European critical tradition" - within which Marx has a central position - would be a more appropriate definition of their position. (I shall come to this broader tradition later on.) However, I have not changed the term, since many respondents - as will be seen - used the term Marxism when they discussed the backgrounds of the departments.

[9] The heyday of the radical movement in Finland was between 1968 and the late 1970's (Allardt 1995a, 110; Häyrynen et al. 1992a). According to Allardt (1995a, 116-117), the emphasis of student radicalism changed towards Marxism-Leninism around 1969-1970; the movement also became more dogmatic, and isolated itself from other schools of thought. Marxism as a research tradition was only in a state of formation at the Finnish universities during the early 1970's (Eskola 1973, 306-313), and it did not have a strong position among the paradigms of Finnish sociology of the era. However, by that time the movement had already led to polarization of the views of the conservative and radical parties (chapter 2). According to my respondents, student radicalism did not have a comparably strong impact in departments of physics and biology. The movement affected history, but not to a same degree as sociology. (In that respect, the situation seems to has been similar in UK and USA; Becher 1989b, 264-265). During the 1980's the differences in political activity of the students in different fields have narrowed (Häyrynen et al. 1992a; 1992b). However, a sociologist held that the issue is not yet discussed and worked through in a manner that would lead to an emotional emancipation from it.

oppression and 'false consciousness' (Marxism) or internal, subconscious conflicts (psychoanalysis)[10].

Although modified, the themes of power, repression and emancipation are present in critical theory (Horkheimer 1991; Kotkavirta 1991; see also Denzin 1994, 509) and in the more recent writings of Foucault (1979), Lyotard (1984) and Bourdieu (1993), who have, in diverse ways, also questioned and criticised the ideas of orthodox Marxian tradition, and attempted to broaden its perspectives (see Hammersley 1995, 22-43)[11]. When the

---

[10] There are also differences between the approaches. The situations in therapy and the struggle for political power between different classes are dissimilar in many ways (Habermas 1978, 286-279; Kangas 1989, 16). However, the general idea of emancipation remains an underlying theme which seemed appealing to the generations who celebrated their youth during the 1960's (chapter 2). Instead of seeking to maintain the current state of affairs, both Freud and Marx held the promise of providing a wider range of self-expression by self-reflection.

[11] "Bourdieu's social theory belongs to the tradition of theories of social reproduction like that of Marx as opposed to those of actions and systems" (Huber 1990, 247). Unlike Marx, Bourdieu identifies many forms of capital (economic, social, cultural, and symbolic). People compete - partly subconsciously - for different forms of capital in different fields (e.g. politics, economics, science): "rational investment and competition do not belong to the economic sphere alone" (Huber 1990, 247-250).

The Marxian utopia of society without inequalities is strong in Bourdieu's early work (Bourdieu & Passeron 1979, 71-76). Bourdieu and Passeron explicitly set the "true democratizing of education" as the ultimate goal. They make an optimistic assumption that "a truly rational pedagogy" could make all or most of the individual differences (which they view as social constructions based on differences in social background) in ability and motivation disappear. Since the success of the privileged class and the ideology of gift is based

> essentially on blindness to social inequalities in schooling and culture, mere description of relationship between academic success and social origin has a critical force (Bourdieu & Passeron 1979, 71).

In his more recent work, Bourdieu (1985; 1993) still emphasizes the critical perspective, analyzes the underlying power and interest struggles in the field of intellectuals, and speaks for the emancipatory task of the sociology of studying their activities (Bourdieu 1985, 74-80).

Generally speaking, the basic emphasis of the scholars representing postmodern approach (e.g. Foucault, Lyotard) seems to remain close to the ideals of democracy and emancipation, while efficiency, control and instrumental reason are criticised (see chapter 2). Hammersley (1995, 33) notes:

> While poststructuralism and postmodernism writing has had a considerable impact on those advocating critical approaches in the social sciences, it does not provide a more effective epistemological grounding for critique than critical theory. Indeed, while often retaining a 'critical' commitment, it generally denies any possibility of grounding, or the need to ground, critique epistemologically. On the contrary, the focus of critical attention becomes precisely such attempts at epistemological grounding, which are seen as the source of modern political repression.

Foucault (during his late 'genealogical' period; Burrell 1988) views power and knowledge as intertwined - there is no social existence without, or outside, the network of power relations. Whereas Marxians think of power negatively - as domination and repression - Foucault (Nietzscheans) views power as producing positive or creative as well as negative effects (Hoy 1989). Foucault seemed to be sceptical about the Marxian total revolution and the ideas of truth and progress, but he still attempted to raise the voice of the oppressed, to improve the status of prisoners and of representatives of sexual minorities. "Foucault's political theory is a 'tool kit' not for revolution but for local resistance", although, given his nihilistic stance, he does not give us

picture is painted in broad strokes, it can perhaps be noted that the emphasis in critique has shifted towards instrumental reason and enlightenment, the issues of efficiency and control, hidden power-games and institutionalized, disciplinary forms of power/knowledge (see Hoy 1989; Pirttilä 1993). Kincheloe and McLaren (1994, 139) describe the background of a broad critical approach[12] - which can be shared by scholars from different disciplinary fields and areas of enquiry - as follows:

> Many academicians who had come of age in the politically charged atmosphere of the 1960s focused their attention on critical theory. Frustrated by forms of domination emerging from a post-Enlightenment culture nurtured by capitalism, these scholars saw in critical theory a method of temporarily freeing academic work from these forms of power. Impressed by critical theory's dialectical concern with the social construction of experience, they came to view their disciplines as a

much reason to assume that any new moral codes and disciplines would be better than the existing ones (Hoy 1989, 141-142; Walzer 1989). Lincoln and Denzin (1994b, 579) note (in relation to their discussion of - among others - Foucault's texts):

> If validity is gone, values and politics, not objective epistemology, govern science... A post-structural social science project seeks its external grounding not in science, in any of its revisionist forms, but rather in a commitment to a post-marxism and a feminism with hope, but no quarantees... (Lincoln & Denzin 1994b, 579; see also Poster 1984).

Lyotard (1984) defines postmodernism as incredulity towards the meta-narratives which have legitimated science, such as the hermeneutics of meaning or the emancipation of the rational or working subject or the creation of wealth. However, his argumentation is in line with the critical tradition when he reveals the goals of increasing "performativity" of research and schooling (Lyotard 1984, 41-53):

> The State and/or company must abandon the idealist and humanist narratives of legitimation in order to justify the new goal: in the discourse of today's financial bankers of research, the only credible goal is power. Scientists, technicians, and instruments are purchased not to find truth, but to augment power (Lyotard 1984, 46).

Similar emphasis is obvious when he calls for "an idea and practice of justice, which is not linked to that of consensus" (Lyotard 1984, 66-67). In the foreword of Lyotard's (1984) book Jameson (1984) still ranges Lyotard - a former Marxian, but "no longer a revolutionary of the traditional kind" - to the tradition of the French eighteenth century and the French Revolution, for which "philosophy is already politics".

[12] Kincheloe and McLaren (1994, 139-140) define criticalist "very broadly and hermenistically" "as researcher or theorist who attempts to use her or his work as a form of cultural criticism and who accepts certain basic assumptions" including the following: all thought is fundamentally mediated by historically and socially constituted power relations; facts can never be isolated from the domain of values or some form of ideology; that the relationship between concept and object and between signifier and signified is never stable or fixed and is often mediated by social relations of capitalist production; that language is central to the formation of subjectivity; that certain groups in any society are privileged over others and the oppression that characterizes contemporary societies is reproduced forcefully especially when subordinates accept their social status as natural or necessary; that oppression has many faces (racism, class oppression) which are interconnected; and that mainstream research is generally, although usually unwittingly, implicated in the reproduction of systems of oppression.

manifestation of the discourses and power relations of the social and historical context that produced them. The "discourse of possibility" implicit within the constructed nature of social experience suggested to those scholars that a reconstruction of the social sciences could eventually lead to a more egalitarian and democratic social order.

The current theoretical backgrounds of the researchers in the studied departments were often described as heterogeneous. Some researchers spoke about "methodological differences" and "multiculturalism" (see Kaukonen 1984, 130; Kaukonen 1990, 42-44). The following views by two respondents from different departments emphasize the historical change in theoretical backgrounds:

> in the 1970s, it was Marxism against some other orientations, this was the dominating theme, to which all kinds of divisions and questions of power could be connected... nowadays there are multiple theoretical orientations, and confrontation between two different camps does not build up... people can co-operate although they have different views

> Marxism was in a hegemonic position, if you can put it in this way, during the 1980s, and now we have younger researchers who are sceptical at least towards that kind of Marxism-Leninism which was taught here in the 1980s... certain philosophical and theoretical debates are continuously going on...

However, a certain critical stance with an emphasis on democracy and emancipation, as well as an accompanying preference for change over status quo was still evident in many cases, especially when the above mentioned, currently powerful generation of sociologists was in question. One respondent noted that broadly speaking his faculty identified with the "critical school". When compared to other disciplines at a general level, the interviewed sociologists tended to be more sensitive to power issues and political consequences of actions and ideals.

A professor considered that the current emphasis on individual leadership is in line with right wing ideology (chapter 2). He worried that the trend may decrease the status of professionals such as professors (see Lyotard 1984, 53). This kind of criticism was not expressed by the respondents in the other disciplines studied. One sociologist held that democracy has been a permanent topic in cultural debate at least 2 500 years, and will stay in that position despite the collapse of socialism. He believed that their relative peripherical location makes it possible to maintain certain theoretical perspectives despite changing fashions in the field. According to another researcher, the disciplinary rhetoric may change quite rapidly, but some underlying basic themes of inquiry are more stable.

In both studied departments of sociology most of the important decisions have been made on the basis of collective discussions. My interpretation is that the sociologists' obvious dislike of strong individual leadership can be understood partly on the grounds of the ideal of academic freedom and the nature of research in a soft and rural field. and partly on the basis of their critical value-orientation and background. This position shows in the following quotation:

> The idea that collective decision-making is inefficient is an interesting and frightening one... thus, democracy is inefficient and totalitarian rule, fascism is absolutely more efficient... it is an idea which is, in my view, terrible, especially when it is put forward by universities... it certainly takes time when people think together, but that this is defined as wasted time is, in my mind, inconceivable. And that differing views and interests are seen as hindering the development of university is terrifying...

Some younger researchers felt that in some cases collegial decision-making takes too much time and can involve persons who have nothing to do with the matters under discussion (see Aittola 1984 and 1987; section 3.3.). Generally speaking, however, they also valued democratic leadership based on discussion, and did not see any alternatives. Most researchers agreed that disciplinary and departmental history has played a major role in determining their preferences concerning departmental decision making and leadership. However, one respondent stressed that there are differences between individuals and schools of sociology, and such preferences are not necessarily shared by every sociologist. He gave an example of a previous professor who did not favour collegial decision-making nor a critical approach.

Ylijoki (1991) has analyzed the student culture in a department of social psychology of a Finnish university, which seems to combine the broad critical approach favoured by many sociologists with the individualism mentioned by Kleinman (1983). According to Ylijoki (1991, 7-9), the main features of this field (which is closely related to sociology) are critical thinking, resistance to all attempts to increase efficiency or performativity, and distinction from other disciplines, except from sociology. The collective norm is that each student must find his/her own voice *within* this broad critical frame.

5.2.3. The Exact Knowledge of Physics

All respondents agreed that physics is the most exact empirical science (see Kantele 1990). The language of physics is mathematics. Some respondents stressed that it is different from soft sciences in the sense that physics is an international science - there is no local or national physics. Instead, methods, standards and procedures of physics are similar everywhere and similar results can be reached in every laboratory. "The corpus of knowledge is universal" even if "the process of building up the subject is parochial" (Becher 1990b, 8)[13].

However, a professor of theoretical physics held that there is also a great "heuristic component" involved in physical research. According to him, the results are based on

---

[13] The physicists interviewed by Becher (1990b, 7-8) also identified some differences "in the ways the discipline is interpreted and practised in different countries".

assumptions, which seem to be - at least so far - in line with our knowledge of the processes in nature. He continued that sometimes new findings do not match with the existing theoretical models or suppositions. Consequently, researchers may be forced to change their basic assumptions, which can lead to scientific revolutions (Kuhn 1970; Becher 1990b).

Some respondents expected new scientific revolutions, while others, especially experimental physicists, did not believe in further revolutions in established areas. It was acknowledged that there is also a certain inaccuratecy involved in physics. For example, in atomic processes strict causality has been rejected; we can only project *statistically* what effect might succeed what cause (Traweek 1988, 48).

During the interviews, I discussed with eight physicists about the impact of chaos-theory on a physicist's world-view. A certain perceived uncertainty does not seem to have a major impact on their belief in general exactness and underlying order in their specialisms, at least when physics is compared to humanities and social sciences (see Becher 1990b). One researcher mentioned that all the experiments made so far have been in harmony with quantum mechanics, "which was invented about five decades ago". The hard, convergent and urban nature of experimental physics has led to "secularization" of research. Experimental physicists do not spend their time developing revolutionary ideas, but instead carry out studies which offer small, linear developments to the existing knowledge (see Becher 1989a, 153; 1990b, 6; Kantele 1990, 112). As one respondent put it:

> I would say that the physics I am doing is secularized science. In that sense, you could say that leadership matters; we do not sit in a chamber and develop revolutionary ideas. Instead, we work from certain premises towards a certain direction... It usually develops in that way that we push the frontiers forwards step by step. Then when things do not go right and we start to circle around a certain problem... I mean, this is the place where revolutions may occur, when somebody realizes what is wrong... But basic work is needed: Einstein's invention that time is relative did not come out from nowhere, but there were experiments which showed that something is wrong... In that sense, if we think that researchers would be free to do anything they liked, there would be no revolutions in science...

Physics is grounded on causal propositions and cumulative findings. But what kind of consequences does this have for social relations and leadership issues within the departments? It seems that some, especially young physicists prefer hard knowledge so strongly that they do not see much value in soft knowledge, which is more subjective and connected to human values (see also Traweek 1988, 91-92). As one professor put it:

> Afterwards, I have wondered that our students, only our good students have this feature... they are interested only in their own subject... they love physics, they do not see they world around them, and they do not value

fields and research which is based on opinions... this self-made emphasis laid on our own discipline is typical for physicists.

Could it be that the hard logic and rationality of your field affects people? Yes, and it may be the case that it screens certain types of people, and those who are successful in this area adopt such features... those who become teachers are usually ordinary people of various kinds; but every now and then we have students who are interested, say, in the general theory of relativity, and they have a strong self-esteem... anything else is nothing, not even chemistry; only mathematics is seen as sensible. This is a typical trait of a good physicists.

The professor held that "on average" scholars in their field begin to get interested in things and fields other than physics only in their middle age. In line with this, the interviewed senior physicists seemed to respect the topic of my study, while some young physicists had a hard time understanding what is the point in studying "subjective things" such as leadership[14]. But it is obvious that this kind of taken-for-granted opinion is itself value-laden, since it leads to the devaluation of social, psychological and philosophical issues which are hard to measure and quantify, like moral choice, democracy, emotions, etc.

Whether or not exact knowledge is to be considered more important than inexact is dependent on situational factors and the values of the observer. When exact knowledge becomes a part of social practice, it becomes involved with our values. For example: should we use nuclear power? Are the possible negative or positive consequences of genetic manipulation more important? The natural perspective of experimental physics seems to leave this kind of social and philosophical issues aside - or at least they are not discussed very often at the studied departments. One of Becher's (1990b, 6) respondents explained that

> the typical physicist's approach is pragmatic and *ad hoc* rather than philosophical: things do not just have to look neat (important though that is), they have to work.

"Most working scientists are realists at heart" (Trigg 1993, 163) and from the realists' dualistic perspective (Alvesson 1993, 1007) social issues do not belong to the realm or sphere of the measurable physical world. Traweek (1988, 17) notes that (particle)physicists "have a passionate dedication" to a

---

[14] Traweek (1988, 13-14) had similar experience during her fieldwork among high energy physicists. Senior people "invariably expressed interest" in her study and "gave thoughtful responses" to her questions. By contrast, young researchers usually showed more disregard: they usually left the doors to their offices open and spoke to her as if they were "free-associating".

vision of unchanging order: they are convinced that the deepest truths must be static, independent of human frailty and hybris. Simultaneously, they believe that this grand structure of physical truth can be progressively uncovered, that this is the highest and most urgent human pursuit.

In hard fields available methods tend to determine the choice of problems (Becher 1989a, 153; Traweek 1988, 49), and the methods are planned to solve experimental and empirical issues.

Differences Between Physicists' and Sociologists' Perspectives

When the views of interviewed physicists are compared to those of sociologists (in an idealtypical form), some interesting differences in perspectives appear. The disciplinary logic seem to be different, at least as far as some researchers are concerned: while hard science leans heavily to classic logic and causal propositions, some sociologists, but not all, maintain that attempts to force experience into logical categories leads to contradiction (e.g. Koski 1993, 158). The former orientation is connected to realism and objectivism while the latter is often more prone to (at least weak) relativism (chapter 4). Both groups have a tendency to apply their own perspective to *both* the social and physical spheres: critical sociologists often view reality (and, indeed, also science; Pinch 1990; Trigg 1993) as socially constructed, while physicists seem to stress the law-like nature of reality (Kantele 1990, 107). In the physicists' case linear thinking, preference of measurability and exact knowledge (Mäenpää & Mäkinen 1989, 105-106) appear to affect their preferences concerning leadership.

Among critical theorists, there is a tendency to stress power issues and the political consequences of leadership philosophies, while experimental physicists seem largely to ignore such aspects. In the terms of Habermas, many physicists tend to share a technical interest in knowledge, while sociologists tend to stress a critical-emancipatory interest in knowledge (Habermas 1978, 308; Kangas 1989, 10-17). This also means that physicists tend to be far less critical in relation to leaders and leadership. For them leadership has in many cases a taken-for-granted nature, and their approach is more pragmatic and straight-forward: leadership is good as long as it works properly and is not severely against personal values and departmental or disciplinary traditions. If there is nothing to complain about (the threshold of complaint seems to be quite high), physicists prefer to concentrate on their work, where shared methods and standards of the discipline reduce the possibility of conflicts, and where most problems can be solved empirically. Especially many young physicists seemed to hope for accurate, well-working, straight-forward leadership, which would help them to maintain their jobs.

Traweek (1988, 162) describes the world of high energy physicists as

> an extreme culture of objectivity: a culture of no culture, which longs passionately for a world without loose ends, without temperament, gender, nationalism or other sources of disorder - for a world outside human space and time.

Leaning on Traweek's (1988) study, Pinch (1990) claims that elite groups of particle physics are very hierarchic:

> Despite the air of casualness and fun which these physicists promulgate, the hierarchy could scarcely be more rigid. Everyone knows who to defer to over the crucial issues, and they don't simply defer on grounds of hierarchy. The person they defer to must present himself as the cleverest person in the lab; if he doesn't, he won't hold the respect of the group for long (for a counter-argument, see Becher 1990b, 16).

The approach of critical sociology, on the other hand, is to make the use of power visible, to criticise the status quo, to provide alternative view-points and to make the voice of the oppressed heard. When this kind of emancipatory approach is connected to soft knowledge, it easily leads to fragmentation and questioning of existing 'truths' rather than to cumulative knowledge (see Jameson 1984, ix; Gergen 1989, 475-476)[15]. It is easy to assume that a group of staff with this kind of emphasis might be a hard nut to crack for an effective result-oriented manager, since his/her attempts to 'organize' work would be easily seen in a negative light as 'oppression', as 'use of power', or as an uncritical approval of the established ideology.

Moreover, scholars who adopt a critical value-base might stress that "disadvantaged classes" (Bourdieu & Passeron 1979; see Huber 1990) should be given priority when students are recruited, while most physicists - and indeed representatives of many other fields - would probably prefer to recruit their students on the basis of the candidates' demonstrated ability and their high motivation to work in the area in question. Because of the limited job opportunities, "any aspiring entrant in physics has to be 'very good and very dedicated'" (Becher 1990b, 9).

When such different value-orientations and perspectives are connected to soft social issues, disagreements usually become obvious. Take for example the recent budget cuts (chapter 2). Sociologist adopting a critical perspective may be tempted to criticise the cuts by trying to reveal the societal (macro level; see Sackmann 1991, 15) power

---

[15] The notion that every aspect of intellectual life "is reducible to sociological considerations" often, and problematically, "goes hand in hand with an uncompromisingly relativist world view" (Becher 1987a, 177-178). As Trigg (1993, 168-169) shows, it is problematic to relativise science on the basis of extreme constructivism and yet, at the same time, put this argument forward as an objective truth claim or knowledge: "If science is socially constructed, so is social theory, and our theory of social theory and so on". Moreover, the view that science is a purely social exercise fails to explain "why it is in principle possible to repeat the same experiment in different social settings" (Trigg 1993, 159). The fact that the applications of science (e.g. cars, nuclear power, cd-players) really work in a technical sense suggests that science has indeed been able to capture some of the basic processes in the physical sphere, nature and matter. However, at the same time we may have different arguments and opinions whether, and to what degree, this success is good or bad, valuable or undesirable, whether we should put our efforts elsewhere, or whether the 'fruits of industrialization' should be divided in another way. In this sense, the value-orientation of critical sociology demonstrates one (but only one) alternative way of thinking (chapter 4).

structures and ideologies which are behind such acts. On the other hand, physicists might adopt a 'realistic' (micro level) perspective and take the broad circumstances as they are, without hoping to change them at the societal level. They perhaps will attempt to work harder, publish more and get more external funds. In doing so, the scientist also - as a critical sociologist might put it - reproduces and maintains the circle of competition and 'symbolic violence' without (perhaps) even noticing it. But those who refuse to contest for declining resources (while others continue to do so) run the risk of becoming the first victims of the budget cuts. Dilemmas like this seem to be an integral part of everyday life. Scholars from different disciplines and with distinct cultural backgrounds usually hold different, even strictly opposite views and preferences concerning them, since such aspects are also connected to our values, ideals and perspectives[16].

Specialisms Studied in Physics

The research in *nuclear physics* is based on group work, and so is the leadership in the studied department of that area. In the department I studied, the important decisions are made in the leading group which consists of professors and the leaders of the research projects, totalling about ten persons. According to the head of department, the tradition of collegial decision making based on discussions in the leading group originates from the initiative of a nowadays retired emeritus professor. But given the nature of their work, this choice seems to be quite natural in their specialism. Some researchers stressed that a similar kind on practice is adopted also in other laboratories around the world[17].

Another feature of the specialism is shift work during the experiments (so called beamtime). Some researchers have to be present even at night to watch over the process by the accelerator. In practice, this leads to exceptionally long working days, which was often seen as a special feature of the field. One interviewed physicist even claimed that he had worked approximately 15 hours a day for nearly twenty years, before he changed his specialism. He was at work during summer vacations, weekends and even on Christmas eves - and nonetheless managed to maintain his family relations. In retrospect, he saw scientific ambitions, hard competition for permanent posts and the example given by the respected leaders as the main reasons for such hard but enthusiastic work. Inspiring international contacts and normative pressure of the research group were other main factors: each individual has to perform his/her own part so that the international project

---

[16] One example is the recent debate about whether more resources should be given to top research units (chapter 2). Different views are held by those who value 'democracy' as opposed to those who speak for 'efficiency' (see Lyotard 1984). Disciplinary differences may play a role in the debate, since rapid cycles of publishing are far easier to maintain in hard urban fields than in soft rural areas (Becher 1989a, 84-86). But such conflicts may exist even between the scholars of the same discipline, as has been the case in sociology between the broad critical tradition and the system theory inspired by Parson's functionalism emphasising the "optimization of performativity" (Lyotard 1984).

[17] There seems to be some national differences. According to Traweek (1988, 91) American physicists emphasize that science is not democratic: "decisions about scientific purposes should not be made by majority rule within the community, nor should there be equal access to the lab's resources". On both these issues, however, "most Japanese physicists assume the opposite".

remains on schedule. According to the respondent, there was no in-betweens; either you worked hard or sought another career path.

Working on a common project within a hard, cumulative and urban field leads to close interaction between researchers. There seem to be preconditions for a good working climate, since the studied departments of physics have not faced hard budget cuts (Kekäle 1995c; Traweek 1988), and since the field generally enjoys a high level of convergence, that is: physicists seem to share a collective ideology and even a common world view (Becher 1989a, 155). Indeed, the researchers in nuclear physics often pointed out that their department is known for its excellent social climate, while in the other department of physics the working climate was characterized as more "businesslike" or "matter-of-fact"[18].

Another studied department of physics represents a different specialism, *optical physics*. The department is increasingly moving towards applied science with intense contacts with industry. The department has also undergone significant changes during the past five years, changing from an department of pure science with peaceful, rural-like working manners towards a dynamic, urban department of applied science (section 6.4.3.). Research is conducted in small projects. The head of the department considers that his task is similar to the task of a project manager in a company or in a Research & Development unit (he has worked on that kind of task before). He assembles research groups, provides funding, gives each group its research tasks and ensures that the tasks will be completed on time. One younger researcher noted:

> The most important function of the departmental head is to create opportunities for work within the department... this means providing money and setting goals for teams. It aids motivation when the department is led in an effective way...

In recent years, nearly all decisions concerning the department have been made by the head of department, who is also considered to be a very competent researcher. As a respected expert in an urban, convergent and hard field, he is generally considered to be capable of making the relevant decisions[19].

5.2.4. Biology: Green Values and Environmental Issues

Another example of a department with an exceptionally good social climate can be found in biology. In the department of biology at university A, all important decisions are made on the basis of discussions by virtually the whole staff. The interaction among the

---

[18] There seem to be social issues connected to departmental history which have probably contributed to the climate; these will be discussed in the next chapter.

[19] After an interview, one young researcher even suggested that the leadership of a single individual would be suitable for society, since in that way we would avoid lengthy and "unnecessary" discussions.

staff seems to work on a daily and a very open basis, during meetings and coffee breaks. They have at least two common disciplinary features with nuclear physicists: close interaction and some shared 'inherent' disciplinary values.

Although biology as a discipline has been categorized as less convergent, less hard and more rural than physics (Becher 1989a, 156-158), the researchers of the department in question seem to share some strongly held beliefs, such as 'green' values and a concern for environmental issues. Biologists seem to have had a major impact on the acknowledgement of such issues in society: according to Jamison et al. (1990, 302), environmental movements in most western European countries started to form in the 1960s as "primarily biological scientists and naturalists" pointed out the negative consequences of postwar industrial and agricultural development.

The concern for environment was said to unite biologists in general to some extent, but this was most obvious among ecologists. It was frequently stressed that many students with this kind of orientation are "conservationists already before their studies". One respondent noted:

> soft values are prevailing even before studies... they are connected with a concern for environmental issues but also with a certain human softness, I suppose...

Some professors mentioned that it is difficult to get students to participate in more academic research projects, where they cannot put the 'green' values directly into practice. Such values are usually further strengthened during their studies because of the close interaction between teachers and students. Biologists stressed that their interaction already has this characteristic during their basic studies due to the frequent and fairly lengthy field courses. As one respondent explained:

> the students in biology are highly motivated, partly because it is difficult to get inside to study biology... students and teachers have natural relationships, since we have to work with each other during field courses and in laboratories...

Generally speaking, the researchers in the both departments seem to share 'green values' to some extent, but they seem to be much more moderate in their views and more critical towards their own thinking than the students of biology which I interviewed previously (Kekäle 1991; 1995b). One might say that the researchers seem to share consciously hold and preferred values, while some of the students held taken for granted basic assumptions (Schein 1985; Kekäle 1995b; see Wakeford & Walters 1995; footnote 3 in chapter 1). As a professor of biology noted:

> actually a scientist should not discuss value issues, but sometimes this is inevitable in connection with environmental issues... if I for example say that a lake is polluted, the word polluted has this kind of value load... one has to take a value position... it is the best and the right solution. In biology

we have to deal with this kind of issue, in other words, we have to take a
critical role and maintain that we cannot do this... [keep on polluting our
environment... biologists...] try to persuade political decision-makers,
environment planners... since biologists are aware of the [ecological]
consequences... I have tried to speak to students about these issues,
because they will face them anyway... but economic aspects often are in
conflict, the different emphasis comes into play...

It was also noted that questions such as bio-diversity are complex and
multidimensional. However, in broad outline, the trend is clear and objective:

...a living organism can react in multiple of ways to foreign matters or
toxic... these are complex issues which makes it, when they are connected
to expectations of simple and easy answers by the public, too easy for
simplifiers to play their games...

*But can we, despite of the complexity, say that the condition of the
environment is getting worse?*

Yes. We cannot go wrong in the issues of such a larger scale.

So, this is a fact?

Yes it is.

According to the respondents, the green values go hand in hand with a non-anthropocentric world-view, "respect for life in general", "soft-values", a low interest in
"economical values", "status anxiety" or "ratrace". It is easy to understand that this kind
of perspective is quite natural for a discipline which studies life, bio-diversity,
ecosystems and species in general. Some researchers in department A held that their
social interaction and their dislike of strong leaders, management or "hard-hearted
economic calculation" mirrored these values:

...management is, I think, a foreign issue in an academic context and
especially in our department... biologists are not economically oriented in
any way, neither are they inclined to influence society in other than
environmental issues, in which we are active... the idea of management is
not close to our way of thinking...

But, as already noted, there also seem to be differences according to specialism (as
well as by country; see Becher 1987a, 182). *Department B of biology* was more clearly
divided into different specialisms, which were in some cases forced to compete for
resources with each other because of the budget cuts. In harder specialisms such as
molecular biology, biochemistry and cell biology, the value orientation of the staff and

students is, according to some respondents, "more academic" and less connected to environmental issues. One professor stressed that the exactness of these specialisms is connected with methodological issues and the development of research instruments and devices. In this department, many central members of the staff were explicitly for a stronger individual leadership:

> I personally feel that we should have a professor who would be the administrative leader of the department on a permanent basis... an economic leader who would be a scientist, and who would seek to benefit the whole department...

The decisions are usually made in leading groups consisting of professors, associate professors and leaders of research groups, but recently the influence of the head has increased. According to biologists in department B, recession has affected especially their costly (hard) experimental laboratory research, which cannot be carried out "with a pen and a piece of paper". Because of lack of resources the leaders had to face the hard task of setting priorities among areas of research and giving notice to some members of the staff (this theme will be discussed further in section 6.4.6.).

5.3. SCHOOLS OF THOUGHT AND INTELLECTUAL DIVISIONS

In chapter 4, I argued that social and cultural phenomena can be considered as processes, potentially changing and evolving, but that some aspects or layers of these processes (typically characterized by a strong commitment and a taken-for-granted nature) tend to be more enduring than others (Kekäle 1995b). So far, I have viewed specialisms as somewhat coherent entities, by trying to pin-point some broad aspects which give a certain degree of continuity to the specialisms and groups in question. Most of the discussed value-orientations seem to be broadly shared by scholars in different countries, which makes it possible to speak - at a general level - about disciplinary or specialism-based leadership cultures. However, it can be argued that some aspects of the specialisms may be more fluid; that is, more prone to change as the argumentation and specialization in different fields proceeds. In the following two sections, I will try to highlight such dynamic and changing aspects. They may help to clarify the scope for academic leaders in directing research. They may also indicate the potential degree of integration or fragmentation of different disciplinary cultures.

Law (1976, 147) has made a distinction between theory-based, technique- or methods-based and subject matter specialities on the basis of their central orientation and main source of solidarity. The three types of specialism are not necessarily separated in practice (Becher 1989a, 49). But if we loosely follow this distinction, it is fair to say that in this section my emphasis will be on knowledge- and (especially) theory-based specialities among the studied disciplines. In other words, I will concentrate on different schools of thought and other intellectual divisions. In the following section (5.4.), the methods-based specialisms will also be under discussion. The descriptions concerning schools of thought in this section are based on the discussions with twelve physicists, eight historians, three sociologists[20] and nine biologists, while the following, closely related section 5.4. is based on the views of eight physicists, five historians, three sociologists and five biologists.

Becher (1989a, 157) describes *sociology* as a "fissiparous and fragmented" discipline with not much agreement on problems or perspectives. One sociologist I interviewed held that terms like "school of thought" or "paradigm" do not describe the current practice of sociology or the human sciences very well. First, there is a considerable overlap with neighbouring fields. Youth studies or women's studies are currently practised by scholars from many fields such as sociology, anthropology and psychology. Kaukonen (1990, 51) notes that in such areas interdisciplinary contacts have become "more active and intensive than between sociologists in different sociological sub-fields" (see also Becher 1989a, 36-40; Becher 1994, 63). Second, there seem to be fashionable themes of discussion (such as the body in sociology) which often change quite rapidly, while some underlying research topics (e.g. power, social divisions) and traditions seem to have a considerable continuity.

Changes in such a turbulent disciplinary environment are not easy to predict. There may be a sudden breakthrough after a long career by a relatively unknown scholar (e.g. Ulrich Beck). Furthermore, as one sociologist mentioned, the actual importance of the work of a scholar becomes evident only after decades, and even a classic may be viewed in a considerably different light by different researchers and during different times (e.g. the tides of Marxism from the 1960's to the present). Since multiple, even contradictory paradigms exist permanently abreast, the notion of normal science and its crisis becomes problematic (Kuhn 1970). Rather than causing a revolution, new thoughts are likely to add to the complexity of the mosaic of knowledge. However, as noted, we may still find some broad unifying themes within certain specialisms.

According to my respondents, the Marxian tradition has affected the research of *history* as well, but lately the impact has diminished (see Ylikangas 1990). Some other broad schools like idealism and positivism which are based on the works of Hegel and Comte and have, like the Marxian tradition, affected the human sciences in general. The Annales school was mentioned once as a broad school of thought in history (Becher 1987a, 183; Becher 1989a, 49). In Finnish history, some scholars have emphasised the influences from the west while others have stressed eastern influences. However, the majority of the respondents, especially in department B stressed that nowadays there are different alignments in history, but strong and distinct schools of thought with different background assumptions are difficult to identify.

It was also stressed that strong schools of thought do not easily develop - in Becher's (1989a) terms - in soft and rural disciplines where the research topics are broad and

---

[20] The number of respondents in sociology is low when these themes are concerned. As noted, this is partly due to the fact that I have studied sociology myself and had better knowledge of the classics and the history of this particular discipline. Consequently, I concentrated more on

diverse, and where researchers are interested in particular[21] and local issues. Also the individualistic tradition of history underlines this trend and affects academic leadership (section 5.2.1.). However, four respondents gave a looser definition to the term 'school' and saw multiple schools of thought or research traditions in history. Typically those who follow these traditions show some kind of continuity, are interested in the same time period or region, and build upon the work of a certain professor. However, only a few respected researchers have been able to establish schools in history.

Physics was seen by the respondents mainly as a uniform and a coherent (hard and convergent) discipline without deep intellectual divisions[22]. There are different research orientations, but when it comes to the basics of physics, there seem to be few fundamental differences. However, it was sometimes stressed that physics has not solved all its problems. The fusion of the general theory of relativity and quantum physics has not been achieved yet, but this does not seem to result in deep disagreements among scholars. Instead, the theories are usually seen as mutually supportive.

Schools of thought and fundamental differences in views are likely to occur in softer, more philosophical or metaphysical and less experimental topics, which deal with such issues as the genesis of the universe. Experimental researchers do not usually want to speculate on such issues. Rather, such questions are left to theoreticians who are specialists in astronomy. One respondent echoed a common view that religion should not be mixed with science, but he also mentioned that there are few dissidents even among respected researchers. There seems to be a shared belief in the unity, rationality and simplicity of nature (Traweek 1988; Becher 1990b, 16). Where the issues that interest experimental scientists are concerned, empirical measurements, the reproducibility of experiments (see Traweek 1988, 157-162) and the hard logic of mathematics seem to solve the potential disagreements. Consequently, a professor of physics stressed the sense of commonality among physicists (see Becher 1989a, 155).

Shared values, hard logic, uniform standards and procedures, and group work which are inherent in hard, urban and convergent experimental physics provide a completely different leadership environment as compared to that in soft rural areas of enquiry. In the former case, the disciplinary basis gives much clearer guidelines for scholars and academic leaders when directing academic work. An example can be found in a book bringing together the future perspectives on research of leading Finnish scholars in different disciplinary fields (Perko 1990): a professor in nuclear physics noted that there are still "few missing links" in his area of enquiry (Kantele 1990, 108); a historian

---

departmental features during the interviews. The departments of sociology were the smallest in my sample (section 4.6). I interviewed altogether nine sociologists in the two departments.

[21] One professor of history considered the view that historians claimed interest in particular issues (as opposed to general laws) too simplistic: there are many counter-examples to this rule, since general patterns can be found in most historical events (see Becher 1989b, 268).

[22] Becher (1987a, 183) points out that this view of disciplinary coherence (which is important in intellectual terms, but also in terms of institutional credibility and status) is constantly put forward by physicists, although "there is little intercommunication among different specialties", and despite the fact that "the scholarly community is becoming increasingly fragmented as knowledge advances".

considered that the choice of research topics in his field largely a "subjective" issue (Ylikangas 1990, 27); a sociologist emphasised the lack of authorities and guidelines, relativism, and a need for re-evaluation in sociology in a post-Marxian situation (Alapuro 1990, 69).

Biology was seen as a heterogenous discipline by biologists. There is mutual antagonism between those who study structures and processes and those who deal with organisms or communities (Becher 1989a, 156). Numerous different alignments, specialisms and research orientations can be found. A professor of biology mentioned plant biology and zoobiology, cell- and molecular biology and ecology as examples of special areas with inherently different perspectives. He claimed that biology is among the most heterogenous of sciences.

However, respondents agreed that although biology in general is not as exact a science as physics and mathematics are, it is not as likely to develop fundamentally different subdivisions and schools of thought as arts and social sciences (see Becher 1989a; section 5.1.). As noted, there are considerable differences in specialisms in biology. In hard urban areas (such as biochemistry) the research comes close to other basic hard and convergent experimental sciences. Researchers gather around their instruments in laboratories. Reliability of findings in these areas is closely connected to the development of methods.

As in physics, respondents held that there are more intellectual divisions and schools in softer areas of biology (or around fundamental questions, such as evolution). The respondents generally agreed that in softer areas such as ecology there are more variables to control, variations increase and predictability becomes more slender. However, one professor remarked that we have not reached ultimate and final truths in any field of inquiry. That is why there is a tendency towards intellectual divisions, which may nevertheless be more frequent in soft fragmented disciplines and specialisms. On the other hand, the green values (section 5.2.4.) unite biologists especially in softer areas such as ecology.

5.4. Choice of Specialisms and Mobility Between Them

It was frequently stressed by respondents from different fields that one needs scientific reputation in order to be accepted and respected as an academic leader. Griffith and Mullins (1972, 961) have made a conceptual distinction by separating *organizational* leadership (arranging times, funds and facilities) and *intellectual* leadership (provided by respected researchers). While respect may be more essential in the case of intellectual leadership, some amount of respect from researchers is needed to support the position of organizational leader and make his/her work easier. Respect is perhaps most often connected to scientific reputation. As one physicist who is an academic leader put it:

> ...you have to have gained respect within your community on the basis of your scientific merits... this is very important, since without it you will

never get enough of the prestige you need [as an individual academic leader] on the basis of leadership methods and means alone...

Especially in rural sciences such as sociology and history, carrying out a study is often a lengthy business (Becher 1989a, 154). A lot of reading is usually required before one becomes familiar with a research tradition in social sciences or the historical data in history, and can make a significant research contribution (Becher 1989a, 72) - and gain a respected position as an academic leader. A researcher's professional identity is formed in the process of specialization, and specialisms may considerably limit the scope of issues which one is expected to comment on and 'manage'. Because of this, specialization becomes an essential issue, not only in research, but also in leadership.

According to *sociologists*, researchers in their field tend to stick to a single chosen (sometimes broad) area of specialism because it is easier to get funding as a known scholar in a certain field. According to a respondent, a researcher's comments are not taken seriously if he/she is not expert in that particular area. It is even against professional norms to express views on issues outside one's own specialism.

In sociology there may be political and ideological issues involved in the choice of specialism or perspective. One respondent mentioned that once one has become a part of some tradition or camp, it may be difficult to change one's specialism and orientation, since a researcher is known on the basis of his/her work. Nowadays, young researchers increasingly find their specialism by joining research projects. These projects are started by senior researchers who have already built some reputation in that field, and who consequently assume power and a certain (at least initial) leadership position within their research groups. Their leadership role they are expected to perform is affected by the norms and values of the specialism or orientation in question (sections 5.2.2., 6.4.1. and 6.4.2.).

Respondents in *physics* stressed that researchers choose their specialism from areas where there is some opportunity to get funding. Such grounds for choice of specialism have become more important due to the recession (chapter 2). One respondent held that nowadays it would take "an enormous self-assurance" to follow one's own instincts and to ignore external and economical realities. According to the respondents, most physicists choose their specialisms while working on their master's thesis or doctoral dissertation. In physics and other hard, convergent and urban areas, the equipment and methods available as well as the ongoing projects closely direct the choice of topics of young researchers. These considerations emphasize the influence on specialisms of project leaders, since the young scholar usually has to follow the path already chosen by the staff, the founder(s) and leaders of the department or project - or to move to another laboratory/department.

Within a broad specialism (e.g. nuclear physics), new developments and innovations direct the process of research in both pure and applied areas. However, there is a minority of researchers - usually described as skilled and independent - who will change their research areas, but even some of these come back to their original field later on. Becher (1989a, 69) categorizes academics who are prone to move into new fields in three groups: 1) those who are highly mobile by temperament or profession, 2) individuals who have become "disenchanted with their current line of research" and who are thus looking for a new departures, and 3) novitiates with no fixed loyalties, willing to move to new and previously unexposed territories.

In hard pure areas it appears to be relatively easy to identify promising new issues (see previous section). Because of that fashion takes a particularly intense form in these disciplines (Becher 1989a, 14; 69; Becher 1990b, 15).

It seems that *historians* often continue to work on the themes of their master's thesis and doctoral dissertation. At least, these themes usually remain quite close to the core of the orientation of the researchers. According to the respondents, this is the most economic and the least time-consuming way in their - to use Becher's (1989a) terms, soft and rural - area of inquiry, where the average age of doctorates is still quite high. Although students are expected to find their topic by themselves, the expertise of their possible supervisors directs his/her choices in practice (Becher 1989b). The pattern of staying with certain themes is also connected to individualistic tradition of the discipline (section 5.2.1.), although a similar kind of pattern can also be found in other, less individualistic fields (like physics).

However, one professor held that it would be worthwhile to change specialisms in history, since would-be holders of chairs are expected to be quite versatile in their studies. Multi-sidedness seems to be a feature which is also respected by other researchers. Current external pressures such as budget cuts are severely challenging the tradition of stable specialisms. Some researchers held that nowadays one should be able to move between specialisms, since continuity of funding is not necessarily guaranteed in any particular special field.

Also in *biology*, the starting and ongoing projects direct the choice of specialism. Projects are connected to expertise and special fields of the department. One respondent claimed that "like in other processes in nature", random patterns affect the choice of specialism, but also personal interests and especially the special areas of the leaders of the projects are important. Three biologists held that mobility between specialisms has been increasing recently, since "artificial" boundaries between special fields have been breaking down. Increasing mobility and a strong emphasis on group work were seen to go hand in hand. Biology is also an area, where the heavy decline of resources has forced researchers to change their specialisms. One example of such fusion is a shared project in fields of ecology and cell biology. However, the process of change is still slow. As noted, the strong value-based choice of specialisms in ecology was seen as hindering mobility between areas, since students of ecology are often unwilling to work on topics related to other areas of biology.

In summary, it seems that in all studied fields the topics of the starting and the ongoing projects direct the choices of specialism of scholars. As suggested in the previous section, different disciplines seem to provide more or less clear guidelines for academic work and leadership. There are disciplinary differences in the scope for academic freedom[23] and senior researchers frequently have more freedom of choice than

---

[23] This theme will be discussed in chapter 7.

junior staff when choosing their specialism. But for all academics, the crucial point is that:

> In one way or another, all new areas of scientific investigation grow out of prior research or out of the extension of an established body of scientific and/or technical knowledge (Lemaine et al. 1976, 2).

These aspects indicate the importance of the basic choices by (previous and current) academic leaders at the departmental and team levels. If the broad choice of topic or theme does not provide funding in the long run, the expertise gained in the project by the scholars may become relatively worthless in professional or economic terms - although not in terms of disinterested pursuit of research knowledge. In this sense, the differences with the turbulent business environment are diminishing as the ability to change orientation, react, anticipate and lead changes in fashion and promising research areas becomes increasingly important in the academic environment (chapter 2).

5.5. DISCIPLINARY DIFFERENCES AND LEADERSHIP ISSUES

The perspectives and features of disciplines and specialisms discussed in earlier sections seem to affect the issues of academic leadership, and provide a context for it among broader trends in academia (chapter 2), and among some cosmopolitan characteristics of academic institutions, such as the respect for academic freedom in most specialisms (section 3.2.2.). Local traditions mix with the features of academia, institution, discipline and specialism. Moreover, as Becher (1989a, 16) points out:

> The steadily changing (and, in the long term, transient) nature of knowledge makes it difficult to claim that any attempt at categorizing it can be permanent and enduring. It is not only that what counts as present understanding quite obviously differs with passage of time... Taxonomies... can do no more than take account, more or less effectively, of our existing state of intellectual awareness. Accordingly, they can best be seen as convenient but contingent devices for ordering our understanding of what knowledge is like in all its various forms.

The disciplinary features discussed in this chapter seem - to return to a metaphor used in the previous chapter - not solid but 'viscous', that is, relatively stable anyway. The important point is that classifications of disciplines

> ...nevertheless serve a useful purpose... They also help to show up continuities and interconnections which more minute and localized scrutiny could obscure, or at best, fail to bring to light (Becher 1989a, 17).

Indeed, a perspective on disciplinary cultures seems to fruitfully complement the forthcoming more localized discussion of organizational cultures and academic leadership. On the basis of my data it seems fair to say that the cultures of disciplines and specialisms play a significant role in moulding the leadership cultures of the departments. The distinct value-orientations of specialisms seem to be in line, generally speaking, with the findings and descriptions of many foreign studies. The impact of some research orientations (e.g. the broad critical perspective in social sciences; emphasis on exact knowledge in physics) on leadership is likely to be international in nature: that is, scholars in different countries may adopt such view-points. "Ideals and practices of academic communities are intimately bound up with the nature of knowledge they pursue" (Becher 1989a, 169).

Leaning on Bourdieu's (1988) work, Häyrynen et al. (1992a, 19) note that different disciplinary communities sustain diverse value-bases. A certain disciplinary field appeals to entrants with corresponding habitus and value-orientation, and the interaction of students and scholars with similar enough interests and values is likely to result in a circular reinforcement of the core values of such cultural units.

In similar vein, Traweek (1988, 21) notes that many physicists "have been committed to being scientists since early adolecense, and their training teaches them to regard physics as a calling, not an occupation". In this chapter, it was noted that many ecologists are "conservationists already before their studies" (section 5.2.4.), "good students" (would-be researchers) in physics "are interested only in their own subject" and in hard, exact knowledge (5.2.3.); and that many sociologists have shown consistency in their basic (critical) approach since "the politically charged" era of the 1960s (Kincheloe and McLaren 1994, 139; chapter 2; section 5.2.2.). Such a long-time commitment seems to be an obvious feature of the typical value-orientations of disciplinary areas and specialisms. Indeed, it is difficult to imagine how one could become an expert in a disciplinary field without a strong and enduring commitment. Yet, at the same time a strong commitment to disciplinary values may direct perception so that other important aspects or spheres are left aside (chapter 4).

Generally speaking, the intellectual cohesion of specialisms seems to vary according to hard - soft, convergent -divergent, and urban - rural continua (Becher 1989a). Disciplines and specialisms located at the right end of the continua, such as sociology, are prone to produce differing scholarly views. However, in the small departments of sociology under study show consistency and integrating cultural values seem to affect leadership. According to my interpretation, this is due to the disciplinary orientation, and homogenous backgrounds of the key researchers (sections 5.2.2.), and also, as will be seen, local departmental history (sections 6.4.1. & 6.4.2.). Hard, individualistic, result-oriented management would be in direct conflict with the inherent values of the critical perspective: values such as emancipation, democracy and collectivism sustain the current departmental decision-making patterns (see Middlehurst 1995, 75). Other value-orientations of specialisms/disciplines seem to affect the departmental leadership as well.

In all studied fields, the observation that the topics of researchers' starting and ongoing projects seem to direct the choices of specialism underlines the importance of the basic choices by academic leaders at the departmental and team levels. The expertise and ability displayed in a given discipline or specialism is an important source of respect for any scholar or an academic leader. That is why most respondents thought that external professional managers and leaders would not be successful at the university context. The long schooling of the researchers often means that they have, to a degree, internalized the central perspectives and values of the discipline and academia (Gerholm 1990). Leaders with a strong disciplinary background understand the nature academic work, and are also unlikely to violate the basic values of the disciplinary and academic community.

We can perhaps compare the orientations and working patterns of studied disciplinary specialisms by borrowing metaphors from sports world[24]. When the specialisms are viewed in this light in the era of Management by Objectives (chapter 2), the central (value) orientations and cultural characteristics of the studied departments might be perhaps classified as follows:

Hard, urban and convergent specialisms (both the departments of **physics**, and department B of **biology**) are, in a sense, similar to fast team sports. The researchers work as a team and compete against other teams. Interestingly, the staff in the department of nuclear physics have competition rowing (crew race) as their hobby. Although all these departments seem to share this general orientation, the role and the position of the individual 'captain' of the team is stronger in the two other departments.

The working atmosphere in department A of **biology**, where the orientation is somewhat *softer*, can be compared to a team sport as well. However, its cultural characteristics remain more the features of country walk, where the main idea is not so much to compete, but to be together, enjoy good company and admire the beauty of the nature and the landscape (see section 6.4.5.)[25]. However, dark clouds in the form of budget cuts have forced the party to increase their speed. Because of their value orientation, the change of climate seems to affect the mood of this party more than that of the participants of crew race, who are all too busy with the rowing and their competition to observe the weather and the environment around them.

The characteristics of *soft, rural, convergent* **history** as well as some areas of divergent **sociology** remain jogging. It belongs to the tradition and to the very nature of these sports that each participant is competing on his or her own, and not directly against others for a prize. Moreover, the distance between the start and finish is relatively long, and the speed is fairly low when compared to sprint distances. Since there are many interesting paths to follow in the woods and through the cities, it is sometimes difficult to get the participants to stay on the same track, to reach the same destination, or even to participate in the same competition.

---

[24] The metaphor is an apt one, since nowadays results are measured in the world of science as they are in sports.

[25] This does not imply that the staff are not doing their jobs; the metaphor refers only to the general atmosphere within the department (section 6.5.5.), as well as to its value orientation (section 5.2.4.).

Finally, it seems that at least the most radical **critical sociologists** tend to act as sports commentators of a highly subversive kind: instead of participating in the race, they try to show that the rules of the game favour some competitors. Because of this, those who are in a disadvantageous position should be given some kind of compensation - or they should be even placed first in their turn. These radical critics tend to question the whole idea of competition because it provides inequality. In fact, their contest seems to be the following: the ones who are the most successful in providing criticism and alternatives to current competitions, as well as in revealing hidden biases and rules, will be the most respected members of the community.

The point is that the positions and tasks of the 'coaches' and 'captains' (academic leaders) who are nowadays responsible for the results of these diverse teams are indeed very different in the contexts of different specialisms and disciplines. Also the results of the teams differ essentially on the basis of the nature of the task ('sport') they are involved with (see Becher 1989a, 162-166). Given the autonomous position of researchers and the relatively 'viscous' or stabile nature of the disciplinary value-orientations, academic leaders must usually take such idealtypical cultural aspects into account. In critical sociology, the preferred disciplinary leadership pattern seems to be democratic and collegial leadership. This pattern was considered the best alternative also in department A of biology representing soft, ecological orientation. Hard, pure specialisms studied in biology and physics at the university B favour teamwork in research and leadership, whereas the current management culture of hard and increasingly applied department A of physics emphasises entrepreneurship, competition, efficiency and business-like management. The diverse leadership styles in history seem to reflect the individualistic tradition of the discipline.

Such preferred leadership styles are connected to disciplinary perspectives and tasks which differ from each other in many ways. To put the matter very simplistically: sociologists concentrate on the social realm, physicists are concerned with physical phenomena, biologists view life from the perspectives of ecosystems, not from the anthropocentric humanistic perspective of historians. Sometimes ecological and social concerns are mixed, as in the recent writings about 'risk society' by sociologist Ulrich Beck (1995). Indeed, it would seem that when combined, the perspectives would provide a richer and probably a more realistic, but also more complicated view of the world than any single disciplinary perspective (see Perko 1990; Segerstråhle 1990)[26]. But in many cases such a combination of perspectives seems to be difficult to achieve because, among other things, of the increasing specialization and fragmentation of science (Barnett 1994; Becher 1994). This might lead to narrowing, instead of widening perspectives, as many outsiders seem to fear. In Becher and Huber's (1990, 236) words:

---

[26] As noted in chapter 4, during 'normal times' different and relevant - but somewhat restricted - perspectives easily co-exist as scholars draw their main influences from within their own tribe, emphasising certain value-orientations and concentrating on certain spheres and intellectual

> It is suggested that academics lack a proper concern to think systematically, and tend to ignore the social, political and ecological consequences of their research. They must, entrapped each in their own disciplinary culture, be unwilling or unable to relativise their own perspective and to collaborate with colleagues in other relevant disciplines. It is thus left to the outsiders to cope with practical problems in their complexity.

To reiterate: the fundamental differences in disciplinary perspectives mix with, and are filtered through, local traditions. Consequently, the preferred leadership styles should be viewed as idealtypical and tentative: they do not probably exist in a pure form in all departments representing the studied specialisms.

Subtle processes and subdivisions within the disciplines have recently received increasing attention in the field of disciplinary culture research. According to Pinch (1990, 298), the Kuhnian term paradigm has proved to be difficult to operationalize and much more fine-grained processes have reached the centre of attention (see Becher 1990a, 333). The general process of specialization and fragmentation within the disciplines is reinforced by the rapid expansion of knowledge, citation practices, publisher's commercial concerns, and also by the competition between researchers (Becher 1990a, 340). In the following chapter, I shall concentrate on such fine-grained cultural processes by discussing the development of departmental leadership cultures. The emphasis in perspective will move from the epistemological and social features of the disciplines/specialisms to local social-psychological processes. This, I believe, will provide a useful complementary point of view on the relationships between cultural phenomena and academic leadership.

---

territories. However, hard enough ecological, economic or social crisis may bring the respective values (i.e. 'green values', efficiency, democracy) into a sharper focus.

Chapter 6

LEADERSHIP CULTURES IN A HISTORICAL PERSPECTIVE

In this chapter, I shall view departmental leadership cultures from a pluralist and eclectic perspective derived from organizational culture research. My starting assumption is that the disciplinary cultures and features (chapter 5) provide a broad framework, within which the departmental practices may develop in different directions, depending, among other things, on the main actors - the powerful persons - as well as the social processes in the department in question. I assume that the views, values and assumptions that affect current expectations and patterns concerning leadership in the departments can be fruitfully understood from a historical perspective (Schein 1985). Next, I shall concentrate on local[1] and social aspects: the currently preferred styles of leadership within the departments and their local historical and social backgrounds. I will start by providing a general theoretical framework, which will be followed by an empirical analysis of the leadership cultures of the studied eight departments in a historical perspective.

6.1. THE LEVELS OF CULTURE

As I pointed out in the introductory chapter, by the term *(leadership) culture* I refer to a group's distinct set of (leadership) patterns, features and traditions as well as the values and assumptions that these patterns have possibly been based on. I agree with Gagliardi (1986) and Schein (1985; 1991b) that some cultural elements (deeply held values and basic background assumptions) tend to be more enduring and profound than others. This argument can be supported by empirical research evidence (e.g. Schein 1985;

---

[1] Patton (1990, 67-68) links organizational culture studies to the broad tradition of ethnography, generally focusing on question: "what is the culture of this group of people?". However, according to Schein (1987, 385) the concept of organizational culture derives more from theories of group dynamics and group growth than from anthropological theories of how large cultures evolve. My approach is closer to the latter theoretical orientation.

Rossman, Corbett and Firestone 1988; Kekäle 1994a). According to my previous studies (Kekäle 1991; 1993; 1995a; 1995b) this distinction between deep and surface levels of culture is useful in university settings.

Schein (1985, 8) remarks that the word "culture" can be applied to "any size of social unit that has had the opportunity to learn and stabilize its view of itself and the environment around it - its basic assumptions". Therefore, any set of people with some common history and shared experiences, including most university departments (at least the permanent staff), as well as broader research communities and their work - the construction and deconstruction of knowledge, world-views, and assumptions - can be seen from a cultural point of view (see Kekäle 1995b). Because of the strong expectation of logical consistency and reasoning, academic cultures may sometimes be more coherent than many other kinds of cultures.

I share Becher's (1990, 334) view that we may, depending on our purpose, perspective, and level of analysis, legitimately discuss knowledge and academic cultures at a very general level, disciplinary level or at the level of different sub-units. Birnbaum (1989, 75) claims that cultural differences among colleges and universities derive from basic assumptions and beliefs, not from superficial differences in administrative structures. In similar vein, Dill (1982, 303) maintains that academic institutions may best be understood as value-rational organizations grounded in strong cultures, which can be described as ideologies and belief systems.

As noted in chapter 4, scientific action and scientific schools are based on certain presuppositions and background assumptions. Kuhn (1970) has maintained that alternative ways of practising science are often based on future promise rather than on past achievement. Consequently, a decision to support a certain paradigm has to be made on the basis of *faith* that the new paradigm will succeed in spite of the large problems it will face. Kuhn has also supported the view that sociological studies of different scientific communities may be useful in discovering their dominant norms[2], values and assumptions, on which scientists base their work during periods of 'normal science' (see Caldwell 1982, 70-79; 225-226; chapter 5). According to Guba and Lincoln (1994), paradigms of qualitative research are basic belief systems based on epistemological, ontological and methodological assumptions (chapter 4). In chapter 5, I suggested that the value-orientations inherent in specialisms and disciplines may provide a basis for a distinctive leadership culture in each department. Clark (1983, 75-76) maintains that cultures of institutions and disciplines are

> powerful sources of belief, working locally in the department and the subfaculty, as well as in the university or college as a whole, and producing the more specific set of beliefs that academics live by.

International disciplinary cultures seem to be strongly affected by the basic task of knowledge acquisition (where results are published in written form) as well as by

---

[2] Norms are behavioral rules which are implicitly or explicitly supported by sanctions (see Allardt & Littunen 1984, 21-24).

external social forces (see Becher 1990a). The basic direction of change at the disciplinary level is towards fragmentation (Clark 1983; Becher 1990a). This general process of specialization and fragmentation within the disciplines is likely to result in diversification at the departmental level.

However, when we focus on local departmental and leadership (organizational) cultures, the direct face-to-face interaction between actors starts to play a greater role (Middlehurst 1993, 131); and, as I have argued, the immediate scope for leadership and management becomes at least potentially broader (section 3.2.2.). Thus, it becomes relevant to shift the theoretical perspective to the socio-psychological level. At the same time, leadership will be highlighted, since studies on organizational culture often link cultural phenomena to those of leadership and management[3].

6.2. THE FORMATION OF DEPARTMENTAL LEADERSHIP CULTURES

The formation of a departmental leadership culture can be seen as a complex negotiation and learning process. According to Schein (1985), the basic situations in which group learning takes place occur when the group is dealing with the internal and external problems it is facing. Organizational culture is socially constructed by the members of an organization by negotiating - often also in an indirect and an unintended way[4] (see Schein 1985, 167) - a series of agreements on important organizational issues, such as leadership and working habits. In these negotiations the leaders usually have more power than the others.

Common, shared experiences and stable membership are essential in the formation and reinforcement of basic assumptions, since it is through shared problem solving and experiences that people develop shared meanings and, possibly, taken-for-granted basic

---

[3] Starting from an emancipatory, critical perspective, Alvesson (1995, 46-47) speaks about the managerial bias of western culture as being typical of the contemporary organizational culture research as well (see chapters 4 and 5).

[4] In chapter 3, I discussed a model of the formal decision-making process which attempts to integrate anarchistic, political, collegial and bureaucratic features of higher education institutions (Enderud 1980; Davies & Morgan 1983; Bush 1995; Dearlove 1995a). The decision-making process proceeds from an unstructured anarchy with unclear problems; to a political phase where the issues are then discussed and negotiated further between different interest groups; to a collegial phase, where less active members are persuaded to accept the compromise which is potentially reached during the political stage; and finally to a bureaucratic stage, where administrative considerations may affect and modify the policy. The outcome may be a legitimate and operationally satisfactory policy (Bush 1995, 151-153; Dearlove 1995a, 167). Such a decision-making process may also lead to shared and crystallized cultural values. However, cultural models of leadership emphasize the informal and difficult-to-formalize aspects of an organization rather than its official elements. Since cultural learning may take place almost anywhere and any time in a manner which may be difficult to anticipate, no universal phases of the process may be identified. Hidden or interpreted messages and lessons learned during and after critical incidents faced by organizational members may became crucial points in the process (Schein 1985). Sometimes also rites and ceremonies may facilitate and support cultural learning and emotional commitment.

assumptions and values. In Finland, university departments have usually had for decades quite permanent core members of their personnel. However, there is no obligatory and formal training for the departmental level academic leaders in Finnish universities. Traditional academic freedom and the lack of general leadership training give each academic leader and department an opportunity to follow its own ideas, values, visions, and assumptions concerning good and proper leadership (Kekäle 1994b)[5].

Recently, more power has been assigned to department heads (chapter 2). Professors have been traditionally very powerful persons at the level of basic units, since the departments of the Finnish universities were originally built around single chairs and professorships (Järvi et al. 1990; chapter 2). Consequently, many of the early basic choices of the departments (especially those made during the academic traditional doctrine; section 2.3.1.) have depended mainly on the original professor and his/her preferences. If s/he has wished it, the professor has been able to direct or decide the main specialism of the department on his/her own. S/he has been able to assemble the core group of scholars of the department.

Today, professors still have power and influence over such issues as what kind of research will be conducted within their department, what are the expectations concerning the research, and what is the tempo or the manner of work: although researchers may often be rather independent, academic leaders can hinder or help the pursuit of the scholarly activities of the researchers in many ways (Moses 1985, 338). If a leader does not want to 'lead', one possible lesson learned by 'subordinates' may be that everyone may do as he or she pleases, which may turn into a tradition in the long run (Kekäle 1995b). In this sense, the original professor's style, decisions and preferences have usually been important and influential.

As noted in section 3.1., there is a mutual influence between leaders and followers. An unsubtle use of power seldom produces commitment in knowledge organizations. According to Blau (1974, 135), the members of a group will follow a leader's suggestions if they believe that they will gain something valuable in exchange, i.e. if they believe that they will "benefit from doing so more than from following the suggestion of someone whose abilities are less respected". If the visions, beliefs and values which are held by the founders and leaders[6] (or the ones more or less openly agreed on during the negotiation

---

[5] Because organizations are open systems, pressures and factors external to the organization influence both the construction of the culture and the interpretations and negotiations of the members of the organization. For example, in chapter 2 I suggested that dramatic budget cuts and changing higher education policy can cause some kind of re-orientation within higher education institutions. As noted, the value-orientations of different disciplines or specialisms may provide general models for leadership. However, the researchers of the departments studied are, by their training, experts in their own field of study, not in management or leadership.

As a result, leadership practices may diverge at the departmental level not only because of the diverse leadership influences, but also due to local social processes. Tierney (1991) has suggested that the local faculty and institutional culture might have even more impact on the work of academics than the international disciplinary tradition they belong to.

[6] Professors and department heads are the formal leaders, but there may also be informal leaders, such as competent researchers, who are able to create (sub)cultures. Both individuals and groups may fulfil leadership functions (Kekäle 1995b).

process) seem to work from one time to another, they become collectively validated and accepted. This provides shared evidence of their truthfulness for the members of an organization.

Critical incidents - shared occasions which have affected feelings, caused a re-evaluation of practices, or facilitated group learning - may became crucial points in the learning process, which is already 'filtered through' prior world-views, and influenced by selective perception[7]. As a result, 'validated' views may experience a cognitive transformation and become basic assumptions taken-for-granted by the members of the group (Schein 1991b).

Such assumptions do not need to be further discussed. They start to guide group members' perceptions, thoughts and feelings in a self-evident manner. The group may even forget that some of its members were perhaps at first suspicious of the original espoused vision. Alternative views are no longer visible and other premises or behaviour based on them may be considered inconceivable by the group (Schein 1985, 18). Even if the external conditions change gradually, such assumptions continue to guide action in a self-evident manner (Schein 1985). In a mature organization which has developed a strong culture, the culture, to a great degree, defines what is, for example, to be thought of as good leadership or how authority and power are allocated and managed[8] (Schein 1985, 321; Schein 1986, 96).

Negotiated social order may be based on traditions and on more or less conscious leadership influence. Leadership influence on culture may materialize at least in two ways: 1) leaders provide their own assumptions and visions as an initial road map into the uncertain future (Schein 1985, 318; 1991a; Clark 1996, 54), and the assumptions then become validated through shared experiences; 2) leaders promote 'mythical' interpretations of success after it has happened (Gagliardi 1986, 131). What counts as success varies across time and place, and the negotiation over such issues are not

---

[7] Our perceptions are selective. Often unconscious mental models, schemes or assumptions act as 'lenses' and guide our perception processes (Neisser 1976; Schein 1985). Such assumptions are often activated 'automatically' in relevant situations by affecting our moods, guiding our perceptions and even shaping our behaviour to provide reinforcement for the basic assumptions in question (Hawton et al. 1989; Kekäle 1993).

[8] According to Hogan et al. (1994, 493) leadership is persuasion, not domination: leadership can only occur when others willingly adopt the goals of a group of their own for a period of time. This view underlines the importance of the fit between the assumptions and values of academic leaders and those which are held in the corresponding mature culture. There is often a circular reinforcement between these, since cultural units appeal to, and also try to recruit, 'suitable' personnel (section 6.2.; O'Reilly et.al. 1991). Similar values also contribute to the leader's ability to convince others that his/her views are correct and well-grounded.

Birnbaum (1989, 204-205) notes that good leadership in academic settings may call for constant rebuilding, maintaining and self-correcting organizational systems. In other words, academic leaders act as a thermostat: for most of the time "their responsibility is to keep the institution in proper balance, and not to 'run' it" (at least if this is not expected in the culture in question). At times of crisis transformational leadership may become possible and even necessary. But in a mature culture, basic assumptions may direct leaders' perceptions as much as they direct others's perspectives, thus making (even the discussion about) change difficult (Schein 1986, 96).

necessarily open and verbal (Schein 1985; Kekäle 1991). Moreover, leadership influence may be, more or less, a social attribution (see cognitive theories; section 3.1.).

In any case, the relationship between leadership and culture, or the relationship between culture and its outcomes (such as organizational effectiveness), should not be seen in terms of simple and linear one-way causality (see Alvesson 1991; 1995; Kekäle 1995b). Rather, it is more fruitful to "replace linear thinking with an understanding of how elements and subsystems are connected to each other in nonlinear circles of reciprocal interaction and influence" (Birnbaum 1989, 47-51; Gagliardi 1986), or to view the process as a rising or descending spiral. Situational factors and our (preliminary) ideas, assumptions, interests and values - which are often rooted in past experience - guide the action, and the positive outcome of action may strengthen our values and assumptions, make them self-evident and even 'holy' (Gagliardi 1986). This kind of emotional and cognitive commitment can be a very strong unifying and sustaining force, which may penetrate organizational life in its totality (section 5.5.). As Alvesson (1995, 120) notes:

> Organizational culture not only serves 'positive' functions such as fulfilling people's needs for meaning, guidance, and expressiveness but also leads to closure of mind, restriction of consciousness, and reduction of autonomy. Culture provides direction but also prevents us from 'seeing'. Culture reflects and reinforces not only (true) consensus but also hegemony and domination. It is hardly possible to take all these dimensions into account at one and the same time, but the field of study should reflect them by incorporating multiple perspectives.

Shared meanings form, at least to some extent, a necessary basis for mutual understanding and co-operation, as has been stressed by classical sociologists such as Durkheim, Weber and Parsons (Habermas 1984), and also by philosophers such as Gadamer, Arendt, Rorty, and Habermas (Bernstein 1985, 225-226). However, the process of cultural formation is not necessarily an easy one; in many cases it involves compromise, conflict, ambiguity or even a fractionation of the group, since some members will leave (Schein 1985, 222). For example, the dynamics of science may in principle support fragmentation, as well as integration, of academic cultures (e.g. Becher 1987c; Becher & Huber 1990). Recruitment of new personnel or an external crisis may contribute to cultural change, to a diversification of different sub-cultures within a disciplinary unit (e.g. Häyrynen et al. 1992a, 19-20), or even (in conditions of strong contradictions) to a 'revolution' (Kuhn 1970; Gagliardi 1986).

Although departments often have "a greater degree of integrity and cohesion than the university" (Middlehurst 1993, 131), not all faculties necessarily hold shared values and assumptions: there may also exist several conflicting cultural units, as well as cultural ambiguity[9]. Unified visible behaviour is not necessarily based on internalized and shared

---

[9] Meyerson and Martin (1987) and Frost (et al. 1991) have stated that research on organizational cultures has divided into three distinctive perspectives. These are *the integration perspective*

values, assumptions and world-views, in that the level of commitment to different traditions of the departments may vary. As Tucker (1993, 402-403) notes, conflict may be latent or manifest.

In the academic context and elsewhere, factors contributing to cultural formation are not always sharply distinguishable (except for the purposes of essentially simplifying cultural analysis). What may be a unique culture can be seen as a complex result of social interaction, internal potentialities and expectations, external pressures, disciplinary and academic traditions, and possibly reactions to change factors which are very difficult to predict from a knowledge of either the environment or the members (see Schein 1985, 83). People often also misunderstand each other, which adds to the complexity of the process. As a result, the outcome of this process is open-ended and hard to predict, and at least in the long run in a state of change, although deeply held values and assumptions - *if crystallized* - tend to be more enduring or 'viscous' than other cultural elements (section 4.1.1.).

6.3. SOME REMARKS ON THE DEPARTMENTS STUDIED

There are some general features which should be mentioned before embarking on the analysis of departmental cultures (see also section 4.6.). Some departments (such as department B of physics and department B of biology) differ from the rest in that they were divided physically into different buildings. In department A of physics, theoretical and experimental physicists work on different floors. These separate units seem to form "separate camps" in the sense that there is closer interaction inside each unit than between them.

At university A, the official post of the head of department has been established quite recently, during the late eighties: before that many departments had common administrative leaders. In practice, however, the professors were in charge of their departments. Consequently, in many cases some kind of cultural pattern in departmental leadership and decision making has been established. The position of the professors has still remained strong: many respondents stressed that the professor is the de facto

---

(which views the culture as a homogenous, consistent and based on consensus), *the differentiation perspective* (which sees cultural inconsistency; consensus is achieved only within subcultures) and *the fragmentation perspective* (where ambiguity and change is seen as an inevitable and pervasive cultural element, allowing no stabilization of clear organizational or subcultural consensus). Mayerson and Martin (1987) argue that culture and cultural change can be viewed usefully from all three perspectives. Admitting this, Schein's (1985) approach unites integration, differentiation, and fragmentation perspectives on organizational culture research. It is, however, cognitively and emotionally difficult to adopt a three perspective approach. Preference for a single perspective is often emotionally and politically grounded (Tierney 1989, 22-26; Frost et al. 1991, 159-161). In this study, I try to adopt this three perspective view. Although I lay stress on the integration perspective, I acknowledge the fact that there may also be considerable ambiguity and differentiation within departmental cultures, which may also affect academic leadership (Kekäle 1995b; for the fragmentation perspective, see for example Meyerson 1991; Frost et al. 1991; Czarniawska-Joerges 1992, 166-167; Kekäle 1993b; 1995b; also section 3.2.1.).

(scientific) leader of the department, especially if s/he is active and in a senior position (on the basis of the data, my impression is that if the professor has *not* been active, nobody else has taken the leadership role on his or her behalf). The full professor's position is strengthened by the fact that the chair has been permanent (see footnote 11 in chapter 2). Since the posts of department heads were established, in some departments the full professor has taken on the tasks of the head as well, while at others one of the doctors or (associate) professors has been elected as the head usually for three years. However, recently the arrangements have been changing since the power of departmental heads has been considerably increased by legislation (chapter 2). Such external changes have manifested themselves in different ways in different departments, as will be seen.

In what follows, I will present the data in a form of a descriptive review, in an attempt to reflect the way in which the leadership cultures and their historical and social-psychological backgrounds were described by the respondents. As noted, the analysis is essentially my interpretation, on the basis of the respondents' interpretations. I shall, more or less directly, structure the discussion on the basis of the following closely related aspects which stem from my initial research questions (chapter 1): departmental leadership cultures and their historical background; cultural meanings (expectations, values, norms) attached to leadership in the departments; views on 'good' leadership and the main functions of departmental headship[10]; and the potential impact of academic leaders in embedding, reinforcing and changing the organizational cultures of their departments. I am especially interested in the 'informal' leadership cultures and practices of the departments: How are important decisions actually made in different departments? What kind of values, practices, and patterns are connected to the issues of leadership, management and decision-making in the studied departments? I shall return to these questions in the next chapter, in which aspects other than cultural will be also highlighted.

If not otherwise indicated, the empirical analysis in this chapter is based mainly on interviews made during 1994 and 1995 (section 4.6.). I have not illustrated my analysis with many direct quotations from the interviews: the cultural analysis is based on the largest part of my interview data (about 500-700 pages, dealing with the vies of all 56 respondents), and I have tried to keep the descriptions of the cases reasonably short. (Nevertheless, the chapter still is by far the longest one.) Especially in the later parts of the chapter, I shall make comparisons between leadership cultures in order to bring out the local and unique features.

---

[10] I shall concentrate on those functions and tasks of leaders which seem to be connected to the everyday work and practices in the departments studied. I shall not discuss abstract, general and context-free properties or traits attributed to 'good' academic leaders. For lists of the formal responsibilities, tasks and functions of departmental heads, see Moses & Roe (1990, 64) and Middlehurst (1993, 132-137).

6.4. EIGHT CASE STUDIES

6.4.1. Department A of Sociology

In the department of sociology at university A, four of the five holders of permanent posts[11] were interviewed. In this department, leadership and decision-making has been collegial and democratic. In practice, nearly all the *common* issues including administration, the department's scientific profile and economic decisions are discussed and decided with the staff. The full (and only) professor (who also acts as a head of department) signs the official papers after the decisions have been made collectively. He acts as the representative of the department in the faculty of social sciences and elsewhere. However, his power seems to be rather restricted even in scientific issues in a way that comes close to the 'ideal speech situation' (Habermas 1984). According to one respondent:

> the professor is one member when we discuss about reasonable ways to carry out research... but his position is not stronger than others'... He may argue his views, but it is the content of the argument that makes the difference, not the professorial position... he has always let the people to do what they want...

The pattern of democratic and collegial decision-making is not always followed: decisions on questions like certain appointments, where too many researchers have their own interests involved, have been made between the head of the department and the faculty of social sciences; and each researcher takes care of his or her teaching and research tasks independently. Although the researchers have handled their own work and specialization, the professor/head has been supportive when needed, as was acknowledged by the researchers. If consensus concerning common issues cannot be reached among the personnel, the professor/head has sometimes made the final decisions.

As described in chapter 5, some of the key researchers in both departments of sociology share a critical Marxian background. The leadership cultures seem to be connected to the critical value-orientation emphasising collective action, democracy and emancipation. In department A, two respondents viewed their department (and their university) as socially more coherent than institutions of higher education in general. It was maintained that a normal practice in academia is that researchers work at home and visit the department only when needed - e.g. when they give lectures or hold seminars - but in this department they work at the office and have more informal contacts with each

---

[11] The posts for research/teaching staff are permanent, but the holders may be elected either for a period of five years (assistants) or for the rest of their working lives (most professors).

other during the day. Intimate contacts are easy to maintain, since the department is small[12].

In department A of sociology, there has been a certain continuity (based on the nature of their research and on the values already mentioned; chapter 5) in leadership culture over time, despite the recent changes in higher education policy which have increased the potential power of the head of department (chapter 2)[13]. The department became a fully independent and self-governing unit only a few years ago. It was around this time that the head of department was chosen exclusively among sociologists. However, the fact that the chair in sociology was established well before that time has in practice provided continuity in unit's leadership culture, as well as a great degree of independence in decision-making. Becoming a fully self-governing and independent department also in an administrative sense was originally seen as a strategy of survival. (As will be seen, in the other department of sociology, a contrary strategy - a merger - was chosen for the same purpose.) In department A, the head/professor made a major contribution to this process, although the solution was also supported by other researchers. More recently, the professor has taken the view that independence allows the staff to develop the department more freely, but it also causes more administrative work, which he sees as a drawback.

Although the staff explicitly values collegiality and democratic leadership[14], there is also a tension caused by their rather obvious dislike of administrative tasks. Generally speaking, collegial decision-making is seen by all respondents as a good practice as far as important decisions are concerned. But there are also less important routine tasks and decisions which have to be taken care of. Two researchers noted that their current practice of collegial management can be slow and cumbersome and sometimes involves persons who have nothing to do with the decisions - a limitation also pointed out by Bush

---

[12] The size of the department may also affect the leadership culture. As Wolverton (1993, 14) notes:

> Within a small department, where people can truly be themselves, relationships of a personal and professional nature can easily become blurred and work for the greater good or ill of all who compose the department. It is much more likely that a collegial style of administering the department will be adopted, since departmental committees would otherwise be pointless, and an authoritative chairperson would not long be tolerated. The faculty in a small department may therefore display greater homogeneity of interests and outlooks...

On the other hand, one sociologist noted that the collegial decision-making in his department has ultimately depended on the "good-will" of the professor: in principle he could have changed his leadership style at any time. Indeed, the size of the department alone does not seem to determine the leadership style: the values and the potential power of the (key) actors seem to play a crucial role. As will be seen, in the small departments of history authoritative leadership of some professors has been tolerated; and my sample also includes a much larger department (department A of biology) with a strong collegial leadership culture.

[13] The doctrine of management by objectives was seen in a negative light by many respondents; one respondent even commented that this seems be a unifying factor among the staff.

[14] One sociologist expressed this by saying that she was "absolutely against" individual leadership, which does not enable democratic control. The respondent maintained that the leader can easily spoil the atmosphere and the working motivation in a department. Since the researchers are motivated, the leader should let them do their jobs without interference.

(1995, 66-69). Consequently, some respondents contended that the head should conduct the less important routine tasks and decisions by him/herself[15]. In this way the faculty would get more time to do research, especially since the teaching tasks are quite heavy.

But it was also noted that the problem would then lie in the question: which are routine decisions and which are not? This is a problem, since all the researchers would still like to have their word on at least *important* questions, and it was also stressed that the power of the head should not be allowed to increase considerably. When viewed from a critical perspective, the question is essentially: who has the power to draw the line between the complex and often ambiguous designation of important and less important decisions, and on what basis are such decisions made? There is a risk that the head would make important decisions on his own. The critical value-orientation naturally leads to a desire to make such use of power visible in order to bring the issue under democratic control. This, in turn, easily results in sticking to (basically) collegial decision-making in all questions:

> it is frustrating when routine decisions are discussed three times in the name of democracy. Such decisions could be made without discussion... and then the staff could just be informed about the decisions... But it is extremely difficult to draw the line between important and less-important decisions... if he [the head of department] would make such decisions, soon some not-so-unimportant decisions might also be made by him. It is difficult to know what would happen... Another thing which leads to endless discussion is lack of preparatory work... but then again some issues are such a nature that the motions are best formed through discussion...

Another problem which arises is: who should take care of the routine administration which is viewed as less important? In this department, the head of department was not willing to take responsibility in decision-making about routine administration, and neither, apparently, was anybody else. The conflict between administrative and scientific/teaching tasks is clear in this case (Clark 1983; Hölttä 1995; section 3.2.2.). The professor/head considered collective decision-making during weekly informal meetings as the most economic solution, since the department is small and since he must also take care of the duties of the head of department. He maintained that a stronger leadership role would take too much of his time, since he has to carry out his share of the teaching and research tasks.

---

[15] One respondent held that the attempts to democratize universities - which were promoted especially during the 1970's (chapter 2) - have not been fulfilled. At that time many student radicals hoped to get more power and influence by participating in administration. However, according to him participation in administrative meetings resulted in increased bureaucracy, but not necessarily in democracy (see Aittola 1983; 1984; 1987; sections 2.3.1. and 3.3.). This may have given rise to the disappointment in collective administration. It was also held that nowadays there is not much to dispute about at departmental meetings, since the allocation of money has been made on an equal basis and scarce resources do not allow much latitude in decisions.

There are other conflicting tasks as well: one respondent noted that an important function of academic leaders at the departmental level would be to acquire external funds. But to be successful in this, the leader needs to have a good reputation as a researcher, which in turn tends to cause further tensions between mutually competitive administrative and research tasks. Thus, paradoxically, the dislike of administrative tasks seems to sustain the collegial leadership culture - a pattern which seems to be democratic also in the sense that it causes little harm to everybody instead of directing all the burden of administration to one person.

6.4.2. Department B of Sociology

In the department of sociology at university B, I interviewed altogether five researchers. There were, at the time, seven permanent posts for teaching/research staff, including two professorial posts: a full and an associate professorship. Unlike department A, in this department separate persons acted as the head of department and as the full professor at the time when the interviews were carried out. However, the studied departments of sociology are similar insofar as the actual power of the academic leaders has been quite restricted during the last decade. Although the experience of senior researchers and both the professors is respected when decisions are made in department B, it is clearly expected that all the important decisions should be made collectively, in a democratic manner and on the basis of discussion among the staff. Both the members of the professorial staff deal with the central issues of research, but the academic freedom of the researchers is respected.

In department B, the head of department (usually either a full or associate professor) is mainly responsible for running the administrative bureaucracy within the department. In practice, he or she acts as a convenor, submitter and chairman at the meetings of collective councils within the department. (The departmental head seems to do more preparatory work for the collegial meetings than the leader in department A of sociology.) A key function of departmental headship was seen to lie in maintaining external relations, to the central administration and elsewhere; the head must inform the staff about relevant issues and act as their representative. One respondent held that without such a contribution the central administration might exercise too much power.

The task of the head also includes the final distribution of economic resources, which usually means that he or she signs the papers after the decisions have been made collectively. An exception to the rule has been the appointment of the junior staff, since too many persons have had their own interests at stake. In this department, such decisions have been considered in working groups. The leadership style in the department has not, however, always been collegial and democratic. The following historical background helps us to understand the current cultural preferences concerning leadership.

The last decade ended a period during which the decisions were generally made by a previous full professor. This was described as an "icy period" with an "awful atmosphere" and occasional explicit conflicts along those who were involved. The professor and most of the staff did not get along as individuals, but the leader is said to have had problems outside the department as well. Some researchers held that the contradictions were strengthened by a clash between an "old-fashioned Parsonsian sociology" (as represented by the professor) and the emancipatory interests of the critical Marxian tradition (favoured by most of the researchers in opposition) (see Lyotard 1984; Burrell & Morgan 1985). The conflict took place when student radicalism and political passions were still strong (section 2.3.1): 'conservative', functionalist Parsonsian sociology and the professor's autocratic leadership style were in deep ideological conflict with the critical and emancipatory aims of the radical scholars.

With the passage of time, the situation got worse and contradictions between the leader and staff members with the opposite orientation grew deeper, resulting in a nearly complete breakdown of communication between the parties. The following example describes the atmosphere: a young office employee used to "escape" the conflicts with the professor by taking maternity leave. Over the years she followed this strategy, but when she had already had five children, she finally decided to resign instead.

The tensions within the department were discharged only when the professor retired and the group previously in opposition to the leader was finally able to live by its own values and visions of good leadership. Some other researchers who did not fit into the new collegial leadership culture (that is, the one who had been on the side of the professor) left the department around that time. The problematic period offers a reminder about the potential consequences of a misfit between the deeply held basic assumptions and values of a leader and his/her staff (section 6.2.), and the importance of human relations in general. The conflict affected the functioning of the department. One respondent held that during the worst period, it did not produce any doctoral degrees. The first doctoral degrees were taken only after the situation in the department got better - some twenty years after its establishment!

According to the majority of the respondents, the current strong preference for collegial and democratic leadership and decision making is rooted in the painful experiences during the rule of the previous full professor. It was generally held that the researchers would not tolerate autocratic leadership any longer. It seems that paradoxically the leader had in part helped to construct and strengthen the current leadership culture, although the result seems to be quite different from what was perhaps intended (section 6.2.). The respondents pointed out that in the past ten years they have not had autocratic leaders. The basic values of their culture have not changed because of the recent doctrine of Management by Objectives (chapter 2). Some current researchers have not even met the professor in question, but the legend lives on in organizational sagas (Clark 1983, 83; Schein 1985) which tell the new members what is considered as good and bad in terms of leadership.

Common enemies may unify, as seems to have happened in this case. But the process of cultural formation is not always simple and straightforward (section 6.2.). One respondent held that the shared experience of autocratic leadership might well have led to a "power vacuum" if the staff had grown to appreciate or tolerate its leaders. According to the respondent, the staff would have been quite cohesive even without such experiences, since its members shared similar research interests. In the studied department, however, the majority of the staff was constantly opposed to the "dictatorship" of the professor. Thus it seems that the long fight for emancipation, which was strengthened by the values of critical sociology (chapter 5) and made concrete by everyday experiences, has formed a strong background for the current departmental leadership culture. As noted in one of the departmental interviews:

> *Sociology has a critical tradition which aims at making the voice of the oppressed heard. Do you think this might have affected the atmosphere in your department, to support democratic discussions?*

> That is true, it has certainly affected it, but as I said earlier, there are different kinds of departments of sociology and it has been different here as well... and certainly our past experiences here have been important... that we experienced such a difficult period, it certainly produced an attempt to establish very different practices...

> *So the meanings stem from this kind of background?*

> Yes, very much so...

During the past decade the chair has been mostly held on a temporary basis by acting professors. The headship has been kept from personifying by changing the leaders regularly, often after every year or two. In relation to independent researchers, the position of the academic leaders is reminiscent more of the status of a colleague - or even a servant - than of a master. According to the current head of department, it is strongly expected that the leader should not "lead too much". As one respondent put it: (in their culture) good leadership is invisible and democratic, but the lack of leadership (or bad leadership) would manifest itself in different problems (or in extra administrative tasks for the researchers)[16]. The professors were expected to start new projects, to acquire funding for research and to guide younger researchers on such issues. However, according to a young researcher encouragement is not usually expected from the leaders; he thought that this is a general feature of Finnish culture[17].

As noted in the theoretical introduction (section 6.2.), cultural formation can be seen as a complex, open ended process. It can be said that strong basic values directing leadership have developed in the department. However, the department was facing major changes which might affect the established leadership practices, although the values of

---

[16] Lately, there has been a concern for fewer meetings among the staff. It is expected - in a similar manner as in department A of sociology - that the head would be invisible in the sense that s/he should not bother others too much with "dull duties". This did not seem to raise the same kind of contradictions as in department A (section 2.4.1.); the staff seems to trust that the departmental head will not make important decisions on his/her own. In this department the pattern is that each professor takes care of departmental headship - 'a necessary evil' - in their turn.

[17] However, the head of department A felt that some of the younger researchers need encouragement, since there is a tendency for them to devalue their own work.

democracy, collectivism and emancipation are likely to show persistence and continuity among the core members of the staff.

First, a new full professor had been appointed, but his visions and possible contributions to departmental leadership were not perfectly clear yet. A full professor has a powerful position within a department, and as the departmental history shows, s/he may even contradict the values of the personnel. In this context, such interventions would probably result in resistance and more or less open power struggle, and perhaps even start a re-evaluation by bringing the cultural values into focus again.

Second, some younger researchers seem to be slightly distanced from the rest of the staff as far as their interests and lifestyles are concerned. They seem to be forming a subculture within the department. Some disagreements have been caused by the recruitment of personnel, when one young scholar is to be chosen among colleagues with quite similar backgrounds and merits. If the recession continues, the competition for appointments and resources will get harder, which may affect the social relations among the staff. However, a professor has recently attempted to integrate the younger generation into the collegial culture of the department.

Third, in 1995 the department was undergoing a merger with three departments representing other disciplines or subject fields. The idea of the merger originated as a strategy of survival in the face of budget cuts (department A had chosen an opposite survival strategy before recession by becoming an independent unit; section 6.4.1.), but it was actually carried out in another way than the sociologists had proposed. At the beginning, it was thought that only two departments "with similar identity" - sociology and social policy - would join forces. However, the central administration of the university wanted more departments to be involved in the fusion. One of the fears connected to the merger was that the leadership or disciplinary cultures of the departments might not match with each other. Furthermore, an individual leader would be in charge of the united departments, and one respondent stressed that too much might depend on the personality of that leader. The merger had not yet been completed by the time of the last interviews. Consequently, no knowledge of the outcomes of the experiment was available.

A Note on the Devaluation of Administration

Most of the sociologists interviewed gave the (implicit or very explicit) impression that they were not interested in administrative tasks per se. This seems to be a common orientation among researchers in general (Kekäle 1994b; also Mäenpää & Mäkinen 1989; section 3.3.); as will be seen, this was especially the case in department of A of biology (section 6.4.5.). Some of the sociologists from both departments studied criticised the central administration "which does not understand the work of researchers well enough", and "whose decisions are not within the reach of democratic control". Such criticism was not expressed to the same extent in the other studied departments[18].

---

[18] Three sociologists interviewed stressed that administration is, in practice, necessary. One of them considered that their co-operation with administrators has been handled in a matter-of-fact

The criticism seems to be based on the fundamental cultural (and political) differences in perspectives, values and preferences of researchers and administrators. Clark (1983, 86-87) points out that in universities, subcultures are bound to develop on other grounds than disciplinary location alone:

> There are more general roles, those of student, faculty, and administrator, around which sub-cultures form. As the enterprise grows, sub-culturing around such major roles grows apace, setting student, faculty and administrative worlds further apart and developing further differences within each.

Some critical incidents (Schein 1985) and the respondents' disciplinary-based critical attitudes towards supervision and the use of power (which would prefer emancipation from administration rather than more regulation, increased democracy rather than efficiency; section 5.2.2.) have probably divided the worlds of the staff and administration even more.

The broad critical incidents include disappointment in administrative reform (chapter 2; footnote 15 in this chapter), which, despite the high expectations, seemed to result in increased bureaucracy. There are also more recent examples of frustrating aspects of administrative routines: some respondents held that some of the assignments given by administration overlap with each other, or are otherwise "unnecessary bureaucracy". For example, information and data concerning publications or curricula must be sent to the faculty office or central administration at short notice, although sometimes closely related information has just been transmitted.

The head of department in department B maintained that when the switch to a Graduate school -system took place recently in Finland (see *Higher Education* 1996, 51), it was expected that the reorganization of the whole postgraduate schedule would be carried out in six weeks by the staff. At the same time necessary information about the financing of the teaching duties of the department was lacking. The completion of such contradictory and time-consuming tasks was left to the departmental head and to the administrative secretary. According to the head, it is no wonder that academics show no interest in becoming elected as head of department: nowadays the task means much extra work with only modest extra pay. The heads of both departments of sociology expressed their willingness to resign their headship.

6.4.3. Department A of Physics

As in department B of sociology, two distinct phases in the leadership history of department A of physics can be identified. However, the phases of cultural history are dissimilar - if not in some ways opposite - in these two departments. The department of

---

way. According to the head of department A, it is essential that academics participate in administrative procedures with the administrators.

physics at university A has recently undergone significant changes in leadership and departmental culture. While most of the studied departments have continued with basically similar leadership patterns despite external changes in laws and economic situation (chapter 2), the staff in question has rethought its working patterns quite thoroughly.

The following analysis is based on interviews with ten researchers in the studied department of physics (there were approximately fifteen permanent posts - including one full professorship and three associate professorships - at that time). During the year 1995, I also conducted a minor action research and development project on departmental leadership in this department (section 4.6.). This separate project involved eight additional interviews or discussions with members of staff. The project was connected to a course on organizational consultancy in which I participated.

During the first two decades after its establishment, the department was led mainly by the original full professor and his long-time assistant and colleague who had both worked in the department since its establishment[19]. The founder was widely acknowledged for the choice of the specialism of the department, namely modern optics. This choice was considered as "excellent" by the current head of department, since in this area the department has been able to achieve considerable results in the long run.

The beginning of the research work was not, however, an easy one, since the full professor himself was not originally an expert in this particular field. Instead, he chose to establish his department by starting on a new and promising area of inquiry. According to one respondent, this resulted in a weaker scientific leadership and a quite "diffuse" leadership and departmental culture, since there was no one who could provide leadership and supervision or start research activity effectively. The contribution of the original leaders remained rather weak and indirect (see section 6.2.; on the impact of the founder).

Depending on the person, the leadership culture of the time was considered as a laissez faire, or democratic leadership, which gave the researchers much academic freedom and valued philosophy and education. The administrative decisions were made on the basis of discussions in which the professors had much influence. But the issues concerning research and instruction were left to individual members of faculty to decide. The basic principle of the "low profile leadership" was described by the saying: "let each and every flower blossom". Consequently, on the basis of the respondents' descriptions, the previous culture of this department - which had in fact specialized in an urban area (Becher 1989a) - might be characterized as rural during the eighties: all the researchers worked on their own and at their own tempo. Their pattern of communication was not intense, they had no common meetings, and the personnel were not accountable for their work to anybody. One senior researcher compared the department to his previous department, coming close to the ideas discussed in the theoretical introduction (section 6.2.):

---

[19] Recently, the headship has been taken care of by some of the other professors. The head of department has been elected during "informal" discussions between the professorial staff.

When I came here, I got an impression of a stagnant situation, I mean the posts were granted inspite of the outcomes of work... in that regard the situation has changed... some people have left and new personnel have been recruited... we also connect the continuity of work to the results... [In the late 1980s...] no common seminars were arranged, no common evenings or occasions for the staff to meet each other, but during the last few years the situation has changed fundamentally... however, the old spirit still lives on: although action and co-operation is arranged, the major part of the personnel will not participate... In my previous department, only mortal illness or a journey abroad could have kept people from participating in such social occasions... this really created a certain daily atmosphere in the department...

This is interesting... I have also found that many departments differ from each other. How would you analyze these differences?

I would think that the culture or tradition created by the first leaders of the departments... such tradition is difficult to get rid of... the tradition here is the problem, since you cannot force anybody to be social... but it is not necessarily active passivity; rather they have not seen anything else...

In the early 1990's the department acquired a new leader, who has worked as a head of department and recently also as an acting full professor. He can be considered as a full-time manager of the department. Although some aspects of the previous culture's social atmosphere seem to remain, much has changed, according to many respondents. The new leader's leadership style is more high profile when compared to the style of previous leader. The profile of the department has been raised by "marketing" - by giving the public and potential students more information about the work done in the department. Supervision has become more effective. The research has been organized in a more purposeful way on the basis of common, small projects instead of individual work.

The department has struck a balance between pure science and applied science. Since the funding allocated through university budgets has diminished, the department has been forced to seek sources of external funding. Hard work is seen as a strategy of survival in the department; the vision of the central researchers has been to make the department an internationally acclaimed top unit in their special area. New ways to increase the results of work are considered by the head of department and by the other key researchers. Consequently, the productivity of the faculty has increased remarkably during the 1990's. The head of the department held that in a period of two years they had produced as many postgraduate degrees and international publications as in the previous ten years.

By the mid 1990's, the influence of the collegial councils over the decisions affecting the department had been reduced to a minimum. Nearly all administrative decisions were made by the current head of department, who was also considered to be a very competent researcher. In fact, he sees his task as similar to the task of a project manager in a company. He assembles research groups, provides funding, gives the group its research tasks and ensures that the tasks will be conducted in time:

> I have got a clear vision and harsh measures to carry it through, just as they are carried through in the firms where I have acquired plenty of experience from R & D projects, about how to conduct them on schedule...

According to some of his subordinate staff and himself, the new leader's style is much more direct, effective, and initiative than that of the previous leader, especially in issues connected to the management of the department. The specialism in question seems to favour this kind of more direct leadership[20]. Two younger researchers commented on the change of leader and the new leadership culture in the following manner:

> He [the leader] has been able to stabilize the direction of our department... since then we have arranged seminars, more results are expected, we have got long-time foreign visitors and vice versa... and he has provided funding for the projects, which is of major importance...

> ...it is a clear strategy... results are expected... our strategy of survival is that we have clear annual goals both in terms of degrees and research...

> *Has anybody criticised this?*

> In my view everybody has understood the importance of this... the only thing has been that there has been discussion whether the quality of degrees will diminish if the pressure to produce them is too hard... a common view is that this would be irrational, since it would spoil the reputation of the department...

On the other hand, many of the interviewed post-doctoral researchers of the department seem still to work quite independently and freely on their own projects. According to three senior respondents, the leadership styles of the previous and current heads of departments were not remarkably different, since the previous leaders made the decisions largely on their own. They had not heard many expressions of visions or strategies of survival by the leaders. While the postgraduates saw the increased effectiveness of the department as resulting from the new leadership culture, many senior members of the faculty attributed it more to the pressures of the changing environment such as budget cuts and competition over reduced resources (chapter 2). According to

---

[20] The head of the department felt that academic freedom is valuable in the field of theoretical physics, where, in his opinion, creativity and great ideas cannot be managed. However, according to him "routine research" - in Becher's (1989a) terms, in hard urban applied areas - can and should be managed and organized: it demands lots of work and can have a clear schedule and progress in phases. In the department in question this management of routine research work has been shown to produce good results (see section 3.2.3).

them, the internal changes had started before the change of leader. However, most of the doctors credited the head of the department for his contribution, about which there was no reason for major complaints. It was maintained that the current head of department had supported the changes and advanced the living of the department in an efficient manner[21]. Compared to the previous leader, he also raised more expectations about the productivity or the effectiveness of the projects. The current leader's ability to make decisions was also valued.

Why are the opinions of the doctors and younger researchers somewhat different? One possible interpretation may be that the positions of these groups of researchers is different in relation to the head of department. For most of the older researchers the head of department is a colleague in a position of trust. For the younger researchers he is - in this case - a supervisor and the leader of their research project. As Hersey and Blanchard (1982) have pointed out, direct guidance, support, and leading should diminish when the abilities and competence of the 'subordinates' increases to an expert level. Thus, the leadership style when dealing with these groups should be different (section 3.1.).

One senior respondent pointed out that the younger researchers tend to appraise the contribution of academic leaders on the basis of two aspects: efficiency of supervision and the job opportunities they provide. The younger researchers are likely to be concerned about the continuity of their work, while the senior researchers are already in a quite safe position, and are therefore more interested in leadership in its democratic aspect (see section 2.3.2.)[22]. Indeed, an interviewed young researcher explicitly stressed the importance of the scientific competence of the leaders. He also valued efficiency, as well as a fair treatment of research teams. According to him, the current head of the department is an example of a good academic leader. Two other respondents explicitly shared this view.

All in all, no great criticism was expressed against the current leadership during the first seven interviews in 1994 (see section 4.6.). The main problem in leadership was seen to concern the flow of information, but it was also held that in that respect the situation had been similar throughout the history of the department. Changes in leadership style had been well in line with the expectations and hopes of most of the respondents[23].

---

[21] The head of department held that the recent decision-making culture in the faculty of natural sciences of university A has been similar to his style of management. Consequently, the departments with this kind of headship have been in the best position during negotiations with the dean (see Warren 1993).

[22] Many senior researchers stressed the importance of predictable behaviour, commitment, and some kind of structure in leadership.

[23] Some researchers were still committed to the basic values connected to the previous leadership. One senior member of the staff stressed academic freedom and the cultivating and educational aspects of the university. He contested the view that the university is a commercial enterprise. Instead, it should promote a versatile, philosophical outlook, accompanied by a "healthy, critical perspective" even on the applications and results of science. He was worried that the current trend seems to be towards increasing "technocracy", where everything will be measured by economic values. According to him, the original professor (and his long-time colleague) had similar views about the functions of the university. Two female researchers echoed these values but did not see many alternatives in the recent situation. However, the rest of the staff saw no problems in

However, during the interviews conducted in 1995, some criticism concerning excessively authoritative and "hard" managerialism was expressed by two female researchers, though such aspects were also understood on the basis of recent external pressures and the general difficulty of making changes happen within a department. One respondent noted that the head must nowadays take the main responsibility for the implementation of changes, regardless of how unwanted they might be. Due to its increased funding base, the department was no longer facing clear threats which might affect its survival. Since the worst crisis was over, the motivation of some members to work for change may have decreased, perhaps resulting in a more critical attitude[24].

The aim of the minor development project conducted during 1995 was to help to find solutions to the difficulties experienced in the flow of information and in commitment to the organizational goals. Two years ago, the head had started the following practice: once a year, he discusses with each researcher the expectations and problems concerning the outcome of his or her work. It was agreed that the leader would - after having some consultative discussions and getting acquainted with the relevant literature - take the human relations aspects more into account during the subsequent discussions. Later on, a female researcher held that leadership had indeed become "friendly". According to the head, he and some other members of the staff had found the discussions helpful in solving interpersonal disagreements. The head of department felt that it was time to loosen his grip, since the department was working quite well on its own. He and the faculty were planning to arrange some meetings during which important issues could be discussed. (Unfortunately, my data provides no information about the outcomes of these discussions.) According to the head, the department's specialism is one of the key areas of technology in the EC, so that its economic future seems bright.

Thus, it seems that a quite fundamental cultural change had been taking place in the department and that the process is still going on. According to my interpretation, the relatively successful cultural change so far can be understood in relation to different contextual aspects (Kekäle 1995d; chapter 7): the dramatic budget cuts and external pressures favouring a more effective leadership, as well as accompanying changes in statutes, seem to have contributed to the changes (chapter 2). But as seen in sociology, these pressures alone are not necessarily strong enough to trigger change if they contradict the values of the researchers. In the department of physics, the internal factors

---

promoting increased productivity and efficiency, nor in the increased orientation towards applied research which could help ensure the survival of the department in the long run. Most of them explicitly considered the new leadership style to be better than the previous one, since the expectations were clearer and the performance of the department had increased remarkably in recent years.

[24] These two female respondents tended to emphasize the human relations aspects of leadership (Blake & Mouton 1964). This was not similarly stressed by the male respondents, who for the most part referred to expectations of fair treatment and the competence of the leaders. For example, an interviewed senior researcher was still quite satisfied with the management in 1995. He held that it was no use shilly-shallying endlessly about different matters in teams. Instead, some risks must be taken, since potential opportunities should be seized upon as soon as possible. Accordingly, decisions should be made rapidly when needed, as has been the case in the department.

have also been supportive of the change, since many members of the staff had been hoping for a stronger leadership. The background for this has been partly the dissatisfaction with the previous leadership and departmental culture which was often considered to be too "diffuse" or "ambiguous". The major changes were also supported because of the personal power of the head of the department, which seems to be, among other things, based on his competence and standing as a researcher, as well as his ability to provide funding for the projects at a time of economic depression. It is possible that the developing leadership culture may yet take another course in the future, for example as a result of the appointment of a new full professor.

6.4.4. Department B of Physics

I interviewed altogether eight current members (plus one former member) of the staff in the department of physics at university B. There were twenty-six permanent posts for teaching/research staff, among them four full professorships and seven associate professorships. According to the head of department, the core personnel have worked for decades in the department.

In this department of nuclear physics, all the important decisions have been traditionally made by a leading group which consists of the professors and the leaders of the research projects, totalling about ten persons (see Middlehurst 1993, 120). On some major issues, the proposals of the leading group are further discussed by the whole personnel (over one hundred members -the proportion of (visiting) staff working on temporary projects is high) at the collegial council, but usually no major changes are made[25]. The head of the department is elected by the professors among the professorial staff, which also gives them some kind of collegial control over him/her. When the interviews were carried out, an associate professor acted as the departmental head.

It is the task of the head of the department to call together the leading group when important issues are to be discussed. Not much preparation for the meeting is done by the head, but the issues are thoroughly discussed in the leading group. According to the respondents, the most difficult decisions have concerned the allocation of economic resources and appointments of personnel; such decisions seem to have caused conflicts in the other studied departments as well, since the interests of the faculty are closely involved. In the department of physics under discussion, however, the leading group has been able to make decisions in a manner that maintains mutual trust, although consensus has not always been easily reached.

According to the interviewed researchers - as well as many of the members of staff of department B of biology where a similar practice is used (see section 6.4.6.) - their leadership culture is considered to be good and to work well as it minimizes conflicts in the long run and provides more information for the needs of decision-making. In fact,

---

[25] Having read a preliminary version of my article dealing with the departmental leadership cultures (Kekäle 1994b), the head of department contacted me and stressed the decision-making power of the leading group as opposed to that of the collegial council (see section 4.3.).

nowadays the tradition is so strong that the individual leaders or heads of departments cannot make important decisions on their own. (In the previously discussed department of physics, individual decision making seems to be generally considered as a good and normal practice and to raise no objections.) As in the discussed department B of sociology, only some routine administrative decisions, the signing of papers, and the task of representing the department, are left for the head in department B of physics. According to the respondents in this department, ones departure from tradition would cause objections and complaints, and such individualistic decisions would not be considered valid. Indeed, no such incidents have occurred in the department. The heads have differed in their eagerness or activity in picking up the problems. But as an assistant noted, the general cultural pattern in decision making has not been affected by changes in personnel, nor by changes of the head of department. It was not believed by the other respondents, either, that any external changes would alter the valued leadership culture:

No, I don't think that anything like that would happen...

I sometimes feel that it is a tradition... the way the department functions... it is not affected by appointments, changes of the head of department, or changes of assistants... it just stays the same...

According to the head of department, the tradition of decision making based on discussions in the leading group originates from the initiative of an original full professor who was considered as the founder of the department. The change of the head in periods of (nowadays) two to four years was also attributed to him. As mentioned earlier (in section 4.2.3.), the nature of the specialism seems to favour group work at least in research. In this department, different practices were first tried out, but the staff settled for a leading group.

There seems incidentally to be differences in the position of academic leaders in different countries. According to a respondent who had experience in working in laboratories in the USA, the procedure in their department is relatively "democratic" and "decentralized". The individual professors and the leaders of research groups are not as powerful, since they discuss matters concerning research within their research groups (see Traweek 1988, 91; section 5.2.3.). However, two physicists held that intensive working patterns seem to be a general feature among nuclear physicists - which would be well in line with the urban, hard and convergent nature of the specialism (Becher 1989a; see chapter 5).

The department has a rich history with some shared critical incidents (Schein 1985; section 6.2.), against which the excellent atmosphere and intense working patterns stressed by the respondents can readily be understood. The original full professor was called to establish the department in the mid- sixties. He took some of his students and colleagues with him and together they formed the original research group of the department. The choice of specialty resulted quite naturally from the interests of the professor and his group, since he was already a respected expert in nuclear physics, regardless of his relatively young age. One respondent noted that at that time his leadership was strong and purposeful, while he also wanted to listen the opinions of his colleagues - this was reflected in his preference for collegial decision making in leading groups. His long-time colleague remembers that:

> ...it was not a common pattern at that time that a professor and a head of department would have discussed with others... but he was democratic in that sense. It was that kind of sensible democracy which was not necessarily to the liking of all students in the 1970s. He was not for a 'one man-one vote' principle, but instead he wanted a collegium [a leading group], or what was the name of it at that time... and he specifically wanted the post of the head to be circulating...

A long-time professor held that the excellent atmosphere in the department is largely due to the original professor. The respondents described the professor as a good or superior, "visionary" and "charismatic" researcher, who often set very high expectations for himself and his group. One respondent maintained that the lectures he gave for beginning students would nowadays be judged as too demanding. His commitment and his serious and persistent attitude towards their work became obvious when the department was to acquire the first cyclotron. The professor had assumed the chair on condition that the necessary accelerator for experimental research would be provided. But the complete, ready-to-use cyclotron turned out to be too expensive. Since the manufacturer also had problems with the assembly and the delivery of the equipment, the first accelerator was mainly assembled by the young staff (most of them in their twenties)[26].

The cyclotron was located in the basement of an old laundry, which served as the main building of the department at the time. So, instead of doing research, the postgraduate students found themselves carrying bricks. This phase of intense manual work took years to complete. In retrospect, the professor's contribution during that phase was seen mostly in providing leadership and arbitrating disagreements. The managerial and technical side of the assembly was delegated to an engineer, whose style of management was described as hard and autocratic. Most of all, he made sure that the task was conducted on schedule and that the cost estimate was not exceeded. The unanimous opinion of the respondents was that such management was necessary at the time. Later on, when the second and larger accelerator was built, the engineer's contribution was again very substantial, as will be seen.

The respondents pointed out that when the experiments with the first cyclotron finally started, the "enthusiasm" and the "excitement" among the young faculty were at a high level, as were also the expectations, objectives and "pioneering spirit". The faculty (including the original professor) worked long days and nights. They "took risks" and concentrated on "difficult and long experiments", which could not be carried out in large laboratories because of the short beam-times given to each group. At first these

---

[26] Building and inventing research equipment seems to be a part of the nature of the broad specialism (Traweek 1988, 49).

experiments resulted in dead ends and failures, but such experiences were considered as "extremely instructive" by the staff. The equipment was constantly improved. When they eventually got good results, it strengthened the team spirit and a certain positive 'everything is possible' attitude which had been cherished by the professor and was still expressed by many respondents during the interviews. A general interpretation seems to be that they had, as a team, carried out a nearly impossible task.

One respondent concluded that the enthusiasm and scientific ambitions were further strengthened by hard competition for permanent posts, by the example given by the respected leaders, and by the normative pressure of the research groups (see section 5.2.3.). But the researchers also found the international contacts inspiring, since young researchers in their twenties regularly visited foreign countries and met Nobel prize winners. A former member of the staff held that the resulting enthusiastic atmosphere and strong culture made it impossible to slow down the tempo at work:

> The department was small and we had only few groups... it was not forced, but extremely enthusiastic leaders showed the model and the others followed... when it started rolling it was impossible to slow down... it was an unspoken rule of life...

All the respondents credited the original professor for a major contribution, especially during the early years of the department. A researcher who had worked with him for twenty-five years claimed that no other leader would have been able to make all this happen. Around the time when the experiments were started, a chair in theoretical physics was established, which supported the main specialism of the department. Since then the faculty has grown steadily. According to a respondent, the two full professors of that time were open-minded enough to broaden the scope of research conducted in the department. When the researchers were able to get started with their research projects, the leadership of the professors grew more indirect, allowing the faculty to "fulfil its ideas within certain limits". The professors' leadership style was described as leadership by example: their commitment to the work, as well as their objectives concerning the research, remained high. This was now seen as a feature of current departmental culture.

It seems that the department has found its own way, since there have been no major problems in relation to social relations or leadership (and, consequently, no need to think about such issues; section 6.2.). Many respondents had a hard time pointing out the distinctive characteristics of good academic leaders. They also had difficulty in naming respected individual academic leaders. The respondent quoted previously noted that "during the most active years leadership was not needed" and that "few of the personnel even knew who the leader was" (see Tucker 1993, 60). Another respondent held that since their specialism stresses team work, individuals do not stand out as clearly as in other fields[27]. Still another physicist claimed that on a normal working day one needs the

---

[27] According to Traweek (1988, 101), each accelerator laboratory "is thought by physicists to reflect the necessarily powerful personality of its director". For example, Traweek (1988, 3-4) describes the influence of the leader and the founder of the first major American accelerator at the

advice of engineers and technicians, but not necessarily that of academic leaders. It seems that the clear, well-working models of research originate from an exact area of inquiry with uniform standards and procedures (Becher 1989a, 154) which are learned within the department as well as through numerous international contacts. All in all, the culture of the department provides a certain continuity, some unquestioned values (commitment to work, priority of exact knowledge, etc.) and common meanings and a well-working leadership pattern to lean on.

In the late eighties, a new accelerator laboratory was built (again, largely by the staff). This major investment was made because of the good reputation and results achieved by working with the old equipment. Traweek (1988, 1-3) has pointed out that high energy physics - which is closely related to nuclear physics[28] - has had a particularly strong position in western societies: "The expansion of the resources of the physics departments is the envy of other disciplines". During the construction process, the previously mentioned "hard" manager was again in charge. One researcher stressed that the huge project was carried out on schedule and - regardless of inflation - the actual costs were lower than the original cost estimate.

In thirty years, the department has grown from a minor group which worked under "primitive conditions" and was led by one full professor, to a widely respected and acclaimed international research unit with a staff of over one hundred members. Besides the post of head of department, there is nowadays also a post of leader of the accelerator laboratory. According to the latter, the research groups have currently many foreign members, which demands an ability to deal with cultural differences. His own solution - which has so far worked out quite well - has been to be open, co-operative and helpful when dealing with the members of the group.

A great deal of the time of the leader of the accelerator laboratory goes to participating in meetings and to writing applications and reports. All the proposals for experiments (the proposals may originate from different countries) are evaluated by an international body. On the basis of this evaluation, the leading group of the accelerator laboratory (which is not the same as the leading group of the department) decides the amount of beam-time given to each experiment. The proceedings of the experiments are followed up on an annual basis by a separate group (see Traweek 1988, 4-5). The leader of the laboratory takes part in both these groups as chairman. The managerial and administrative tasks are a growing part of his work, although major decisions are, as before, made in leading group.

University of California at Berkeley as long-lasting. Ernest Orlando Lawrence was "indefatigable in his search for money to support the lab": "his public appeal that physics should be funded because it ultimately enhances the public good has been copied by today's physicists". Moreover, Lawrence's role in design, construction, research, and funding "established a style in laboratory research that is maintained now throughout the particle physics community".

[28] By working with great accelerators, particle physicists (high energy physics) deal with the basic constituents of matter and the elementary forces between them - the components of the nucleus. Nuclear physicists deal with the relations between nuclei; the main implications of their work lie in nuclear energy, material science and medicine (Traweek 1988, 3-4).

The professor who acts as the leader of the accelerator laboratory has especially tried to provide funding for research projects - a task which he has succeeded in. Some applied projects have been started in the department in order to broaden the funding base. But, in fact the department has not been in financial difficulties during the general recession, since the budget cuts have been compensated by extra funding from foreign countries. Flexible allocation of resources between projects has also helped the department to overcome the recession without noticeable damage to its essential functions (see Kekäle 1995c).

6.4.5. Department A of Biology

I interviewed altogether ten biologists in the department of biology at university A. There were approximately twenty permanent posts for research/teaching staff - two posts for full professors and three for associate professors. In this department, decisions are made on the basis of discussions by virtually the whole staff. If consensus cannot be reached among the personnel, the head has the final word. At least some kind of compromise is always aimed at. The interaction among the faculty seems to work on a daily and a very open basis, during meetings and coffee breaks. The atmosphere was considered as excellent by the researchers and by the students as well (Häyrynen et al. 1992b; Kekäle & Kuittinen 1993).

In everyday communication, status hierarchies are not stressed or respected. Rather, a spontaneous reaction to "showing off" would be joking and laughter. It is in keeping with this attitude that the departmental leaders are respected as human beings, but their work - or management/leadership in general - is certainly not idealized. As described in section 5.2.4., most of the researchers share the disciplinary (green) values, and the close interaction is in part a typical feature of the field. One respondent maintained that funding for the projects in the department comes from different sources, which means that there is less competition and fewer potential contradictions among the faculty. However, some respondents stressed that a good working atmosphere is not necessarily a typical feature of the departments in their field.

When discussing good leadership, the interviewed professors stressed the importance of assertiveness and the ability to make decisions *when needed*, but, generally speaking, no major differences of opinions were found. The researchers presented fairly unanimous opinions on the leadership culture of the department and on their respect for academic freedom, as well as on the valuation of the democratic leadership and decision-making based on discussions open to the whole staff. The members of staff stressed that a strong individual leader would not be successful in their department because of the existing leadership culture: that kind of leader would spoil their excellent atmosphere. On the other hand, decision making by professors in *leading groups* (which was favoured in the department B of physics) would not be accepted either. In some cases it had been tested, but some members of the staff were clearly against. It was felt that the procedure violated the central values of democracy and open participation, and threatened to split the faculty into separate camps. One respondent expressed the view that the practice was indeed "extremely inconsistent" with the valued pattern of decision making:

> ...it has happened that professors have retired to their great wisdom and made decisions on their own... it has not happened often, but usually it has resulted in conflict and deterioration of the spirit within the department... such practice is extremely inconsistent, if all the appointments made have so far been made in a democratic manner and on the basis of competence, and then suddenly this does not seem to happen... but after all we have got good researchers in that way too, so this is more a matter of principle...

It seems that a strong leadership culture has been constructed by the core members of the staff, some of whom have been working in the department since its establishment. Their mutual co-operation has been unproblematic from the beginning. Some researchers were colleagues (or, as one researcher put it, good friends) even before they started their work in the department. The leadership of the long established professor (who has also worked as the head of department for most of the time) as well as other important members of the staff has been democratic, friendly, supportive and broad-minded all the time. It was sometimes explained that at first the current leader adopted a more "traditional professorial role", but he very soon found common ground with his colleagues. Later he became a full professor, but he still continued to lead in an open and democratic manner.

The leadership can be described as follows: it is not direct but leadership from the background, it values people and academic freedom, and emphasizes human relations and necessary work conditions, though not so much administration. An associate professor held that a well-working headship is one factor behind the department's success. The respondents commented that the original full professor has always used his power "for and with the faculty", not "over" or "against" it. There have been no other "power-greedy" persons in the department. The professor himself held that each researcher in the department is powerful. His explicit leadership philosophy comes close to McGregor's (1961) *theory Y*: since the researchers are internally motivated and very capable, the leader should 'unchain' them and let them work freely along their interests within a certain loose framework, structured by the very broad scope of research in the department[29]:

> a leader should let the people's own talents come out... so that they will be able to do their best, yet at the same time making sure that it will not meander too much... you have got to let them be free, and then results will

---

[29] The research interests and specialization in the department were described as very broad, covering nearly all areas of biology (which are often divided elsewhere into separate departments, such as zoology, botany, ecology and genetics; see section 5.3.). According to the respondents, the professors have not tried to direct or frame the specialisms of the individual researchers. This solution has been well in line with their supportive approach. Lately there has been strong external pressure to set some kind of priority among the research topics (chapter 2).

be achieved... chaining them too much is one of the worst mistakes which a leader can make...

in my view, the role of the head of department is to create opportunities for people to do decent work... so that administration would not interfere too much with their work, so that it would not spoil good peoples' work (laughter)...

It was generally accepted that the human relations and leadership aspects (Blake & Mouton 1964) have been handled "intuitively" in a very good, or even in the "best possible way" by the original professor and by some other core members of the staff. Their social skills have found good use when supervising students who have problems with their studies. The professor/head seems to be highly trusted among the staff. It was said that he even knows quite well the private matters of the researchers. The professors of the department are respected on the basis of their active research contribution.

However, some respondents expressed a mild criticism in remarking that the administrative and managerial tasks have not been taken care of in an equally excellent manner, since decisions tend not to remain on schedule. The professor and two other interviewed biologists (all of them had acted as a departmental head or dean) held that it would be very difficult to succeed equally well in all the different roles of academic leaders, related to the diverse tasks of research, teaching and administration (a conclusion in line with the findings of Mäenpää & Mäkinen 1989; see section 3.3.). Instead, it was said that professors and departmental heads tend to concentrate their efforts mainly on some of these roles[30].

At the time when the interviews were conducted, another researcher was acting as the head of department on a temporary basis. He had basically continued the valued democratic leadership tradition (which would, as he admitted, be very difficult indeed to alter), but he had also been more precise in dealing with the administrative procedures. The recent budget cuts[31] seem in fact to have increased the valuation of good administrative management among the staff. One respondent mentioned in 1995 that the continuity of the work of the researchers was more tightly connected to the results and efficiency of the projects. This new trend is due to the budget cuts and the general financing policy which emphasises measurable results. However, in this department the new demands have been expressed in an "indirect" and a "soft" manner by the professors.

---

[30] Such orientations are usually connected to the personality, competencies and values of each leader. The fundamental question is: if there is not enough time to get every possible task done in a best possible way, what should I concentrate on? What are the most important (or the most interesting) aspects of my work? In the university context, the answer has usually been fairly obvious, since academics tend to value research over teaching and administration (Mäenpää & Mäkinen 1989; Kekäle 1994b; see section 6.4.7.).

[31] According to the head of department, the suggested budget cuts for 1994 related to their annual part-time teaching budget in the proportion of 3 to 5 (where three stands for the cuts, while five equals to the money previously needed for part-time teaching on an annual basis). According to

A Critical Incident

The preferences concerning departmental decision-making and leadership seem to be comparable in this department with those in the departments of sociology. In all three departments, important decisions are made in open and democratic discussion. However, it is also suggested that the head of the department should take care of routine administration without bothering the researchers too much. The permanent faculty in the department of biology is considerably (three to four times) larger than the faculties in the departments of sociology. However, the 'disciplinary profile' of the soft areas of biology seems to be rather similar to that of sociology, when they are compared on the basis of Becher's (1989a) disciplinary dimensions (chapter 5).

The basis of the similar preferences concerning leadership nonetheless seem to be different: for critical sociologists the democratic values have a largely political and theoretical/ideological background (see section 5.2.2.). In biology, democracy and open participation were strongly preferred as a good departmental practice, but the biologists' political aims seem to lie elsewhere. Both biologists and critical sociologists seem to favour alternatives to the status quo in society, but biologists are inclined to criticise society on the grounds of the environmental problems, while the critical sociologists have found their main reason for protest in the inequalities concerning wealth, power or opportunities (chapter 5). But even so, perhaps an indirectly common political framework for these leadership cultures can be discerned.

According to the original full professor of biology, their leadership culture was established during the process of degree reform (chapter 2). It is not necessarily a coincidence that the values of open participation and democracy were stressed during the reform, whose ideological background has been claimed to be that of Marxism-Leninism (Häikiö 1977; section 2.3.1.). Some of the main principles of the reform were to increase democracy and the participation of students and the whole staff in decision-making (Paukkunen 1977) - features which are highly valued in the department of biology.

The critical attitude towards administration seems to have strengthened during the degree reform (e.g. Kivinen et al. 1993; chapter 2) of the late 70's, which has become, in many ways, a major critical incident (Schein 1985) in the history of the young department. The reform faced strong resistance in the department, since the changes were brought "from outside". Although the staff considered the reform as "unnecessary" and "laborious", it had to conform to the changes which were supported by legislation. Many respondents claimed that the reform has unified the staff by offering a common enemy in the form of "unnecessary bureaucracy". This general attitude seems to be still quite strong among the staff, but there remain slight differences between individuals. The "devaluation of formalities" and administration was seen as a general feature of the departmental culture by some biologists.

In the light of current experience, however, it was felt that the staff were right after all, since some of the "forced decisions" were reversed later on. All in all, although the reform was resisted, it seems by the same token to have selectively strengthened the

---

him teaching was the only area where the massive cuts might be directed, but of course, research would suffer from such cuts. too.

'soft' values of democracy and open participation: only those aspects which were in line with the emergent culture, and with which the staff could easily identify, were absorbed (see chapter 5; section 6.2.).

6.4.6. Department B of Biology

I interviewed altogether six biologists in the department of biology at university B. There are twenty permanent posts in the department (five full professorships and three associate professorships). The department has many divisions or lines of study, each structured around full or associate professorships: the respondents were chosen to represent harder specialisms such as biochemistry, cell biology, molecular biology and hydrobiology (Becher 1989a; chapter 5)[32].

In this department, the decisions concerning important issues are discussed in a leading group (called a collegium) which consists of professors and the leaders of research projects. According to three respondents, the head of the department makes the final decisions, but practice has been that very strong grounds are needed if s/he is to oppose the will of the collegium. Some issues are discussed further in meetings by the whole faculty. The collegium itself is not an official decision- making body. Its main purpose has been to provide democratic control, to stimulate discussion about the decisions, and to spread information concerning the decisions and important issues to the rest of the staff. Especially when the collegium is not unanimous, the power of the head to make the final decision increases.

This leading group practice is somewhat similar to the one used in department B of physics. However, the position of the head has been potentially stronger in this department of biology, since in practice s/he takes the final responsibility for the decisions in both official and unofficial terms. The interviewed head of department and another respondent saw that the actual power of the head depends much on the person and his/her willingness to contribute to decision making. Moreover, consensus is not aimed at as eagerly by the collegium and the time-budget of the meetings seems to be more tight in this department.

The position of the head has been further strengthened by the following procedure: in addition to the collegium, the department has a minor body which undertakes the preparatory work for meetings and submits the agenda for the collegium, which then discusses the propositions. In the department of B of physics, the important issues were discussed without much preparation in the leading group; similarly, no preparation before the collegial decision-making is usually done in department A of biology and department A of sociology.

---

[32] There were only a few (2-9) permanent posts in each division. One to two key respondents were interviewed in each of them. I shall discuss leadership practices on the level of the department as a whole.

The minor submitting body of department B of biology consists of the head of the department, his deputy and an assistant, whose contribution seems to be actually quite significant. Some urgent tasks and negotiations have been delegated to this body or to other working parties. The collegium was enlarged to its current composition (the professors, the leaders of research projects and an assistant) at the beginning of the decade. The 'body of three' which submits the plans to the collegium was also established during that time. Respondents held in 1994 that the practice had so far worked "reasonably well".

Nowadays, the head of department is elected for a period of three years. According to the respondents, the leadership styles of individual heads have varied substantially in the past. The current head considered the post as necessary, but held that it is not easy to find willing persons for the task - a view widely shared by the respondents. According to him, the expectations of the faculty can be quite high, although no schooling for the task is currently provided. The two interviewed professors and the assistant were not at all against a stronger managerial position for academic leaders, nor were they against increasing the efficiency of the research groups, although - at the same time - some collegial discussion and democratic control were considered as valuable. These respondents seemed to share a common vision of a stronger and more effective academic leadership, where the emphasis would be on assembling research groups and providing funding for them. Nor were the basic principles of Management by Objectives resisted. A professor noted:

> I accept the principle that economic resources are allocated to those groups which produce something in return... projects and groups with weak outputs must be either terminated or re-activated so that they produce something... this is a very difficult issue, and I do not accept Management by Objectives completely without reservations, but I still feel that it is a better system than the previous one...

Having observed different leaders, all the respondents were convinced of the importance of effective academic leadership. The following example was given: approximately one dissertation in ten years was produced under the supervision of a professor, while under the leadership of his follower the same department produced ten dissertations in one year. In fact, all the respondents connected the whole long-term success and vitality of the specialism and the department to the manner in which the leadership (especially the chair) was handled. According to one respondent, this impact is evident especially when opposing extremes of leadership styles are compared. A professor maintained that:

> the task of the head of department is a demanding one... the better s/he works the better the department functions; the worse the contribution of the head is, the worse the functioning of the department is. The importance and meaning of the head of department has not been fully recognized and understood within universities...

However, in those departments (like department B of physics) which have had for a long time a well-working and un-problematic leadership culture (which has eventually become taken-for-granted), leadership and the functioning of the department were not connected in a similarly direct manner.

In department B of biology, a professor held that the head should delegate the routine tasks to other members of staff (instead of the others delegating them to him/her, which would seem to be a more natural option or practice in the departments of sociology and in department A of biology). He also proposed that the teaching and research tasks of the head should be diminished so that s/he would be able to concentrate on the strategic and important issues of developing and managing the research and instruction in the department.

Another (acting) professor proposed temporary posts for professors: the continuity of the work should not be taken-for-granted - as it nowadays seems to be - but the re-election should depend on the results of the research. According to him, the professor determines the pace of work for the whole group, but he acknowledged that the "happiness" of the staff does not necessarily increase if they work harder. The respondent would also prefer to leave the departmental administration and management to a permanent "administrative" or "leading" professor so that the researchers could be enabled to concentrate on research. Such a professor should have a strong scientific background, and preferably a degree in administrative or economic sciences as well. S/he should work to benefit the whole department, not just certain groups. According to him this model (used in some departments in Germany) will be increasingly necessary in the future because of the growing competition and demands for efficiency. Surprisingly, such a person seems to match some of the characteristics of a most unwanted leader in department A of biology.

The decisions concerning the allocation of resources have been made on a collegial basis in this department. The different divisions led by the professors have used the money according to their own preferences; the divisions have traditionally worked quite independently. In line with the vision of stronger and more effective leadership, the trend has recently been towards increasing coordination and integration between research projects. Some of the most difficult decisions have so far concerned the priority of research topics and areas. The disagreements have been brought to the forefront by the fact that the department has recently faced financial difficulties. Adequate resources for teaching were not easy to find and there was considerable pressure to discontinue some temporary posts as well[33]. Such issues were discussed in collegium and also by the whole staff of about sixty persons. Naturally, it has proved difficult to reach a consensus about which activities should be discontinued, since everyone considers the issue from his or her own point of view.

These tensions have recently affected the working atmosphere, which has so far been quite good according to most of the respondents. Two interviewed members of non-professorial faculty felt the threat quite strongly and bitterly. They held that at least three posts would be terminated, but the staff are kept in uncertainty about their future. The

---

[33] The economic situation did not seem to be quite as bad in the other studied departments.

general discussions have not led to any solutions. According to one of the respondents, the final decision ultimately depends on the head of the department. It was suspected that the specialisms currently without a permanent professor - or with a passive professor - would be in the worst position when the cuts were implemented (see Wolverton 1993, 10-12).

The doctors have traditionally continued to work in the department, but nowadays they are increasingly expected to find a job somewhere else. The temporary posts will for the most part be allotted to new postgraduates who - when taking their doctoral degrees - will simultaneously provide some additional funding for the department. This may lead to a contradictory and paradoxical situation, since some older doctors find themselves competing for the same low-paid posts as the students they are supposed to supervise. The head of the department and two other respondents criticised the recent politics, where the postgraduates are expected to take their degrees rapidly but where the continuity of their work is not taken care of. According to them, more mid-level posts should be available, but the resources are scarce. One professor of sociology expressed the same worry about the job opportunities of post-doctorals. Indeed, such problems, connected to the reward structures in higher education, seem to undermine the current doctrine of Management by Results, since the rewards are not, after all, strictly connected to the results (section 2.3.2.).

6.4.7. Department A of History

Five of the eight holders of permanent posts were interviewed in the department of history at university A. (Nowadays, there are two full and two associate professorships in the department.) Previously, a case study dealing with organizational cultures of the department had been carried out (Kekäle 1993a; section 3.3.). Like the other departments at university A, the department had a common administrative leader with some other departments in the faculty until the late eighties. It was only after that time that the first actual head of department was elected in departmental council. There are two separate divisions or lines of inquiry, which have traditionally been led by separate (at first associate, later full) professors: General history and Finnish history.

According to the respondents the long-standing professor of General history had clearly orientated himself to the tasks outside the department. Consequently, he did not have time to concentrate on the tasks in the department, such as the supervision of research, which also resulted in a lack of academic followers. A respondent maintained that it was largely expected and accepted that the professors of the time would take part in larger questions in society, but need not be too concerned with the everyday matters in their departments.

The leadership style of the professor was described as "impulsive" and "autocratic" during the periods he worked in the department. One respondent noted that he preferred "individualistic" research, not projects. After the full professor retired, the application process for the professorship took years to complete, as it usually does (Airaksinen 1995). Consequently, the leadership of the division of General history was handled, for a long time, on a temporary basis by different (acting) professors. The respondents generally held that this interregnum has had an adverse effect on the long-term development of the division. The head of the department pointed out some aspects of the problem:

> I would say that co-operation and social relations have been weaker on our side than on the other side of the department... we have not had a similar kind of continuity as far as the holders of key posts are concerned...

There seems to have been cultural differences within the two divisions which were, according to the respondents, connected to their different leadership histories (Kekäle 1993; 1995b). The culture of the division of General history was described as quite individualistic at the beginning of the 1990's. For example, the students interviewed in the previous research pointed out that they were expected to work on their master's thesis on their own, as had at times been explicitly stated by the supervising teachers. Among the staff, there seemed to be a preference to concentrate on their own business. As mentioned earlier, such individualistic modes of work seem especially typical of history as a discipline (chapter 5). It has moreover been (historically) quite common in Finnish academic culture to stress the importance of academic freedom and the importance of the individual's own work and talents when appraising academic success (see Häyrynen et al. 1992b, 17-18).

The division of Finnish history has had the same professor for nearly twenty years, which has provided a certain continuity to the leadership. The long-established leader of the division has criticized the traditionally individualistic nature of basic academic studies. From the very beginning he stressed the importance of effective supervision and support of graduate students[34]. Since then, the students have been encouraged to consult their teachers at any time during the day with their problems. According to the respondents, the teachers in this division have tended to have a closer interaction with each other and with the students than the teachers of General history. One respondent

---

[34] However, his opinion was that postgraduate studies require more independence: researchers must carry out their studies by themselves, no matter how much discussion or supervision there might be. According to him, the reasons why a study does not reach completion are only excuses, since researchers have always had to work in their own time. He held that the best way in which an academic leader can support the work ethic of the staff is to recruit motivated postgraduate students and researchers; people either have motivation or don't. According to him, given that the results of the work are of necessity important, the current trend towards increased efficiency is fully justified:

> when the MBO is criticised... that the business world is moving away from it... I don't believe this at all. In my view, since we are using decreasing public funding in the academic world, some kind of results have to be achieved. How will the results be measured if not by checking what has been done? This is not bad at all; on the contrary, it motivates the departments which have previously shown good results. If no attention is paid to the results, it would be nonsense....

All in all, the values of the professor seem to be quite explicit and he also practices what he preaches: it should be clear to everybody that hard work is respected in his division.

described the leader as a hard worker, who manages effectively to handle the basic tasks of the department: research, supervision and instruction - a rare feature according to three interviewed biologists (see section 6.4.6.).

But according to the professor himself, he is not interested in administrative tasks, or in being the head of the department. He holds that it would be "ridiculous" to discuss good academic leadership at a general level in the department. Instead, the results of the work speak for themselves. The feedback should be given, and the problems should be discussed during the relevant situations at work: good leadership is "invisible". Indeed, his colleagues respect him as their "natural leader". Although the administrative tasks are not especially liked, the central teachers of the division explicitly value both the teaching and research tasks of the department. They prefer to work in the department, as the professor has done, within easy reach of the students.

The teachers of the division hold that the more effective supervision and the example given by the professor have contributed remarkably to the growth of the numbers of annually graduated students. Statistics show that Finnish history produced annually between 1,5 and 4 times more graduates than General history during a period of several years around the shift of the decades[35]. One respondent held that all the students starting Finnish history actually take their degree.

But during the mid-nineties, the division of General history has shown good results. General history has finally acquired a new full professor, and the process of change is going on. A respondent stressed that previously the productivity of the department was not considered as important as it is nowadays, when funding depends on the measurable results of the work. However, in many ways the exact direction of the changes is not yet clear, since the two leading figures of the division have quite different preferences and visions about the future and the key areas of research, and their power-relations seem to be uncertain.

Currently the department has ceased to function as two separate divisions. Instead it is viewed as a whole, as a one administrative unit with a single head of department. However, his position and contribution seems to be controversial; and the leadership culture as well as the expectations concerning leadership seem ambiguous or diverse (section 6.2.).

The head of department maintains that the independent researchers need not be led after all. Instead, the head must listen to his/her colleagues, give them all the information needed, and act on the basis of their views. Two other respondents acknowledged that the leadership has been democratic, since the important decisions have been discussed with the staff. The head has not 'bothered' the staff with administration, which was considered as an ideal state of affairs by one respondent[36]. According to all the leading figures of the

---

[35] This should not be attributed only to the different leadership histories of the divisions. In both departments of history, it was suggested that it is more difficult to acquire source material for research in General history: the subject area is broader, too, and the source material is written in a foreign language. These factors have probably contributed to the differences in productivity.

[36] The head of department also felt that nowadays there is too much administration and too many administrative tasks. According to him, researchers should not be "burdened" with such "secondary" tasks. The priority of research was shared by all the respondents.

department - the head of department and the two interviewed full professors - authoritarian leadership does not work in a university context, since it diminishes the commitment of the faculty and causes conflicts between the researchers. A full professor maintained that because of the concern for academic freedom, the leaders should not try to affect the basic solutions concerning the work of the researchers. However, he also held that the budget cuts are forcing the faculty to find common themes in research.

Not all the respondents were satisfied with the current management. Criticism was expressed about economic decisions. Three respondents held that detailed information concerning the economic situation of the department has not been given to the faculty. Instead, the head has reserved this side of decision-making largely for himself. According to one respondent, open discussion and criticism concerning the goals of the department are not promoted or accepted by the head. Another respondent called the faculty meetings "therapy" sessions, where no real decisions are made. An interviewed full professor admitted that the head of department usually discusses relevant issues with him in the first place, but that the most important decisions are made with the staff. He thought that any resulting disagreements could be fruitful, and that the flow of information has been so far quite unproblematic in the department.

The head of department held that there has been an attempt recently to integrate the research topics of the researchers more closely. He considered that the best strategy of survival would be to acquire more external funding, to start broad international research projects, and to review the teaching methods in the department. But it was also stated that the current leadership is not likely to increase the sense of integration in the department. One respondent held that he could not remember any conflict that would not have been - in one way or another - connected to the head of department himself. The respondent wanted the headship to be more fair. According to him the current "meeting mania" does not necessarily indicate that everything is under control or that the decision making is democratic. A head should be able to provide dynamic leadership and some kind of common direction "during difficult times", to defend the interests of the faculty, and to do his best to develop the department. Two other younger researchers also expected some kind of vision, policy, or strategic choices which would indicate a direction leading to a brighter future.

Birnbaum (1989, 197-198) notes that much leadership consists of carrying out routine tasks when things are going well and making minor adjustments when problems are noticed, but that at times of crisis and problematic situations more direct leadership may be required. These respondents clearly waited for this kind of stronger contribution: the worst economic crisis ever experienced calls for action instead of endless discussion. The main underlying sources of conflict lie in the positions of younger researchers (with temporary agreements) and the positions of the head and other professors (with permanent posts): the latter traditionally make the final decisions, while the former are currently in a position in which they pay the price for failed decisions or, indeed, lack of decisions (section 2.3.2). Their posts are the first ones to be discontinued if nothing is done and the economic situation keeps getting worse. Moreover, the junior staff would need funding, which would require initiating research projects and some kind of decisions about the priority among research topics. However:

the department lacks a clear strategy, we are just following the old paths...
no new orientation in research will materialize unless somebody takes the
task seriously and starts to work on it...

The younger researchers seemed to feel that enough is not being done, but that they
were powerless to search for the ways out. During the interview the head of department
considered that a more unifying and co-ordinating role might be appropriate for a leader.
But so far he has largely followed a pattern traditionally considered as good in university
settings: namely respect for the academic freedom of the researchers. According to this
tradition, the basic tasks and their solutions are left largely for the researchers themselves
to decide.

Furthermore, unclear power relations and power struggles have led the existing
members of professorial staff to a state of indecision. Two respondents held that the well-
respected full professor of Finnish history is not willing to take charge, since he has
become more "diplomatic" over the years. It is not, in any case, easy to start large
projects in a soft, rural field (Becher 1989a) with traditionally individualistic modes of
work (chapter 5). The departments of hard, urban physics are in a much better position in
that respect. The departments of physics have also managed to find dynamic leadership
responses to the crises and challenges they have faced during the assembly of the
accelerators (department of B of physics; section 6.4.4.) or because of the recession
(department A of physics; section 6.4.3.).

6.4.8. Department B of History

I interviewed six members of the staff in department B of history. The department
had eleven permanent teaching/research posts at the time when the interviews were
carried out; three for full and two for associate professors. The interviewed researchers
represented Finnish history and General history, as was the case in the other department
of history.

The head of the department B has been elected from the different divisions by turns.
According to three respondents, the professors of the older generation were very
powerful in the department. They mostly made the decisions by themselves, in a way
they preferred, and without any consultation with the other members of staff. Their task
was made easier by the fact that a greater part of the administrative tasks were handled by
the central administration in the sixties and seventies. The leadership styles of the
professors and the heads have varied considerably, depending on the person. The
following accounts may shed light on the issue.

During the first decades, the department was led by a powerful professor, who was
described by one researcher as "very dominating", "energetic" and "productive". One
respondent remembers that the staff had one short meeting at the beginning of term, once
or twice a year. The allocation of teaching duties and the themes of dissertations were
decided briefly in these meetings. Then each researcher worked on his or her own for six
months or a year, until the next meeting was held in a similar manner. The professor

preferred to concentrate on research and larger issues, while the assistants handled the practical routines in the department.

Another full professor adopted quite the opposite approach, since she wanted frequent discussions with the staff. Some researchers had already become accustomed to the nearly complete academic freedom, so that the professor had difficulty in getting in touch with the staff. The style of her successor was, once again, more "distant", with not much interaction with the staff. The leadership of one short-lived head was described as autocratic. It was also thought that he advocated his own interests too much, which caused criticism among the staff.

A respondent held that the approaches of each leader were quite fixed and permanent, although they may have differed fundamentally from one another. Two other respondents suggested that the previous leaders either delegated all the tasks to somebody else, or made all the decisions (usually very slowly) by themselves.

During the late sixties (when the higher education system was expanding rapidly; chapter 2), a new generation of researchers - about half of the current staff - started to work in the department. One respondent held that they were all interested in history, had a similar kind of social background, and were about the same age. Consequently, the social interaction among them has been intense. Having worked in the department for twenty-five years, this 'collegium' is currently in a powerful position. In practice, many decisions are made by them.

During the late sixties and seventies, the radical movement (section 2.3.1.) affected somewhat the administrative processes in the department. A full professor described that as a period during which the amount of discussion increased and the students participated in administration, but "not much changed" in the "conservative" department after all, since "the energy of change drowned into discussions" (Aittola 1984; section 3.3.). He felt that the past three years have been a period of more important and dramatic change. However, in his view it is still quite difficult to evaluate this ongoing development, since we do not yet have the necessary historical perspective.

In questions concerning teaching and research, the freedom of the members of the faculty is respected in this department, as in department A. One respondent commented that he was "free as a bird" to arrange his own work. Another considered this freedom as a necessary precondition for work motivation. The previous head of the department (who was interviewed in 1994) held that independent researchers need not be led per se: the task of the head of department consisted mostly of day-to-day matters and routine administration.

Recently, a new professor has been appointed, who also acts as the head of department. Two respondents held that the change of leader has given rise to some optimism among the staff, since the head has tried to be open and democratic in his leadership. The full professor is also a long-time colleague of some of the researchers (the previously discussed 'collegium'). This long-standing friendship has been an obvious advantage according to him, since he knows the expectations of the staff quite well. His open and impartial leadership was acknowledged by the staff. Among other things the flow of information has become better. He has been able to calm down some very long-lived conflicts between colleagues. Three respondents considered that in the light of their experiences, the personality of the individual who is in charge of the department is an important factor as far as the general atmosphere and working conditions are concerned:

> I think that the head of department has a significant impact... if he prosecutes mainly his own aims... or when he takes into account the staff, tries to be fair in every way, is open and tells us what is going on, that creates a nice atmosphere...

Once again, the impact of leadership becomes visible because revealing comparisons can be made between sharply contrasting examples (see section 6.4.6.).

Interestingly, the approach and leadership philosophy of the current head of department (who was interviewed in 1995) seems to recall fuzzy logic (Kosko 1994; section 4.1.1.); it is not either-or, neither black or white, but emphasises the in-between and 'grey' aspects. For example, the leader is ready to discuss decisions with the staff, but is also able to make decisions in conflicting circumstances when needed. He emphasised reflection and flexibility, but also some kind of priority in the strong areas of research; open and collegial decision-making (especially within his own division), but without too much hesitation; the importance of a team, but also of the individuals in the collective. Striking the balance between opposites may be difficult task at times, but the approach may provide a flexible leadership, which takes the situational factors better into account (section 3.1.).

Because of the lack of historical continuity, the new departmental leadership culture is still in a state of formation and the practices and opinions are ambiguous and conflicting (section 6.2.). As a result, it is difficult to get a clear picture of the state of affairs. Some researchers held that most of the decisions are currently made on the basis of discussions by the faculty, although the 'collegium' of old workers seems to be most powerful in that respect. The preliminary work for the meetings has often been delegated to a working team or to assistants.

But the different divisions seem to have different practices. One respondent stressed that the departmental head has considerable power in economic issues, but the current head himself maintained that he has, to a significant extent, delegated economic decisions to the different divisions. This has been the practice according to two other respondents. They stressed the power of the full professors, who currently represent different generations and diverse leadership traditions. Nonetheless, the professors and the representatives of the different divisions meet once a week. During this meeting the economic situation is discussed.

It seems clear that the junior members of staff are likely to suffer most from the recession in this department as in others. One respondent emphasised the insecure future of the assistants who are working on a temporary basis for periods of six months at a time. This representative of the assistants worried about the seemingly "permanent insecurity" of their work. The criticism was however not as strong as in the other studied department of history, or in department B of biology.

Chapter 7

CONCLUSIONS

Having now analyzed academic leadership in the context of disciplinary and departmental cultures, it seems to me that the two cultural perspectives can be usefully viewed as complementary. The perspective on disciplinary cultures (chapter 5) and the more localized analysis of organizational cultures (chapter 6) are partly overlapping, but they also highlight slightly different aspects of the phenomena under study.

The *disciplinary perspective* discussed in chapter 5 is valuable in pointing out broad social and epistemological features which seem to affect academic leadership in a given disciplinary context. The nature of the intellectual tasks and traditions of discipline obviously direct departmental leadership. Academic tribes also have their chieftains (Ylijoki 1994): scholars who are more influential than others in affecting and directing the disciplinary culture in question, or even academic culture in general. Disciplinary analysis is able to provide some (at least tentative) generalizations concerning preferred disciplinary leadership styles, which seem valid as long as the relevant conditions, such as intellectual orientations and tasks (especially the commitment to the value-orientations and perspectives in question), remain similar enough (section 5.5.).

In contrast, the analysis of *departmental cultures and leadership* helps to shed light on more localised aspects and variations which may not be reached by a more general discussion of disciplinary features and leadership, but which makes it difficult to formulate generalizations. From this perspective, generalizations are not the main concern, since the focus is on local and particular aspects (Alasuutari 1994, 206-209). In all cases leadership practices differ at least slightly even within a given basic disciplinary field (physics, history, sociology, biology), as the staff in question succeed in inventing (partly unique) solutions and patterns in response to their managerial problems. The departmental leadership cultures resulting from complex social processes (section 6.2.) can be characterized by some common patterns and values, by diverse subcultures or by cultural ambiguity. Examples of each of these predominant types, as well as mixtures of them, can be found within my sample.

In effect, both perspectives add something to the cultural analysis of academic leadership, in part because of their different levels of discussion: broad and international vs. local and particular (section 3.2.3.). Both view-points are useful but partial. To quote Becher (1987c, 271) again :

> To see the whole is to see it in breath, but without access to the particular; to see the part is to see it in depth, but without a general overview.

In practical leadership situations in departments, disciplinary and local aspects mix with each other. In the theoretical introduction to chapter 6, I described the formation of leadership culture as a complex learning and negotiation process, where the leaders have more power than others in affecting the outcomes. The values and views of the leaders and faculty are affected by disciplinary and academic traditions and influences, which are, in turn, filtered and interpreted through the 'lens' of personal or shared values and assumptions of members of the staff. While some broader historical and disciplinary aspects (chapters 2 and 5) provide a general framework and a background for departmental leadership, the tradition of academic freedom and the lack of leadership training have given each leader and staff more or less broad scope to follow their own ideas, visions, and assumptions about good and proper leadership[1]. (see sections 6.4.3., 6.4.7. and 7.1.3.).

In the beginning of the study, I had some initial questions in my mind (chapter 1). In what follows I shall discuss these themes, starting with the questions connected to the 'informal' leadership cultures and practices of the departments: How are important decisions actually made in different departments? What kind of disciplinary and departmental values, practices, patterns and assumptions are connected to the issues of leadership, management and decision-making in the studied departments? What is (are) the main function(s) or tasks of departmental headship in different departments? How is 'good' academic leadership seen in different disciplinary and departmental contexts?

Since these questions are interrelated, I shall discuss them in connection with each other, by concentrating on aspects which seem to be connected to the everyday work and practices in the departments studied[2]. In the forthcoming sections, I shall come to my other initial research questions: which of these cultures have been effective in supporting the academic work in different disciplines (section 7.2.); and how (and in which circumstances) are the heads of departments and informal leaders able to embed and reinforce the organizational cultures of their departments - if they lead this culture at all (section 7.3.)?

---

[1] Prior social interaction at the departmental level (which involves both disciplinary and local aspects; section 3.2.3) is an important source of leadership influence (section 6.2.). On the basis of interviews it seems that the models, views and values concerning good leadership have often been based on the leader's and the faculty's experiences. Leadership models have been adopted either by identifying with a respected role model, or by abandoning a model which has been considered as adverse or negative in the light of individual values and experiences.

[2] I shall not discuss abstract, general and context-free properties or traits the respondents sometimes attributed to good academic leaders (see chapter 3). For general lists of the formal responsibilities, tasks and functions of departmental heads, see Moses and Roe (1990, 64) and Middlehurst (1993, 132-137).

7.1. TYPES OF LEADERSHIP CULTURES

I shall discuss the issues framed by the first set of questions by providing a summary of each main type of leadership culture: collegial and democratic structures, leading groups, strong individual leadership, and differentiated or ambiguous leadership cultures. It should be noted that the categorization is inevitably simplified and idealtypical: while it describes essential features of the leadership cultures at a departmental level, some of the cultures studied were changing and might be (soon) classified in another way. The discussion concerns important administrative and strategic decisions and departmental leadership cultures at the departmental level on the basis of my data (chapter 4). I do not intend to discuss all the subtle differences between the departments (see chapter 6).

7.1.1. Collegial and Democratic Leadership Cultures

In departments A and B of sociology and department A of biology, the central cultural values and expectations are the respect for the academic freedom of the researchers, and the strong expectation that all the (important) decisions should be made collectively and democratically in open discussion among the whole staff. In these departments, the scope for spontaneous decision-making by the head is limited to some routine administration and to signing papers after the decisions are made by the staff. The role of leadership is seen as supportive to academic basic tasks: good leaders create and develop the conditions of academic work, but they do not dominate or make decisions on their own. This view comes close to Dearlove's (1995a, 167) contention that good academic leaders are modest "learning leaders" who facilitate and organize, but do not dictate the decision-making process. In department A of sociology and department A of biology the original full professors have acted also as head of department for the most of part of the department's history (sections 6.4.1. and 6.4.5.). In these departments, the staff have tended to share most administrative routine decisions, although many respondents in both departments recently expressed a wish to leave such decisions to the departmental head. In the sociologists' case the professor/head has not been willing to take responsibility for them, and the staff have not been willing to allow the power of the head to increase (section 6.4.1.). In department B of sociology, much of the routine administration was left for the head to undertake.

My interpretation is that the *sociologists'* obvious dislike of strong individual leadership can be partly understood on the grounds of the tradition of academic freedom (Russell 1993; Kekäle 1994b) and the nature of research in a soft and rural field. Becher (1989a, 157) has described sociology as a "fissiparous and fragmented" discipline with not much agreement on problems or perspectives. The soft, rural and divergent disciplinary environment of sociology does not provide as clear guidelines for leadership and research as does the hard, urban and convergent experimental physics (section 5.3.; Alapuro 1990). Consequently, the role of power becomes more explicit in departmental decision-making in sociology, and it is also emphasised in the critical disciplinary perspectives.

Indeed, sociologists' cultural preferences concerning leadership seem to be connected to the critical (Marxian) background of many key researchers in the departments studied (section 5.2.2.). In broad outline, the current diverse critical approaches lay emphasis on values like democracy and emancipation; they aim at the increased empowerment of subordinate groups and resist instrumental rationality and managerialism (Kincheloe & MacLaren 1994, 139-140; sections 5.2.2. and 6.4.2.). The critical approaches can be shared by scholars from different disciplinary fields and areas of enquiry in arts and social sciences (Kincheloe and McLaren 1994; chapter 5), but in the other disciplinary groups studied critical theory did not have a comparably strong position. Historically, the critical orientation in sociology seems to be connected to the international student radicalism and the national administrative and degree reforms which attempted to democratize universities in the 1970s (section 2.3.1.). Departmental histories and social processes also appear to have affected the current leadership patterns. For example, in department B of sociology, the long-standing conflict between a professor (representing a structural-functionalistic orientation) and critical scholars seems to have strengthened the current collegial leadership culture (section 6.4.2.).

The staff in *department A of biology* have similar expectations and preferences concerning departmental leadership. Although biology represents a harder disciplinary area than sociology, they both come close to the divergent and rural ends of the social dimension (Becher 1989a; section 5.1., table 1.). The leadership culture in department A of biology seems to be connected to certain values and orientations inherent in ecology in particular. The respondents pointed out that these include 'green' values and a concern for environmental issues, a non-anthropocentric world-view, "respect for life in general", "soft-values", and a low interest in "economical values", "status anxiety" or "the ratrace". Some researchers held that their close social interaction and their dislike of strong leaders, management or "hard-hearted economic calculation" mirrored these values (section 5.2.4.).

The personalities and the close interaction among key members of staff seem to have directed the process of formation of the leadership culture: it was sometimes explained that at first the professor/head adopted a more "traditional professorial role", but his colleagues directed him towards his current leadership style. It was generally accepted that the human relations and leadership aspects (Blake & Mouton 1964) have been handled "intuitively" in a very good, or even in the "best possible way" by the original professor and by some other core members of staff. But perhaps an indirect link with the critical approach can be identified as well: according to the original full professor of biology, their leadership culture was established during the process of degree reform (section 2.3.1.). Some of the main principles of the reform were to increase democracy and the participation of students and the whole staff in decision-making (Paukkunen 1977) - features which are nowadays highly valued in department A of biology (section 6.4.5.).

7.1.2. Decision-making in Leading Groups

In department B of physics and department B of biology the important decisions are made by a leading group. Both the areas represent experimental, hard and pure sciences. Recently, department B of biology has been moving in the direction of stronger individual managerialism, while the department B of (nuclear) physics has remained true to the leadership culture based on decision-making in the leading groups, a pattern which has proved to be suitable for its members.

In *department B of physics* the leading group consists of professors and leaders of research projects, totalling about ten persons. On some major issues, the proposal of the leading group is further discussed by the personnel (over one hundred members) at the collegial council, but major changes are seldom made. The head of department calls together the leading group when important issues are to be discussed. Not much preparation for the meeting is done by the head, but the issues are discussed in the group. In addition, the head makes some routine administrative decisions and represents the department on different occasions. According to the physicists, their leadership culture is considered to work well, in that it minimizes conflicts and provides the necessary information for decision making. Individual leaders or heads of departments were expected not to make important decisions on their own (section 6.4.4.).

The choice of departmental specialism was based on the work of the original full professor. The departmental tradition of rotating headships, and the tradition of collegial decision making in the leading group also originate from the initiative of the original full professor. The urban, hard and convergent nature of the specialism seems to favour group work at least in research (Becher 1989a; section 5.2.3.). Some researchers stressed that a similar kind of practice is adopted in other laboratories around the world, but Traweek (1988, 91) has pointed out some national differences (footnote 17 in chapter 5). In this department, different decision-making patterns were first tried out, but the staff settled for a leading group.

The specialisms in *department B of biology* represent hard areas of inquiry (e.g. molecular biology, biochemistry and cell biology). Department A of biology is more heterogenous in its scientific profile, and the ecological value-orientation seems to get a stronger emphasis there. The approach of the staff and students in department B is, according to some respondents, "more academic" and less connected to environmental issues. Also the current expectations concerning leadership are much more in line with economic values and managerialism. This emphasis is likely to be connected to the different values and to the changed external conditions (chapter 2) which have affected the department: because of the recession, the academic leaders have faced the hard task of setting priorities among areas of research and giving notice to some members of the staff (section 6.4.6.).

In this department, the decisions concerning important issues are discussed in a leading group, which consists of professors and the leaders of research projects. However, the group is not an official decision-making body. According to three respondents, the head of the department makes the final decisions, but the practice has been that very strong grounds are needed if s/he is to oppose the will of the leading group. When the collegium is not unanimous, the power of the head increases. His/her position has been further strengthened by the following procedure: the department has a minor body (consisting of the head of the department, his deputy and an assistant), which undertakes the preparatory work for meetings and submits the agenda for the leading group, which then discusses the propositions[3]. Some urgent tasks and negotiations have been delegated to this body or to other working parties. Thus, although the pattern is somewhat similar to the one adopted in department B of physics, the position of the head is potentially stronger, since s/he is expected to take the final responsibility for the decisions, and to play a considerable part in formulating the propositions to be discussed.

The leadership styles of individual professors have varied substantially in the past. Having observed different leaders, all the respondents were convinced of the importance of effective academic leadership, and they connected the long-term success and vitality of the specialism and the department to the manner in which the leadership (especially by the chair) was handled. Many central members of the staff shared a common vision of a stronger and more effective individual leadership, where the emphasis would be on assembling research groups and providing funding for them (section 6.4.6.).

7.1.3. Strong Individual Leadership

The leadership culture in *department A of physics* comes closest to individual managerialism and decision-making. In the 1990s, the influence of the collegial councils over the decisions has been considerably reduced. Nearly all the strategic and administrative decisions concerning the department are made by the head, who is also considered to be very competent researcher. He considers that his task is similar to the task of a project manager in a company: he assembles research groups, provides funding, gives the group its research tasks and ensures that the tasks will be conducted in time. According to some of his subordinate staff and himself, his style of leadership is much more direct, effective, and initiative than that of the previous head of department, especially on issues connected to the management of the department and his research groups. Depending on the person, the previous leadership culture was considered as a laissez faire, or democratic leadership, which gave the researchers much academic freedom (section 6.4.3.).

On the basis of the respondents' descriptions, the previous culture of this department - which had in fact specialized in a hard, convergent and urban area (Becher 1989a) - might be characterized as rural during the eighties: all the researchers worked on their own and at their own tempo. Their pattern of communication was not intense, they had no common meetings, and the personnel were not accountable for their work to anybody. However, during the 1990s, the profile of the department has been raised by "marketing" - by giving the public and potential students more information about the work done in the department. Supervision has become more effective. The research has been organized on

---

[3] No preparation before the collegial decision-making is usually undertaken in department of B of physics, department A of biology and department A of sociology.

the basis of common, small (urban) projects instead of individual work. The department has struck a balance between pure science and applied science: since the budget funding has diminished, the department has been forced to seek sources of external funding - a task in which it has succeeded (section 6.4.3.).

Changes in leadership and departmental culture had been well in line with the expectations and hopes of most of the respondents. However, during the interviews conducted in 1995, some female physicists expressed critical views about authoritative managerialism. The head of department felt that it was time to loosen his grip, since the department was working quite well on its own and the worst crisis was over. He and the faculty were planning to arrange some meetings during which important issues could be discussed, but my data provides no information about the outcomes (section 6.4.3.).

7.1.4. Differentiated or Ambiguous Leadership Cultures

The leadership cultures in both departments of history can be characterized as differentiated according to individual professors, or even as ambiguous, when viewed at the departmental level. This seems to be connected to the individualistic tradition in history (and the humanities more generally) which was stressed by all respondents in the discipline (section 5.2.1.).

Department A of history has two separate subjects or main lines of study. Their different leadership histories seem to have produced some cultural differences between them (section 3.3. and 6.4.7.). The division of Finnish history has had the same professor for nearly twenty years, which has provided a certain continuity to the leadership, whereas the leadership of General history was handled, for a long time, by different (acting) professors. Nowadays, the department functions as one administrative unit with a single head of department. However, his position and contribution seems to be controversial; and the leadership culture as well as the expectations concerning leadership seem ambiguous or diverse. For example, two respondents acknowledged that the leadership has been democratic, since the important decisions have been discussed with the staff. However, three respondents held that the head makes economic decisions largely by himself. It was maintained that open discussion concerning the goals of the department is not promoted or accepted by the head, and that real decisions are not made in the faculty meetings. Some junior researchers felt that their department lacks a clear strategy, since everyone concentrates solely on his or her own work.

According to my interpretation, the interests and positions of junior and senior staff are liable to be in conflict when resources are declining (in this and in many other departments facing budget cuts). The professors are traditionally in the best position to make decisions, while the junior researchers have to pay the price for failed decisions or, indeed, lack of decisions, since their temporary posts are the first ones to be discontinued (section 2.3.2., 6.4.6. and 6.4.7.)[4]. However, it is not easy to develop a departmental

---

[4] The pattern seems similar to that found in department A of physics (section 6.4.3.), in which the resources have not declined: the younger researchers are likely to be concerned about the

strategy, since all the respondents still value academic freedom (see Häyrynen et al. 1992b, 17-18). This value-orientation is reinforced by the individualistic (soft, rural; Becher 1989a) nature of the department's work, and by the diffuse power-relations of the professorial staff, who have conflicting ideas, values and visions of the future (sections 5.2.1. and 6.4.7.).

The leadership culture in *department B of history* (section 6.4.8.) also seems fairly ambiguous or differentiated. During its history, the department has been led by very different individuals. A respondent held that the approaches of each leader have been quite fixed and permanent, although they may have differed fundamentally from one another. As a result, the staff members seem tolerant of different leadership styles - perhaps because of both the professors' independent and powerful position and the individualistic tradition of the discipline.

Some consistency has recently begun to appear because of the appointment of a new professor (who also acts as the head of department), whose leadership style was described as open and democratic, and was acknowledged and valued by the respondents. Some researchers held that most of the decisions are currently made on the basis of discussions by the faculty. The preliminary work for the meetings has often been delegated to a specific team or to assistants. In practice, many decisions are made by those researchers - about half of the current staff - who started to work in the department in the late sixties. The social interaction among them has been intense, since they share some similar interests and a common background (section 6.4.8.). However, different professors still seem to behave according to their own preferences, and the outcome of process is not yet clear at the level of the department as a whole.

7.2. DIVERSE LEADERSHIP CONTEXTS

The leadership cultures and ways of reaching decisions are indeed different in diverse disciplinary and departmental contexts. The functions and tasks the head of department is expected carry out in these departments seem to range from undertaking the whole management of the department on a full-time basis, to signing some papers after the decisions are made collectively by the staff (see Tucker 1993, 66-70)[5]. Some leadership cultures seem to differ in the way they emphasise human relations or leadership functions (e.g. departments A of biology and sociology) or task oriented management behaviour (department B of biology, department A of physics). These dimensions are distinguished in Blake and Mouton's (1964) famous managerial grid. Starting from the assumption of 'one best way' of leadership, they maintained that the leaders often stress one of these

---

continuity of their work, while the senior researchers (who are already in a quite safe position) expect democratic leadership.

[5] Different higher education doctrines (chapter 2) may be reflected in these leadership cultures, which can be classified along the continuum of collegial/democratic vs. individual/professorial decision-making and leadership - a dichotomy underlying the doctrines connected to polarized political ideologies in the 1970s.

approaches at the expense of the other, although both aspects of leadership should complement each other (Lönnqvist 1985, 10). Indeed, both aspects seem to be important and neither should be completely neglected.

But if the background assumption of one best way of leadership is abandoned - as is the case in more recent leadership theories (section 3.1.) - it can be simply stated that many departments have produced a working pattern which would not necessarily fit well into a different departmental context, and that the values and perspectives of different research collectives may be diverse and even conflicting (chapters 5 and 6). Moreover, there is usually no close interaction between the researchers in the different fields: physicists do not read the writings of sociologists; biologists and historians do not consult each other (see Clark 1983, 14-15). Consequently, it would be difficult and unnecessary - as far as leadership at the departmental level is concerned - to achieve any general consensus about best leadership: no such simple 'one best way' to lead has been found in research on the topic either (chapter 3; Bush 1995). But even though there may not any be universal and eternal best way, that does not mean that there could be no local or temporarily well-grounded solutions. Many departments have indeed found working solutions and leadership patterns which have allowed them to function in an efficient way, and which have been seen in a positive light by the majority of the staff[6].

As already noted, it is possible to point out some idealtypical and tentative leadership patterns which derive largely from disciplinary tasks and perspectives (chapter 5). Such disciplinary patterns may be preferred in terms of disciplinary norms (or they may be seen as natural in the given specialism), but the actual leadership cultures may still vary in different departments depending on local aspects and processes. In (soft, pure, divergent and rural; Becher 1989a) critical sociology and ecology, the preferred leadership style seems to be democratic and collegial leadership; the emphasis is on 'soft' values and emancipation rather than on increasing efficiency and hard result-oriented management. In harder specialism of biology and physics, the valuation of measurability, exact knowledge and linear thinking (Mäenpää & Mäkinen 1989, 105-106) appears to

---

[6] It is difficult to evaluate leaders. On the basis of the research literature, Hogan et al. (1994, 495) claim that the best way of evaluating them is on the basis of both the performance of the team and the ratings by subordinates, peers or supervisors. Empirical literature suggests that these features are correlated. There are however problems connected with this kind of evaluation. The data needed to make the first kind of evaluation are often difficult to obtain or badly contaminated by other factors (Hogan, et al. 1994, 496). In universities, where the duties are not clear, the problem is how to measure performance (Birnbaum 1989, 11; chapter 2). But as Aarnio et al. (1995) note, this does not mean that some rough indicators cannot, or should not, be found. The departments studied in university A scored higher than the average of their faculty when the working years of professors (or working years of professors and assistants) were compared to the number of postgraduates produced (Kekäle 1993c; section 4.3.). Also the studied departments of university B gave an impression of unproblematic functioning and increasing productivity on the basis of the numbers of basic and postgraduate degrees produced. This impression was reinforced in the course of the interviews. Many of the diverse leadership patterns were considered to be good and productive by the subordinates. Consequently, if these rough indicators of performance and ratings by subordinates are accepted, there seem to be multiple ways to achieve good leadership. In fact, examples of good leaders and leadership patterns can be found from departments representing each of the different basic categories of leadership cultures (section 7.1.).

give better grounds for managerialism (section 5.2.3.). In such areas, the exact methods and hard convergent nature of the disciplinary knowledge provide clearer guidelines for management and academic work. The approach to leadership seems not to be critical, but pragmatic and straight-forward: leadership is good as long as it works properly and is not against their personal values and departmental or disciplinary traditions. As noted, the studied hard, pure specialisms in biology and physics at the university B favour teamwork in research and leadership, while the management culture of hard applied department A of physics emphasises entrepreneurship, competition, efficiency and business-like management. The individualistic tradition of soft, pure, convergent and rural history leaves more room for individual leaders to choose their style, although leader's contribution to the well-being of his/her department is obviously valued.

However, departmental leadership and the position of different departmental leaders becomes more complicated if the changing external environment is taken into account (Kekäle forthcoming). An established leadership culture provides an unproblematic leadership situation only as long as the leaders remain in their expected role, and as long as there is no need for change. For example, in the departments which have collegial and democratic leadership cultures (section 7.1.1.), the potentially problematic questions in relation to leadership might be: if the recession continues and it becomes necessary to cut the funding from some areas, or to determine narrower strategic core areas of research, in which way will this be done? Which kind of order of precedence will be set, by whom and on what grounds? It may be difficult to reach consensus on such issues, since the core interests of the researchers are too much involved. To make matters worse, the established cultural values (democracy, equality, academic freedom) and the weak power position of the head do not seem to allow him/her to make difficult decisions. But according to the current statutes (section 2.4.), the final responsibility over such decisions is his/hers alone. Similar tensions may occur if there is a need to increase productivity and the performance of the department. The leader is officially responsible, but the informal culture and his/her weak power position make it difficult to do anything about the situation without giving rise to internal conflict (see the discussion on transformational leadership in section 3.1.).

In contrast, the head of department B of physics (section 6.4.4.) seems to be free of such potential conflicts. The department's economic resources have not diminished recently. The equipment and laboratory buildings are relatively new and there is no need to invest in them further in the near future. The main specialism is coherent and the research is naturally based on team work. The strong leadership culture of the department has worked well and provides a clear framework, as well as professional support, for the head of department. The departmental culture strongly supports hard work, and the nature of the hard, urban and convergent specialism (Becher 1989a) makes it easier to produce measurable results quickly. Consequently, there are no strong pressures to increase productivity. Things are going well, and the head is in a position in which he is expected to carry out routine tasks and perhaps, if needed, to initiate minor adjustments (Birnbaum 1989, 197-198) which are then, in this case, discussed and decided in the leading group.

Thus it seems that the leadership task may vary from relatively easy to downright stressful and difficult according to the pressures which largely derive from the context and from the leader's own position in the field. In some cases the head may unproblematically continue the cultural pattern which has been accepted within the department or specialism; in other cases there are no such established guidelines, or the cultural expectations are conflicting, or they may clash with the external realities. This complexity makes general views about good academic leadership problematic (chapter 3). The same kind of leadership may result in a different (positive or negative) outcomes in different contexts (Birnbaum 1989; Kekäle 1994b; Kekäle forthcoming).

7.3. LEADERSHIP AND CULTURAL CHANGE; DOES LEADERSHIP MATTER?

In the beginning of my study I was interested in the question: how (and in which circumstances) are the heads of departments and informal leaders able to embed and reinforce the organizational cultures of their departments - if they can affect them at all? A leader's ability to shape the culture may depend on multiple contextual aspects such as his/her relative power-position in department, his/her competence, and the values of the staff. External or situational factors (laws and statutes and economic pressures; chapter 2) or crises may contribute to cultural change (Kekäle 1995d). Consequently, it seems difficult to answer this question on a general level, although the theme has been much discussed among scholars. For example, recent perspectives on learning organizations have generated the idea of flexible reflection and change of cultural values and assumptions (Kuittinen & Kekäle 1996). On the basis of the research literature on organizational cultures, it appears controversial whether the change of an existing strong culture can be intentionally engineered or controlled by leaders and managers (see for example Schein 1985; Clark 1987a; Meyerson & Martin 1987; Schafritz & Ott 1987, 378; Alvesson 1990).

Some relevant considerations can be provided on the basis of my study. As described in section 6.2., I have viewed culture as a socially constructed reality. Departmental culture evolves - often in an indirect and an unintended way - in a dynamic and complex learning process which involves both internal and external factors (Schein 1985; Gagliardi 1986; Gerholm 1990; Hatch 1993; Kekäle 1995b; section 6.2.). In time, the scope for alternative views and models diminishes sharply as the current cultural patterns become self-evident and taken-for-granted, and as the staff's commitment to them increases (Schein 1985; Gagliardi 1986; section 6.2.). On the basis of my data, deeply held cultural values frame and direct academic leadership (chapters 5 and 6; section 7.1.).

As my case studies indicate, cultural values can be pervasive and stable[7]. Despite the considerable increase in authority which has taken place during the worst recession ever

---

[7] Although deeply held cultural values and assumptions are largely socially constructed (within a broader context; chapter 4), they are not necessarily easy to change: too great a deviation from current social and psychological identities may cause change initiatives to be perceived as unattainable, while change causing too little deviation may be considered as unnecessary (Reger et al. 1994).

(chapter 2), the leadership and working patterns had not changed much in the departments which had produced a strong culture. But when strong arguments support the need for change, it is often seen to be the leader's responsibility to try to bring it about. One problem may be that at that point s/he might have become too deeply involved with the existing cultural perspective to be able to see alternatives.

Academic leaders (professors) seem to have most influence on the leadership culture when the department is young and the culture is still developing, or has not yet consolidated. It seems that some founders of departments as well as other strong academic leaders have clearly contributed to the formation of the departmental or leadership culture (Clark 1987a; Kekäle 1995a). As pointed out in section 6.4.7., the first leader of a division in department A of history criticized the traditionally individualistic nature of humanistic and academic studies. He stressed the importance of the effective supervision and support of graduate students. Because of his position as a respected researcher and a "natural" leader, he has been able to contribute to a more efficient supervision pattern (section 6.4.7.). As another case in point, the leadership style of the current head of department A of physics seems to differ significantly from the leadership of his predecessor, at least as far as his own projects are concerned. The leader, who is also considered to be a very competent researcher, acts as a full-time manager of the department (section 6.4.3.).

Although the leadership styles of these two (a historian and a physicist) have been different in many ways, they also have several things in common. As noted, both have been able to bring about change. In particular, both have strong merits as researchers and are respected on that basis. Both have been successful in acquiring funds for research projects, an achievement which has supported their leadership position. During the interviews, both expressed clear values, assumptions and visions much more often than any other respondents in their field[8]. Both seem to be highly committed to their task; they practice what they preach. Moreover, both leaders are highly interested in results and have concentrated on the well-being of their department.

There are other examples which indicate that leadership matters[9]. Department B of sociology was paralysed because of the social conflicts between the leader and staff members (section 6.4.2.). In department B of physics, the founder was said to have directed the group to their current specialism and manner of working. He also initiated the decision-making pattern based on leading groups, which is well suited to the nature of the specialism (section 6.4.4). Having observed different individual leaders, many

---

[8] In 1994, when both leaders were interviewed, the professor/head of department A of physics verbalised his values 29 times: all the other physicists did so 7 or less times during the interviews. Only 5 expressions of value could be scored for the department head of department B of physics. Similarly, the professor of history in department A expressed - usually clearly and strongly - his values and philosophies 20 times during the interview, as opposed to 15 times by a departmental head of history, and 6 or less expressions of values by the other history respondents.

[9] Hogan et al. (1994, 494) conclude their discussion of leadership studies as follows:
> In summary, a growing body of evidence supports the common sense belief that leadership matters. Consequently, psychologists need to better determine when,

respondents in department B of biology (section 6.4.6.) and department B of history (section 6.4.8.) were convinced of the importance of effective academic leadership. The biologists frequently connected the whole long-term life and vitality of their department to the manner in which the leadership (especially by the chair) was handled.

The most radical cultural changes have perhaps occurred in department A of physics, where a new and powerful head of department was elected at the beginning of this decade. As noted, the working patterns within the department have changed to a great extent (section 6.4.3.). I have argued that these changes can be understood in relation to different contextual aspects: they were possible because of the personal power of the head of the department, which seems to be, among other things, based on his competence and standing as a researcher, as well as his ability to provide funding for the projects at a time of economic depression. Furthermore the external pressures and the accompanying changes in statutes, as well as the hopes of many members of the staff for a stronger and clearer leadership, caused by a previous incoherent or ambiguous culture, seemed to contribute to the changes. The current emphasis on effective team work is well in line with the nature of the departmental specialism; the previous working patterns of the researchers were rather individualistic and slow, as they characteristically worked in a soft, rural research field (see chapter 5; Becher 1989a).

Thus, there were both internal and external pressures and expectations leading towards the present situation. A competent and powerful head was able to support and initiate changes in keeping with his own values and visions, and with disciplinary norms in general. However, the changes did not necessarily touch the deeper elements of the culture (section 6.1.), namely the values of the majority of the staff. Instead, the leader was able to fulfil some existing expectations concerning stronger leadership. However, this kind of leadership would have been in direct opposition to the values of the staff in both departments of sociology and in department A of biology. As a result, the consequences of such leadership would have been very different in these departments.

7.4. A NOTE ON POWER, LEADERSHIP AND ACADEMIC WORK

In section 6.2., I connected the issues of power[10] to the formation of a departmental leadership culture. Professors have power and influence over the kind of research

---

where, and how leadership affects organization effectiveness and help organizations to choose better leaders.

[10] Power is context- and relationship- specific: a person is not powerful or powerless in general, but only in respect to other social actors (individual, subunit, organization) in specific social relationships (Pfeffer 1987, 311; Middlehurst 1993, 28-36). Power can manifest itself in at least in three different ways (see section 3.1.):

1. Ability to get one's own views and ideas through in situations where conflicting views are present,
2. power to keep certain topics or views outside the debate or discussion, and
3. power to shape others' views and opinions about what should and can be done (Weber 1980; quoted in Järvi et al. 1990).

conducted within their department, the expectations concerning that research, and the tempo or the manner of work: although researchers may often be rather independent, academic leaders can hinder or help the pursuit of the scholarly activities of the researchers in many ways (Moses 1985, 338).

The academic's contribution to research constitutes a very strong source of personal power and respect in the studied departments (Tucker 1993, 44-46)[11]. Consequently, those heads who are not strongly respected on the basis of their research merits may find it difficult to take advantage of their recently increased authority in a way that would be accepted by their peers (section 5.4.). This does not have to hinder them from contributing to the administration, or to the functioning and well-being of their departments: "Few administrators are charismatic, but all administrators can be competent" (Birnbaum 1989, 204-206)[12].

As this study has shown, depending on the departmental context, important administrative and strategic decisions (Chaffee 1985; Maassen & van Vught 1992) may be successfully made by individual leaders, leading groups, or by the whole academic staff (Kekäle 1994b; section 7.1.). However, some broadly shared limits to leaders' use of power in practical teaching/research tasks can be identified according to my data. The power of the leaders in relation to the activities of experienced and competent researchers appeared to be rather restricted in all the studied departments: senior researchers in large part take responsibility for their everyday work, regardless of the department or specialism. This seems to be the case even in department A of physics, where the head of department has considerable power in most departmental decisions. As Dearlove (1995b, 13) notes:

> Precisely because fundamental research involves going beyond the frontiers of established understanding, good researchers can hardly be told what to do.

The strong position of competent experts is based on academic traditions and on the fact that they are difficult to replace by someone else. Their expertise forms the knowledge capital of the department or of the knowledge organization to which they

---

[11] Only one respondent spontaneously mentioned good teaching as a source of respect among colleagues. Teaching is a private matter, since other scholars do not usually observe each others' ways of teaching (Kekäle 1994a). But probably this also reflects the relatively common undervaluation of instruction as opposed to research. Administrative tasks are equally undervalued (section 6.4.2.).

[12] It should also be noted that research contributions and leadership skills do not necessarily go hand in hand. On the basis of respondents' descriptions it becomes clear that many great scientists of the past would not have been good organizational leaders. Instead, as one physicist put it, they seemed to consider many aspects of everyday life as trivial. It was maintained that Newton was not capable of love or friendship, Galileo was nearly burnt at the stake - and was poor and disgraced when he died; and Einstein was temporarily expelled from the university of Zürich. A biologist stressed that Darwin was an "unpopular person". In many cases the intellectual leadership provided by great researchers of the past has materialized only after a long delay, or even after the death of the scholar.

belong (Sipilä 1991, 52). This holds especially true in specialisms where the academic work has strong theoretical and innovative components. In such areas, self-management (Sims and Lorenzi 1992) and a considerable autonomy for scholars seem to be a normal and fruitful pattern, especially when intellectual leadership is not needed or cannot be provided.

Indeed, a loose connection can be noted between the significance given to academic freedom and the intellectual tasks in the specialism in question. Among my respondents, the tradition of academic freedom was valued especially highly in the soft pure and rural fields of sociology, biology (university A) and history. According to a full professor in biology, and full professors in both history and sociology, freedom of thought is essential in academic work: research topics and issues are open to discussion and argumentation, but it is not the responsibility or the right of academic leaders to censor, control, or use their power over these issues (Kekäle 1994b). In contrast, the hard, urban department of (optical) physics with an increasing orientation towards applied research (and - according to some respondents - similar departments of biology), and direct co-operation with the industrial sector, seem to be more inclined to adopt strong individual leadership roles patterned after the models of the business world. The head of department A of physics considered that academic freedom is valuable in the field of theoretical studies, where, in his opinion, creativity and great ideas cannot be subject to management. However, he thought that routine research can and should be managed and organized: it demands lots of work, can have a clear schedule and can progress in phases (see section 7.2.).

7.5. CONCLUDING REMARKS

In this research, my contention has been that although there may not be one best way to lead an academic department, it is certainly not irrelevant how an individual chooses to lead. Departmental academic leadership involves a complex network of influences, pressures and possibilities. The knowledge of this field, as well as an ability to work with both its symbolic and concrete, established and ambiguous aspects seems to be a crucial ingredient in defining good leadership practices, to identifying future priorities, or to overcome previous problems. As Mintzberg (1991, 22) notes: "Any good vision of the future has to be rooted in an understanding of the past".

I have sought to understand how different disciplinary perspectives, departmental cultures and broad trends in society affect academic leadership. Although the contexts for departmental leadership vary across nations and institutions, they are not necessarily always (or completely) dissimilar. Some idealtypical features which seem broadly shared within a certain specialism could be identified (chapter 5), and identical trends (declining resources, increased assessment and demand for accountability) have occurred in many European countries (Middlehurst 1995; Crosthwaite and Warner 1995; Kuoppala 1995). Because of such broad international similarities in the leadership context, it may be that departmental leaders in different nations can see at least some connections between their own situation and the cases I have discussed (see Crosthwaite and Warner 1995, 6).

This said, it should be acknowledged that my sample consists only of eight minor and relatively young departments (section 4.6.) which were studied in a short historical period (even though I have tried retrospectively to trace their cultural backgrounds). In many countries universities have much longer and more complicated traditions. There was some variation between the leadership patterns and practices of the departments studied in a particular disciplinary field; such differences are likely to be broader still as the national and institutional contexts change (section 3.2.3.).

The interpretation of the leadership cultures I have studied is likely to be more complex than the one I have been able to offer, since for the sake of simplicity I have had to exclude many trends and aspects in academia. For example, the social status of different universities and disciplinary departments - and the cultural capital accumulated in them - varies; I have not analyzed nor taken into account such differences, nor the changes in them, which seem nonetheless to affect at least student-teacher relationships (Häyrynen et al. 1992b).

Allardt (1980, 4-5) has pointed out that different historical eras affect academic cultures along with disciplinary traditions. He identifies three types of scientific community, which in fact come close to the types of leadership cultures identified in this study, and which may be found in diverse disciplines: the democratic and non-hierarchical type, the traditional type which is built around a respected professor, and the liberal type in which scientific assessment is at least formally carried out by senior researchers. This suggests that the dynamics of leadership cultures may be more complex than my description allows. In any event, academic leaders may be able to learn something from these cases and from the resulting study of academic leadership.

The cultural context of leadership is not static, although some elements of it (if established) seem to be rather stable (chapter 4, section 6.2.). To some degree, leaders may affect contextual factors, or act as a thermostat (Birnbaum 1989) by resolving the tensions between different pressures in order to rebuild and subsequently maintain organizational systems (Kekäle forthcoming). In such cases, much depends on the leader's standing within the department, power position and competence as a leader and a researcher, ability to negotiate with the researchers and with other relevant parties, and ability to get funding research projects. Combining such diverse tasks may be difficult, but it is also possible to delegate different leadership functions to different individuals or groups.

An individual's leadership qualities and the way they are regarded may change. By trying to modify the leadership culture of a department a leader may gain or lose respect. Forced and failed changes may damage the organization and downgrade the status of the leader, which may make it more difficult for him/her to lead in the future, whereas successful changes help to support his/her position. Even if a process of necessary reform is initiated by a powerful academic leader[13], the commitment of the staff to change and its contribution to the academic enterprise are critical factors, since the performance of a

---

[13] According to my case studies, strong individualistic managerialism and leadership patterned after the models of the business world are best in line with the disciplinary cultures of experimental, hard, urban (applied) specialisms (Becher 1989a).

department is based on the work of the researchers, whose reputation has to be maintained. As an experienced consultant, Berry (1994, 44), notes: "I have yet to see any major change occur successfully without commitment from those whose jobs are affected". Commitment may be achieved if the grounds for the change are sufficiently strong for the researchers to recognize their validity, or if the changes are supported by external pressures.

The perceived fairness of decision making, the practical reasonableness and success of the choices, visions, ideas and assumptions of the leaders, as well as their ability to inspire others and get support from them, seem to be among the required leadership qualities in the management of meaning. In self-regulative and autonomous academic organizations, where motivation is intrinsic to the nature of work, and where positive responses to radical changes are unlikely to be readily forthcoming (Middlehurst 1993, 36), leadership may not always be seen as a virtue in its own right, but it may nonetheless significantly support and benefit academic work.

Chapter 8

REFERENCES

Aaltio-Marjosola, I. (1991) *Cultural Change in a Business Enterprise. Studying a Major Organizational Change and Its Impact on Culture.* The Helsinki School of Economics and Business Administration. Acta Academiae Oeconomicae Helsingiensis. Series A:80. 11/1991. Helsinki.

Aaltonen, T.-P. (1993) *Suomen korkeakoulujärjestelmän rakenteen kehitys professuurien avulla tutkittuna. [The Development of the Structure of Finnish Higher Education System Examined on the Basis of Professorships].* A Manuscript.

Aarnio, A., Ylikangas, H., Kanniainen, V. & Kekkonen, J. (1995) *Professori - virka- vai yliopistomies. [Professors - Civil Servants or Academicians?]* Yliopisto 43 (16), 31-32.

Ahonen, P. (1995) *Yliopistojen kannustinongelmat. [The Problems of Reward Structures for Universities.]* In Wiberg (Ed.) Yliopisto uusiksi! Gaudeamus, Tampere.

Airaksinen, T. (1987) *Tiedepolitiikan oikeudenmukaisuus. Tutkimuksen vapaus, tutkijan oikeudet, tieteen laatu ja tuki. [The Fairness of Science Policy. The Freedom of Research, the Rights of Researchers, the Quality of and the Support to Research.]* In Airaksinen, T. Häyry, H. & Häyry, M. Tiedepolitiikan oikeudenmukaisuus ja tutkijan vastuu. Gaudeamus, Helsinki.

Airaksinen, T. (1995) *Mysteerinäytelmä professorinvalinta. [The Mystery Play: the Elections of Professors.]* In Wiberg (Ed.) Yliopisto uusiksi! Gaudeamus, Tampere.

Aittola, T. (1983) *Yliopistoyhteisön jäsenten käsityksiä ja kokemuksia uudesta laitoshallinnosta. [The Opinions and Experiences of Members of the University Community on the New Model of Departmental Administration].* Jyväskylän yliopiston uuden laitoshallinnon seurantatutkimuksia 2. Jyväskylän yliopisto, Hallintoviraston julkaisuja 8.

Aittola, T. (1984) *Laitoshallinto - Demokratiaa vai byrokratiaa? [Departmental Administration - Democracy or Bureaucracy?]* Jyväskylän yliopiston uuden laitoshallinnon seurantatutkimuksia 4. Jyväskylän yliopiston hallintoviraston julkaisuja N:o 14.

Aittola, T. (1987) *Hallinnollinen rationaalisuus ja yliopistoreformit. [Administrative Rationality and University Reforms.]* Unpublished Licentiate thesis. University of Jyväskylä, Department of Sociology.

Aittola, T. (1992) *Uuden opiskelijatyypin synty. [Origins of the New Student Type.]* Jyväskylä Studies in Education, Psychology and Social Research 91. Jyväskylän yliopisto, Jyväskylä. (English Summary.)

Aittola, T. & Aittola, H. (1985) *Yliopisto-opiskelun mielekkyyden kokeminen ja opiskelijoiden elämismaailman perusrakenteet. [Finding Study at University Meaningful and the Basic Structures of Students' Life-World.]* Jyväskylän yliopiston kasvatustieteen tutkimuslaitoksen julkaisuja, N:o 359.

Aittola, H. & Aittola, T. (1990) *Yliopisto elämismaailmana. Opiskelun ja hallinnon muutosprosessit 1980-luvun yliopistossa. [University as a Life-World. The Processes of*

Change in Studying and Administration within the University of the 1980s.] Julkaisusarja 31/1990. Jyväskylän yliopiston ylioppilaskunta, Jyväskylä.

Alapuro, R. (1990) *Suomi, sosiologia, Eurooppa. [Finland, Sociology, Europe.]* In Perko, T. (Ed.) Tiede muutoksen maailmassa. Atena kustannus Oy, Jyväskylä.

Alasuutari, P. (1994) *Laadullinen tutkimus. [Qualitative Research.]* Vastapaino, Jyväskylä.

Alestalo, M. (1995) *Yliopisto tulosnormien kahleissa. [University in the Chains of Result Norms.]* In Wiberg (Ed.) Yliopisto uusiksi! Gaudeamus, Tampere.

Allaire, Y. & Firsirotu, M. (1984) *Theories of Organizational Culture.* Organizational Studies 5 (3), 193-226.

Allardt, E. (1973) *Suomalaisen sosiologian tutkimisesta. [On Studying Finnish Sociology].* In Alapuro et al. Suomalaisen sosiologian juuret. WSOY, Porvoo.

Allardt, E. (1980) *Tiedepolitiikan heiluriliikkeestä. [On the Pendulum Motion of Higher Education Policy.]* A Speech in the 10th Anniversary of Finnish Academy 10.03.1980. A Manuscript.

Allardt, E. (1992) *Korkeakoulut Suomessa vuonna 2010. [Finnish Universities in 2010].* Korkeakoulutieto 19 (2), 15-23.

Allardt, E. (1995a) *Suunnistuksia ja kulttuurishokkeja [Orientations and Culture Shocks.]* Otava, Keuruu.

Allardt, E. (1995b) *Tiede ja olennaiset kysymykset. [Science and the Essential Questions.]* Tiedepolitiikka 20 (4), 5-12.

Allardt, E. & Littunen, Y. (1984) *Sosiologia. [Sociology.]* WSOY, Juva.

Allen, M. (1988) *The Goals of Universities.* The Society for Research into Higher Education & Open University Press, Bury St Edmunds, Suffolk.

Altheide, D.L. & Johnson, J.M. (1994) *Criteria for Assessing Interpretive Validity in Qualitative Research.* In Denzin, N.K. & Lincoln, Y.S. (Eds.) Handbook of Qualitative Research. Sage Publications, Thousand Oaks.

Alvesson, M. (1990) *On the Popularity of Organizational Culture.* Acta Sociologica 1990 (33), 1 31-49.

Alvesson, M. (1991) *Concepts of Organizational Culture and Presumed Links to Efficiency.* Hallinnon tutkimus/Administrative Studies 10 (3), 181-191.

Alvesson, M. (1993) *Organizations as Rhetoric: Knowledge-Intensive Firms and the Struggle With Ambiguity.* Journal of Management Studies 30 (6), 997-1015.

Alvesson, M. (1995) *Cultural Perspectives on Organization.* Cambridge University Press, Wiltshire.

An Introduction to Higher Education in Finland. A Brief Guide for Foreign Students (1994). Centre for International Mobility (CIMO), Helsinki.

Antikainen, A. (1986) *Koulutuksen tulevaisuus ja koulutuspolitiikka. [The Future of Education and Educational Policy.]* Koulutussosiologisia tutkimuksia ja kirjoituksia. Gaudeamus, Jyväskylä.

Bachrach, P. & Baratz, M.S. (1962) *'The Two Faces of Power'.* American Political Science Review 56 (3), 947-952.

Balderston, F.E. (1974) *Managing Today's University.* Jossey-Bass, San Francisco.

Baldridge (1971) *Power and Conflict in the University.* John Wiley & Sons, New York.

Barnett, R., Ed. (1994) *Academic Community. Discourse or Discord?* Jessica Kingsley Publishers, Guildford.

Becher, T. (1987a) *The Cultural View.* In Clark, B.R. (Ed.) Perspectives on Higher Education. Eight Disciplinary and Comparative Views. University of California Press, Berkeley.

Becher, T. (1987b) *Disciplinary Discourse.* Studies in Higher Education 12 (3), 261-274.

Becher, T. (1987c) *The Disciplinary Shaping of the Profession.* In Clark, B.R. (Ed.) The Academic Profession. National, Disciplinary and Institutional Settings. University of California Press, Berkeley.

Becher, T. (1989a) *Academic Tribes and Territories. Intellectual Enquiry and the Cultures of Disciplines.* The Society for Research into Higher Eduction & Open University Press, Bury St Edmunds, Suffolk.

Becher, T. (1989b) *Historians on History.* Studies in Higher Education 14 (3), 263-278.

Becher, T. (1990a) *The Counter-culture of Specialisation.* European Journal of Education 25 (3), 333-345.

Becher, T. (1990b) *Physicists on Physics.* Studies in Higher Education 15 (1), 3-19.

Becher, T. (1994) *Interdisciplinarity and Community.* In Barnett, R. (Ed.) Academic Community. Discourse or Discord? Jessica Kingsley Publishers, Guildford.

Becher, T & Huber, L. (1990) *Editorial.* European Journal of Education 25 (3), 235-240.

Becher, T. & Kogan, M. (1992) *Process and Structure in Higher Education.* Routledge, London.

Beck, U. (1995) *The Reinvention of Politics: Towards a Theory of Reflexive Modernization.* In: Beck, U., Giddens, A. & Lash. S. Reflexive Modernization: Politics, Tradition and Aesthetics in the Modern Social Order. Polity Press, Cornwall.

Bennett, J.B. & Figuli, D.J., Eds. (1993) *Enhancing Departmental Leadership. The Roles of the Chairperson.* American Council on Education. Series of Higher Education. Oryx Press, New York.

Bensimon, E, Neumann, A. & Birnbaum, R. (1989) *Making Sense of Administrative Leadership: the 'L' Word in Higher Education.* ASHE/ERIC Higher Education Report 1., Washington DC.

Bernstein, R.J. (1985) *Beyond Objectivism and Relativism: Science, Hermeneutics and Praxis.* University of Pennsylvania Press, Philadelphia.

Berry, J. (1994) *Executive Commentary on Reger et al. (1994) article: Creating Earthquakes to Change Organizational Mindsets.* Academy of Management Executive 8 (4), 43-44.

Biglan, A. (1973) *The Characteristics of Subject Matter in Different Scientific Areas.* Journal of Applied Psychology 57 (3), 204-213.

Birnbaum, R. (1989) *How Colleges Work. The Cybernetics of Academic Organization and Leadership.* Jossey-Bass, San Francisco.

Blackler, F., Reed, M. & Whitaker, A. (1993) *Editorial Introduction: Knowledge Workers and Contemporary Organizations.* Journal of Management Studies 30 (6), 851-862.

Blake, R.R. & Mouton, J.S. (1964) *The Managerial Grid.* Gulf Publishing Co, Houston, Texas.

Blake, R.R. & Mouton, J.S. (1982) *Theory and Research for Developing a Science of Leadership.* Journal of Applied Behavioral Science 18 (3), 275-291.

Blau, P.M. (1974) *Exchange Theory.* (First published in 1964.) In Grusky, O. & Miller, G.A. (Eds.) The Sociology of Organizations. Basic Studies. The Free Press, New York.

Bourdieu, P. (1985) *Sosiologian kysymyksiä. [Sociology in Question.]* Vastapaino, Jyväskylä.

Bourdieu, P. (1988) *Homo Academicus.* Polity Press, Cambridge.

Bourdieu, P. (1993) *Sociology in Question.* Sage Publications, London.

Bourdieu, P. & Passeron, J.-C. (1979) *The Inheritors. French Students and Their Relation to Culture.* The University of Chicago Press, Chicago.

Bryman, A. & Burgess, R.G. (1994) *Reflections on Qualitative Data Analysis.* In Bryman, A. & Burgess, R.G. (Eds.) Analyzing Qualitative Data. Routledge, London.

Buchanan, D., Boddy, D. & McCalman, J. (1988) *Getting In, Getting Out, and Getting Back.* In Bryman, A. (Ed.) Doing Research in Organizations. Routledge, London.

Burrell, G. (1988) *Modernism, Postmodernism and Organizational Analysis 2: The Contribution of Michel Foucault.* Organization Studies 9 (2), 221-235.

Burrell, G. & Morgan, G. (1985) *Sociological Paradigms and Organizational Analysis.* Gower, Guildford.

Bush, T. (1995) *Theories of Educational Management.* Paul Chapman Publishing, Gateshead.

Byckling, E. (1996) *Millaisessa ympäristössä syntyy hyvää tutkimusta? [What Kind of an Environment Supports Good Research?]* Korkeakoulutieto 24 (2), 20-25.

Caldwell, B. (1982) *Beyond Positivism: Economic Methodology in the Twentieth Century.* George Allen & Unwin. Guildford.

Cannon, R.A. (1983) *The Professional Development of Australian University Teachers: An Act of Faith?* Higher Education 12 (1), 19-33.

Carr, W. & Kemmis, S. (1986) *Becoming Critical: Education, Knowledge and Action Research.* Falmer Press, Lewes.

Chaffee, E.E. (1985) *The Concept of Strategy: From Business to Higher Education.* In Smart, J. (Ed.) Higher Education: Handbook of Theory and Research, Vol 1. American Educational Research Association, Washington.

Clark, B.R. (1983) *The Higher Education System. Academic Organization in Cross-National Perspective.* University of California Press, Los Angeles.

Clark, B.R. (1984) *The Organizational Conception.* In Clark, B.R. (Ed.) Perspectives on Higher Education. Eight Disciplinary and Comparative Views. University of California Press, Berkeley.

Clark, B.R. (1987a) *The Making of an Organizational Saga.* In Schafritz, J.M. & Ott, J.S. (Eds.) Classics of Organization Theory. Brooks/Cole Publishing Company, Kingsport, Tennesee.

Clark, B.R. (1987b) *Conclusions.* In Clark, B.R. (Ed.) The Academic Profession. National, Disciplinary and Institutional Settings. University of California Press, Berkeley.

Clark, B.R. (1995) *Leadership and Innovation in Universities. From Theory to Practice.* Tertiary Education and Management 1 (1), 7-11.

Clark, B.R. (1996) *Case Studies of Innovative Universities. A Progress Report.* Tertiary Education and Management 2 (1), 52-61.

Clark, B.R. & Neave, G.R. (1992) (Eds). *The Encyclopedia of Higher Education.* Vol 1. National Systems of Higher Education. Pergamon Press, Oxford.

Clark, J. (1993) *Personnel Management, Human Relations Management and Technical Change.* In Clark, J. (Ed.) Human Resource Management & Technical Change. Sage Publications, London.

Cohen, M.D. & March, J.D. (1974) *Leadership and Ambiguity: The American College President.* McGraw-Hill, New York.

Cronström. C. (1995) *Anonyymit ilmiannot ja laiskat professorit.[Anonymous Denouncements and Lazy Professors.]* Yliopisto 43 (17), 24.

Crosthwaite, E. & Warner, D. (1995) *Setting the Scene.* In Warner, D. & Crosthwaite, E. (Eds.) Human Resource Management in Higher and Further Education. The Society for Research into Higher Education & Open University Press, Bury St Edmunds, Suffolk.

Czarniawska-Joerges, B. (1992) *Exploring Complex Organizations. A Cultural Perspective.* Sage Publications, Newbury Park.

Dahrendorf, R. (1959) *Class and Class Conflict in Industrial Society.* Routledge & Kegan Paul, London.

Davies, J.L. and Morgan, A.W. (1983) *Management of Higher Education Institutions in a Period of Contraction and Uncertainty.* In Boyd-Barrett, O., Bush, T., Goodey, J., McNay, I. & Preedy, M. (Eds.) Approaches to Post-School Management. Harper and Row, London.

Dearlove, J. (1995a) *Collegiality, Managerialism and Leadership in English Universities.* Tertiary Education and Management (TEAM) 1 (2), 161-169.

Dearlove, J. (1995b) *The Deadly Dull Issue of University 'Administration'? Good Governance, Managerialism, and Organising Academic Work.* A Paper Presented at SRHE -Conference. 12-14 December, Edinburgh.

Denzin, N.K. (1994) *The Art and Politics of Interpretation.* In Denzin, N.K. & Lincoln, Y.S. (Eds.) Handbook of Qualitative Research. Sage, Thousand Oaks.

Denzin, N.K. & Lincoln, Y.S. (1994) *Introduction. Entering the Field of Qualitative Research.* In Denzin, N.K. & Lincoln, Y.S. (Eds.) Handbook of Qualitative Research. Sage, Thousand Oaks.

Dill, D. (1982) *The Management of Academic Culture: Notes on the Management of Meaning and Social Interaction.* Higher Education 11 (3), 303-320.

Eklund, K. (1992) *Asiantuntija - Yksilönä ja organisaation jäsenenä. [The Expert - An Individual and a Member of an Organization.]* Jyväskylän yliopiston täydennyskoulutuskeskuksen tutkimuksia ja selvityksiä 12. Jyväskylän yliopisto.

Elovainio, P. (1974) *Korkeakoululaitoksen rakenne ja yhteiskunnan muutos. [The Structure of Higher Education System and the Change of Society.]* Sosiologia 11 (5-6), 244-265.

Enderud, J. (1980) *Administrative Leadership in Organized Anarchies.* International Journal of Institutional Management in Higher Education 4 (3), 235-253.

Eskola, A. (1973) *Suomalaisen sosiologian uudistuminen. [The Reformation of Finnish Sociology].* In Alapuro et al. Suomalaisen sosiologian juuret. WSOY, Porvoo.

Fontana, A. & Frey, J. (1994) *Interviewing. The Art of Science.* In Denzin, N.K. & Lincoln, Y.S. (Eds.) Handbook of Qualitative Research. Sage, Thousand Oaks.

Foucault, M. (1979) *Discipline and Punish.* Penguin, Hammondsworth.

Frost, P, Moore, L, Louis, M, Lundberg, C. & Martin, J. (1991) Eds. *Reframing Organizational Culture.* Sage Publications, Newbury Park.

Gagliardi, P. (1986) *The Creation and Change of Organizational Cultures: A Conceptual Framework.* Organizational Studies 7 (2), 117-134.

Gergen, K.J. (1989) *Social Psychology and the Wrong Revolution.* European Journal of Social Psychology 19 (5), 463-468.

Gerholm, T. (1990) *On Tacit Knowledge in Academia.* European Journal of Education 25 (3), 263-271.

Gordon, G., Gray, H., Guildford, P., Gunn, R., Hampshire, P., Lovell, B., McNay, I., Middlehurst, R., Partington, P.A., Paulson-Ellis, M. & Wookey, P. (1994) *Higher Education Management and Leadership: Towards a National Framework for Preparation and Development.* Occasional Green Paper No. 9 UK UCOSDA Task Force One. The UK Universities' and Colleges' Staff Development Agency, Sheffield.

Griffith, B.C. & Mullins, N.C. (1972) *Coherent Social Groups in Scientific Change.* Science 177 (4053), 956-964.

Guba, E.C. & Lincoln, Y.S. (1994) *Competing Paradigms in Qualitative Research.* In Denzin, N.K. & Lincoln, Y.S. (Eds.) Handbook of Qualitative Research. Sage Publications, Thousand Oaks.

Habermas, J. (1978) *Knowledge and Human Interests.* Heinemann, London.

Habermas, J. (1984) *The Theory of Communicative Action. Volume One. Reason and the Rationalization of Society.* Beacon Press, Boston.

Hammersley, M. (1995) *The Politics of Social Research.* Sage Publications, London.

Hanson, E.M. (1979) *Educational Administration and Organizational Behaviour.* Allyn and Bacon inc., Boston.

Hatch, M.J. (1993) *The Dynamics of Organizational Culture.* Academy of Management Review 18 (4), 657-698.

Hawton, K., Salkovskis, P.M., Kirk, J. & Clark, D.M. eds. (1989) *Cognitive Behaviour Therapy for Psychiatric Problems.A Practical Guide.* Oxford University Press, Oxford.

Hearn, J.C. & Anderson, M. (1996) *The Changing Demography of University Faculty: A Conceptual Agenda for Research.* A Revised Version of the Paper Presented in 17th Annual EAIR Forum, 27-30 August 1995, Zürich.

Heiskala, R. (1990) *Tulkinnan koeteltavuus ja aikakauslehtien analyysi. [The Testing of Interpretations and the Analysis of Journals and Magazines].* In Mäkelä, K. (toim.) Kvalitatiivisen aineiston analyysi ja tulkinta. Gaudeamus, Helsinki.

Helenius, B. (1995) *Nuoret, työ ja koulutus - selviytymistrateginen näkökulma. [Youth, Work and Education from the Point of View of Survival Strategies.]* Korkeakoulutieto 22 (4), 22-27.

Helsingin yliopisto - historiaa ja nykypäivää (1970) *[The University of Helsinki - Past and Present].* WSOY, Porvoo.

Hersey, P. & Blanchard, K.H. (1982) *Management of Organizational Behaviour. Utilizing Human Resources.* Prentice Hall, New Jersey.

Higher Education Policy in Finland (1994) Ministry of Education, Helsinki.

Higher Education Policy in Finland (1996) Ministry of Education, Helsinki.

Hogan, R., Curphy, G.J. & Hogan, J. (1994) *What We Know About Leadership. Effectiveness and Personality.* American Psychologist 49 (6), 493-504.

Horkheimer, M. (1991) *Traditionaalinen ja kriittinen teoria [Traditional and Critical Theory].* In Kotkavirta, J. (Ed. and Compiler) Järjen kritiikki by Theodor W. Adorno, Max Horkheimer and Herbert Marcuse. Vastapaino, Jyväskylä.

Hovi, R., Kivinen, O. & Rinne, R. (1989) *Komitealaitos, koulutusmietinnöt ja koulutuspolitiikan oikeutus. Ammatillisen ja akateemisen koulutuksen oikeutusperustelujen muutokset suomalaisissa koulutusmietinnöissä 1860-luvulta 1980-luvun lopulle. [The Institution of the Government Committee and the Justification of Educational Policy in Committee Reports].* Turun yliopiston julkaisuja, sarja C osa 73. English Summary.

Hoy, D.C. (1986) *Power, Repression, Progress: Foucault, Lukes and the Frankfurt School.* In Hoy, D.C. (Ed.) Foucault: A Critical Reader. Basil Blackwell, London.

Huber, L. (1990) *Disciplinary Cultures and Social Reproduction.* European Journal of Education 25 (3), 241-261.

Häikiö, M. (1977) *Tutkinnonuudistuksen taustaa: järjestelmäkeskustelua ja tutkintoasetuksia. [Backgrounds of the Degree Reform: Degree Statutes and Debates on the System.]* In Häikiö, M., Rautkallio, H., Tuomikoski-Leskelä, P & Vuorinen, J. (Eds.) Korkeakoulut ja tutkinnonuudistus. KTTS:n julkaisusarja 23. WSOY, Helsinki.

Härö, E.S., Karlsson, K.-P. & Ursin-Iivanainen, H. (1993) *Suomi Euroopassa. Karttoja ja diagrammeja. [Finland in Europe. Maps and Diagrams.]* Maanmittaushallitus, Jyväskylä.

Häyrynen, Y.-P. (1970) *Yliopiston ilmastot. [The Climates of the University].* Helsingin yliopisto, sosiaalipolitiikan laitos. Tutkimuksia n:o 7.

Häyrynen, Y.-P. (1974) *Tutkinnonuudistus Joensuun korkeakoulussa: mitä se merkitsee, mihin se tähtää, mitä se edellyttää. [Degree Reform at the University of Joensuu: What Does it Imply, What Does it Aim At, What Does it Require.]* In Tutkinnonuudistus Joensuun korkeakoulussa. Joensuun korkeakoulu. Monistesarja A 1/1974, tutkimuksia ja selvityksiä.

Häyrynen, Y.-P. & Hautamäki, J. (1976) *Ihmisen koulutettavuus ja koulutuspolitiikka. [The Educability of Man and Educational Policy.]* Weilin+Göös, Tapiola.

Häyrynen, Y.-P., Perho, H., Silvonen, J. & Kuittinen, M. (1992a) *Kaksi opiskelijapolvea, kaksi kulttuuria. Helsingin yliopiston vaikutuksista ja opiskelijain kokemusrakenteesta 1969 ja 1989. [Two Student Generations, Two Cultures of Learning. Comparison of the university experiences and the impact of teaching among students of 1969 and 1989: the case of Helsinki University.]* Psychological Reports N:o 13. University of Joensuu, Faculty of Social Sciences. (English Summary).

Häyrynen, Y.-P., Perho, H., Kuittinen, M. & Silvonen, J. (1992b) *Ilmapiirit, kentät, ja kulttuurit. Suomen korkeakoulutus 1973-1989. [Fields, Cultures and Athmospheres at the Finnish University: A Study of 57 Educational Fields in 1989 and Change of Athmospheres between 1973 and 1989].* University of Joensuu, Publications in Social Sciences N:o 15. (English Summary).

Hölttä, S. (1993) *The University of Joensuu - Implementation of the National Higher Education Policy at a Regional University.* OECD Country Review. Visit of the Examiners at the University of Joensuu. Working Paper.

Hölttä, S. (1995) *Towards the Self-Regulative University.* Publications in Social Sciences N:o 23, University of Joensuu.

Hölttä, S. & Pulliainen, K. (1992) *Improving Managerial Effectiveness at the University of Joensuu.* IIEP, Paris 9th September 1992, UNESCO.

Hölttä, S. & Halonen, M. (1994) *A Changing University in Changing Society: Strategies and Experiences of the University of Joensuu.* A Paper Presented at the 9th International Meeting of University Administrators. Prague, August 21-26, 1994.

Hölttä, S. & Nuotio, J. (1995) *Academic Leadership in a Self-Regulative Environment. A Challenge for Finnish Universities.* Tertiary Education and Management 1 (1), 12-20.

Immonen, K. (1995) *Tiedepolitiikka tieteen ohjaajana. [Science Policy as a Steering Mechanism of Research.]* Tiedepolitiikka 20 (2), 29-36.

Jameson, F. (1984) *Foreword.* In Lyotard, J.-F. The Postmodern Condition: A Report on Knowledge. Theory and History of Literature, Volume 10. Manchester University Press, Guildford.

Jamison, A., Eyerman, R. & Cramer, J. (1990) *Where Do Intellectuals Come From? On the Formation of Intellectuals in the Environment Movement.* In Elzinga, A., Nolin, J., Pranger, R. & Suneson, S. (Eds.) In Science We Trust? Moral and Political Issues of Science in Society. Science and Technology Policy Studies 2. Lund University Press, Lund.

Jetten, E. (1984) *Social Contacts at University.* In Framhein, G. & Langer, J. (Eds.) Student Worlds in Europe. Kärntner Druck- und Verlagsgesellschaft m.b.H., Klagenfurt. Kärntner Universitäts-Druckerei.

Jolkkonen, A. (1985) *Korkeakoululaitoksen muotoutuminen ja uudet tehtävät. Empiirisiä havaintoja suomalaisesta korkeakoulumallista. [The Formation and the New Functions of the University Institute. Empirical Observations on the Finnish University Model.]* Joensuun yliopisto, Kasvatustieteen tiedekunnan selosteita N:o 5. Kasvatussosiologia. English Abstract.

Juuti, P. (1989) *Organisaatiokäyttäytyminen. Johtamisen ja organisaation toiminnan perusteet. [Organizational Behaviour. Basics of Leadership and Organization's Functioning.]* Otava, Keuruu.

Järvi, P. Kivinen, O. & Rinne, R. (1990) *Yliopiston tila ja tahto. Turun yliopiston yhteiskuntatieteellisen tiedekunnan ja hallintoviraston henkilöstön näkökulmia yliopistoonsa. [The State and the Will of the University. The Personnel of the Faculty of Social Science and Administration Office at the University of Turku View Their University.]* Koulutussosiologian tutkimusyksikön tutkimusraportteja 5. Turun yliopisto.

Jääskeläinen, V. (1994) *Kauppakorkeakoulun johtaminen 1990-luvun Suomessa. [The Management of a School of Economics in Finland in the 1990s.]* Korkeakoulutieto 20 (4), 19-23.

Kangas, J. (1989) *Jürgen Habermasin kommunikatiivisen toiminnan teoria. [The Theory of Communicative Action by Jürgen Habermas.]* Tutkijaliiton julkaisusarja 45. Tutkijaliitto, Helsinki.

Kanniainen, V. (1995) *Onko valtiovallan ja yliopistolaitoksen romanssi ohi? [Is the Romance between the State and the Universities Over?]* In Wiberg, M. (Ed.) Yliopisto uusiksi! Gaudeamus, Tampere.

Kantele, J. (1990) *Fysiikan visiota. [Visions of Physics.]* In Perko, T. (Ed.) Tiede muutoksen maailmassa. Atena kustannus Oy, Jyväskylä.

Katz, D. & Kahn, R.L. (1974) *Open Systems Theory.* (First published in 1966.) In Grusky, O. & Miller, G.A. (Eds.) The Sociology of Organizations. Basic Studies. The Free Press, New York.

Kaukonen, E. (1984) *Suomalainen sosiologia tieteentutkimuksen valossa. [Finnish Sociology in the Light of Science Studies.]* Sosiologia 22 (2), 128-138.

Kaukonen, E. (1990) *Theory, Dynamics and Policy of Science.* Acta Universitatis Tamperensis ser A, vol 300. University of Tampere, Tampere.

Kekäle, J. (1991) *Keskusteluilmapiirit Joensuun yliopiston kolmella opintosuunnalla - Laadullinen tutkimus opiskelijakulttuureista. [The Climates of Discussion Within Three Fields of Study at the University of Joensuu. A Qualitative Study on Student Cultures.]* Psychological Reports N:o 11. University of Joensuu, Faculty of Social Sciences. (English Summary).

Kekäle, J. (1992) *Organisaatiokulttuuri koulukunta scheinilaisesta näkökulmasta tarkasteltuna. [Organizational Culture School from a Scheinian Perspective.]* Unpublished Master's Thesis. University of Joensuu, Department of Sociology.

Kekäle, J. (1993a) *Yliopiston ainelaitoksen organisaatiokulttuurit. [Organizational Cultures of a University Department.]* Unpublished Licentiate Thesis. University of Joensuu, Department of Psychology. (English Summary).

Kekäle, J. (1993b) *Organisaatiokulttuurin tutkimuksen kolme näkökulmaa. [Three Perspectives of Organizational Culture Studies.]* Psykologia 28 (5), 320-327. (English Abstract.)

Kekäle, J. (1993c) *Laitosjohtajan ja -johtajuuden vaikutus laitoksen toimintaan, kulttuuriin ja tuottavuuteen. [The Impact of the Departmental Leadership on the Functioning, Culture and Productivity of the Department.]* Unpublished Proposal for a Research Project.

Kekäle, J. (1994a) *Luento-opetuksen kehittäminen. Vähemmällä luennoimisella parempiin tuloksiin. [Developing Lecturing. Better Results with Less Lecturing.]* Korkeakoulupedagogiikan perusmateriaaliprojekti, julkaisu N:o 2. OMP, Oulu.

Kekäle, J. (1994b) *Academic Leadership in Different Disciplinary Contexts.* A Paper Presented in 16th Annual EAIR Forum, 21-24 August 1994, Amsterdam

Kekäle, J. (1995a) *Academic Leadership in Different Disciplinary Contexts.* A Summary version of Kekäle (1994b). Tertiary Education and Management (TEAM) 1 (1), 35-36.

Kekäle, J. (1995b) *Organizational and Leadership Cultures within University Departments.* Administrative Studies / Hallinnon tutkimus 14 (2), 100-111.

Kekäle, J. (1995c) *Ainelaitosten johtamiskulttuurit ja selviytymistrategiat - Strategisen johtamisen mahdollisuuksista laitostasolla. [Leadership Cultures and Strategies of Survival. - On the Possibilities of Strategic Management in University Departments.]* A Paper presented at the seminar 'Strateginen johtaminen korkeakouluissa' [Strategic Management in Universities] 1.6.1995 University of Tampere.

Kekäle, J. (1995d) *Academic Leadership and Change.* A Paper Presented in 17th Annual EAIR Forum, 27-30 August 1995, Zürich.

Kekäle, J. (Forthcoming.) The Field of Possibilities of Academic Leaders.

Kekäle, J. & Kuittinen, M. (1993) *Joensuun yliopiston pedagoginen kehittämishanke. [The Pedagogical Development Project at the University of Joensuu.]* Final Report. JOPKE, Joensuu.

Kekäle, T. & Kekäle, J. (1995) *A Mismatch of Cultures: A Pitfall of Implementing a Total Quality Approach.* International Journal of Quality and Reliability Management 12 (9), 210-220.

Ketonen, O. (1971) *Yliopiston tie. [University's Way.]* Otava, Helsinki.

Kettunen, P. (1994) *Johtamiskoulutus - hengissäsäilymiskurssi korkeakouluille? [Leadership Training - A Course of Survival for Universities?]* Korkeakoulutieto 20 (4), 31-35.

Kincheloe, J.L. & McLaren, P.L. (1994) *Rethinking Critical Theory and Qualitative Research.* In Denzin, N.K. & Lincoln, Y.S. (Eds.) Handbook of Qualitative Research. Sage Publications, Thousand Oaks.

Kivinen, O. (1989) *Valtio, markkinat ja akateeminen yhteisö. Korkeakoululaitoksen tilan ja tulevaisuuden kansainvälistä vertailua. [State, Markets and Academic Community. International Comparisons Concerning the Future and the State of Higher Education.]* In Kivinen, O. (Ed.) Muutoksen pysyvyys. Sosiologisia näkökulmia yhteiskuntaan. Turun yliopiston julkaisusarja, sarja C osa 83. Turku.

Kivinen, O. (1995) *Tutkimuksen, opetuksen ja opiskelun yhteys. [The Connection Between Research, Teaching and Studying.]* In Wiberg, M. (Ed.) Yliopisto uusiksi! Gaudeamus, Tampere.

Kivinen, O. & Rinne, R. (1992) *Vähemmän mutta parempia yliopistoja. [Less but Better Universities.]* Helsingin Sanomat 13. Dec. 1992.

Kivinen, O., Rinne, R. & Ketonen, K. (1993) *Yliopiston huomen. Korkeakoulupolitiikan historiallinen suunta Suomessa. [The Future of the University. The Historical Direction of Finnish Higher Education Policy.]* Hanki ja Jää, Helsinki.

Kleinman, S. (1983) *Collective Matters as Individual Concerns. Peer Culture Among Graduate Students.* Urban Life 12 (2), 203-225.

Kogan, M. (1987) *The Political View.* In Clark, B.R. (Ed.) Perspectives on Higher Education. Eight Disciplinary and Comparative Views. University of California Press, Berkeley.

Koho, A. (1974) *Johdannoksi. [Introduction.]* In Tutkinnonuudistus Joesuun korkeakoulussa. Joensuun korkeakoulu. Monistesarja A 1/1974, tutkimuksia ja selvityksiä.

Kontkanen, L. (1994) *Löyhäsidonnaisuus tieto-organisaatiossa: Esimerkkinä aikuiskoulutuskeskukset. [Loose Coupling in Knowledge Organizations: The Case of Adult Education Centres.]* The Finnish Journal of Business Economics 43 (3), 260-281.

Koski, L. (1993) *Tieteen tahtomana, yliopiston tekemänä. Yliopiston sisäiset symboliset järjestykset. [Required by Science, Created by Universities. The Internal Symbolic Orders of Universities.]* University of Joensuu, Publications in Social Sciences N:o 17. English Summary.

Koski, L. (1994) *Kohti aitoa tosiyliopistoa. [Towards a Genuine and Real University.]* Tiede & Edistys 19 (4), 347-350.

Kosko, B. (1994) *Fuzzy Thinking. The New Science of Fuzzy Logic.* Harper Collins Publishers, Glasgow.

Kota 1992. [A Database Concerning Finnish Higher Education.] Opetusministeriö, korkeakoulu ja tiedeosasto.

Kotkavirta, J. (1991) *Jälkisanat. [Epilogue.]* In Järjen kritiikki by Theodor W. Adorno, Max Horkheimer, Herbert Marcuse. Translated, edited and compiled by Jussi Kotkavirta. Vastapaino, Jyväskylä.

Kuikka, M.T. (1992) *Finland.* In Clark, B.R. & Neave, G.R. (Eds.) The Encyclopedia of Higher Education. Vol 1. National Systems of Higher Education. Pergamon Press, Oxford.

Kuhn, T.S. (1970) *The Structure of Scientific Revolutions.* The University of Chicago Press, Chicago.

Kuittinen, M. (1992) *Ilmapiiri - Tiedettä vai kansantarua? Opintoilmapiirien konsensuaalisuus vs. subjektiivisuus. [Climate - Science or Folklore? How Consensual are University Students' Study Climate Perceptions?]* Unpublished Licentiate Thesis. University of Joensuu, Department of Psychology. (English Summary.)

Kuittinen, M. & Kekäle, J. (1996) *Oppivan organisaation kulttuuri. [The Culture of a Learning Organization.]* Psykologia 31 (3), 182-190. (English abstract.)

Kuoppala, K. (1995) *Euroopan tahtiin muuttuva suomalainen korkeakoululaitos. [Finnish Higher Education System - Changing in Pace with Europe.]* Korkeakoulutieto 22 (3), 61-65.

Kuoppala, K. & Marttinen, K. (1995) *Suomen tiedehallinnon määräytymisestä osana Eurooppalaista korkeakoulujärjestelmää. [On the Formation of the Administration of Finnish Higher Education as a Part of the European Higher Education System.]* Länsi-Suomen taloudellinen tutkimuslaitos, julkaisuja N:o 60. Vaasan yliopisto, Vaasa.

Lahti-Kotilainen, L. (1992) *Values as Critical Factors in Management Training.* Acta Universitatis Tamperensis ser A vol 356. University of Tampere, Vammala.

Latomaa, T. & Vilén, J. (1992) *Korkeakoulujemme pakko uudistua. [Universities Must Reorganize.]* Helsingin Sanomat 1. Sep. 1992.

Law, J. (1976) *The Development of Specialities in Science: The Case of X-ray Protein Crystallography.* In Lemaine, G., MacLeod, R., Mulkay, M. & Weingart, P. (Eds.) Perspectives on the Emergence of Scientific Disciplines. Mouton & Co, The Hague.

Leininger, M. (1994) *Evaluation Criteria and Critique of Qualitative Research Studies.* In Morse, J. (Ed.) Critical Issues in Qualitative Research Methods. Sage Publications, Thousand Oaks.

Lemaine, G., MacLeod, R., Mulkay, M. & Weingart, P. (1976) *Introduction. Problems in the Emergence of New Disciplines.* In Lemaine, G., MacLeod, R., Mulkay, M. & Weingart, P. (Eds.) Perspectives on the Emergence of Scientific Disciplines. Mouton & Co, The Hague.

Lie, S., Malik, L. Harris, D. Eds. (1994) *World Yearbook of Education 1994. The Gender Gap in Higher Education.* Kogan Page, London.

Liiten, M. (1996a) *Tulosohjausta pohtinut työryhmä ehdottaa: Yliopistojen ja ministeriön väliset tulossopimukset kolmeksi vuodeksi kerrallaan. [A Proposal from the Working Group Examining Result Management: Agreements on Results Between Universities and the Ministry of Education Should be Made for Three Years at a Time.]* Helsingin Sanomat 18. sep. 1996.

Liiten, M. (1996b) *Tutkijat kilpailemaan tieteen lisärahasta. Tekes jakaa valtaosan 1,5 miljardin markan potista. [Researchers May Compete For Additional Funding of FIM 1,5 Milliard. A*

Lions Share Will be Allocated by the Development Centre of Technology.] Helsingin Sanomat 18. Dec. 1996.

Lincoln, Y.S. & Denzin, N.K. (1994b) *The Fifth Moment.* In Denzin, N.K. & Lincoln, Y.S. (Eds.) Handbook of Qualitative Research. Sage Publications, Thousand Oaks.

Linna, M. (1992) *Onko korkeakoulujen kehittäminen kiinni vain rahasta? [Does the Development of Higher Education Depend Only on Money?]* Korkeakoulutieto 19 (2), 24-28.

Lockwood, G. (1985) *Universities as Organizations.* In Lockwood, G. & Davies, J. (Eds.) Universities: The Management Challenge. SHRE & NFER-Nelson, Worchester.

Lounasmaa, O.V. (1993) *Paras tieteellinen tutkimus turvattava lamankin aikana. [Best Research has to Be Secured even During the Recession.]* Helsingin Sanomat 15. Jan. 1993.

Lukes, S. (1974) *Power. A Radical View.* Macmillan, Hong Kong.

Lumijärvi, I. (1985) *Johtamistyön sisällöstä. Johtamistyön universalistiset ja yrityspohjaiset kuvaukset valtionhallinnon johtamistyön tulkitsijoina - metodisia ja sisällöllisiä perspektiivejä. [On the Content of the Work of Leaders. Universal and Enterprise-specific Descriptions of Leadership in Public Administration - Perspectives on Methodology and Content.]* Julkishallinnon julkaisusarja N:o 1/1985 A. Tampereen yliopisto, Tampere.

Lyotard, J.-F. (1984) *The Postmodern Condition: A Report on Knowledge.* Theory and History of Literature, Volume 10. Manchester University Press, Guildford.

Lönnqvist, J. (1985) *Johtamisen ja johtajan psykologiasta. [On the Psychology of Leadership.]* Valtion koulutuskeskus. Julkaisusarja B nro 34. Valtion painatuskeskus, Helsinki.

Maassen, P.A.M. (1996) *The Concept of Culture and Higher Education.* Tertiary Education and Management 2 (2), 153-159.

Maassen, P.A.M. & van Vught, F.A. (1992) *Strategic Planning.* In Clark, B.R. & Neave, G.R. (Eds.) The Encyclopedia of Higher Education. Volume 2; Analytical Perspectives. Pergamon Press, Oxford.

Marin, M. (1970) *Tiedekunnat opintoympäristöinä [Faculties as Study Environments.]* Tammi, Helsinki.

Marttinen, K. (1988) *Korkeakoululaitoksen organisatorisista ohjausmalleista. Teoreettisia lähtökohtia. [On Organizational Models of Steering of Higher Education. Theoretical Points of View.]* Vaasan kauppakorkeakoulu, Länsi-Suomen taloudellinen tutkimuslaitos, julkaisuja No 21. Vaasa

McGregor, D.M. (1961) *The Human Side of Enterprise.* McGraw-Hill, New York.

McNair, S. (1993) *Summary Speech.* In Hale, B. & Pope, N. (Eds.) 1993 Edinburgh Conference. Speeches and Papers from the EHE Directors Conference. Enterprise in Higher Education. The Edinburgh Enterprise Centre.

Meyerson, D.E. (1991) *"Normal Ambiguity?" A Glimpse of an Occupational Culture.* In Frost, P, Moore, L, Louis, M, Lundberg, C. & Martin, J. (Eds.) Reframing Organizational Culture. Sage Publications, Newbury Park.

Meyerson, D. & Martin, J. (1987) *Cultural Change: An Integration of Three Different Views.* Journal of Management Studies 24 (6), 623-647.

Middlehurst, R. (1993) *Leading Academics.* SRHE & Open University Press, Bury St. Edmunds, Suffolk.

Middlehurst, R. (1995) *Changing Leadership in Universities.* In Schuller, T. (Ed.) The Changing University? The Society for Research into Higher Education & Open University Press, Bury St Edmunds, Suffolk.

Middlehurst, R. & Kennie, T. (1995) *Leadership and Professionals: Comparative Frameworks.* Tertiary Education and Management (TEAM) 1 (2), 120-130.

Miller, H.D.R. (1995) *The Management of Change in Universities. Universities, State and Economy in Australia, Canada and the United Kingdom.* The Society for Research into Higher Education & Open University Press, Bury St Edmunds, Suffolk.

Minztberg, H. (1991) *Strategic Thinking as Seeing.* In Näsi, J. (Ed.) Arenas of Strategic Thinking. Foundation for Economic Education, Helsinki.

Mintzberg, H. (1994) *The Rise and Fall of Strategic Planning.* Prentice Hall, London.

Moodie, G.C. & Eustache, R. (1974) *Power and Authority in British Universities.* George Allen & Unwin Ltd, London.

Morgan, G (1986) *Images of Organization.* Sage Publications, Beverly Hills.

Moses, I. (1985) *The Role of Head of Department in the Pursuit of Excellence.* Higher Education 14 (4), 337-354.

Moses, I. (1992) *Leadership: Deans and Heads of Departments.* In Clark, B.R. & Neave, G.R. (Eds.) The Encyclopedia of Higher Education. Volume 2: Analytical Perspectives. Pergamon Press, Oxford.

Moses, I. & Roe, E. (1990) *Heads and Chairs. Managing Academic Departments.* University of Queensland Press, Maryborough, Victoria.

Mustajoki, A. (1995) *Professoreiden tutkimusansiot. [Professors and Their Scientific Merits.]* Yliopisto 43 (17), 3.

Mustonen, S. (1995) *Mittauksesta kuvaukseen. [From Measurement to Description.]* Yliopisto 43 (17), 24.

Myllynen, T (1992) *Tulos ja sen mittaaminen. [Results and How to Measure Them.]* Yliopistouutiset 31 (46), 6.

Mäenpää, A. & Mäkinen, J. (1989) *Tuloksellisen johtamisen edellytyksistä korkeakouluissa. [On the Prerequisites of Effective Management in Higher Education.]* Vaasan korkeakoulu, Länsi-Suomen taloudellinen tutkimuslaitos julkaisuja n:o 24, Vaasa.

Mäkinen, R. & Määttä, P., Eds. (1989) *Students and Studying in Higher Education in Finland.* Institute for Educational Research. Publication Series B, N:o 35.

Neisser, U. (1976) *Cognition and Reality. Principles and Implications of Cognitive Psychology.* W.H. Freeman and Company, San Francisco.

Nevala, A. (1983) *Joensuun korkeakoulun perustamisvaiheet. [The Phases of the Founding of a Higher Education Institute in Joensuu.]* Pohjois-Karjalan yliopistoseura, Joensuu.

Nevala, A. (1990) *Mittavat tavoitteet - pienet muutokset? Opiskelijakunnan rakenteen yleispiirteet Suomessa 1900-luvulla. [Large Objectives - Small Changes? General Features of the Structure of the Student Population in Finland in the 19th Century.]* In Jalkanen, H. & Mäkinen, R. (Eds.) Korkeakouluopintojen kulku ja opintoilmapiirit. Kasvatustieteiden tutkimuslaitoksen julkaisusarja B. Teoriaa ja käytäntöä 59.

Nevala, A. (1991) *Mittavat murrokset - pienet muutokset. Korkeakoulupolitiikka ja opiskelijakunnan rakenne Suomessa 1900-luvulla. [Large Transitions - Small Changes. Higher Education Policy and the Structure of Student Population in Finland in the 19th Century.]* Unpublished Licentiate Thesis. University of Joensuu, Department of History.

Numminen, J. (1987) *Yliopistokysymys. [The Question of Universities.]* Otava, Helsinki.

O'Reilly III, C.A., Chatman, J., & Caldwell, D. (1991) *People and Organizational Culture: A Profile Comparison Approach to Assessing Person-Organization Fit.* Academy of Management Journal 34 (3), 478-516.

Orton, J.D. & Weick, K.E. (1990) *Loosely Coupled System: A Reconceptualization.* Academy of Management Review 15 (2), 203-223.

Parsons, T. (1951) *The Social System.* Free Press, New York.

Patton, M.Q. (1990) *Qualitative Evaluation and Research Methods.* Sage Publications, Newbury Park.

Paukkunen, L. (1977) *Jyväskylän yliopiston yhteiskuntatieteellisen tiedekunnan tutkinnonuudistuskokeilusta. [On the Experiment of the Degree Reform at the Faculty of Social Sciences of the University of Jyväskylä.]* In Häikiö, M., Rautkallio, H., Tuomikoski-Leskelä, P & Vuorinen, J. (Eds.) Korkeakoulut ja tutkinnonuudistus. KTTS:n julkaisusarja 23. WSOY, Helsinki.

Pekkala, S. & Rönkkömäki, H. (1991) *Tulosjohtamisen soveltuvuus Oulun yliopiston laitoksiin. [The Applicability of MBO in the Departments of the University of Oulu.]* Unpublished Master's Thesis. University of Oulu, Faculty of Education, Department of Behavioral Sciences.

Perho, H. (1978) *Korkeakouluympäristön laadullinen rakenne ja muutos opiskelija-arvioiden perusteella. [Qualitative Structure and Change of University Environments.]* Joensuun korkeakoulu, Kasvatustieteiden osaston julkaisuja n:o 6. (English Summary.)

Perko, T., Ed. (1990) *Tiede muutoksen maailmassa. [Research in a Changing World.]* Atena kustannus Oy, Jyväskylä.

Pesonen, P. (1982) *Finland: the 'one man-one vote' issue.* In Daalder, H. & Shils, E. (Eds.) Universities, Politicians and Bureaucrats. Europe and United States. Cambridge University Press, Cambridge.

Pfeffer, J. (1987) *Understanding the Role of Power in Decision Making.* In Schafritz, J.M. & Ott, J.S. (Eds.) Classics of Organization Theory. Brooks/Cole Publishing Company, Kingsport, Tennesee.

Pinch, T. (1990) *The Culture of Scientists and Disciplinary Rhetoric.* European Journal of Education 25 (3) 241-257.

Pirttilä, I. (1993) *Me ja maailman mallit. Tiedonsosiologian ydintä etsimässä. [We and Our Models of Reality. An Exploration of the Argument in the Sociology of Knowledge.]* University of Joensuu, Publications in Social Sciences No. 17 (English summary.)

Pirttilä, I. (1995) *Neuvotteleva akateeminen johtajuus. [Negotiatiating Academic Leadership.]* Unpublished Manuscript.

Poster, M. (1984) *Foucault, Marxism and History.* Polity Press, Worcester.

Puuronen, V. (1995) *Nuoret maailmansa tuottajina? Tutkimus nuorisososiologian metodologiasta ja nuorten keskusteluista. [Young People as the Constructors of Their World? A Study of the Methodology of Youth Sociology and Conversations of Young People].* University of Joensuu. Publications in Social Sciences No. 21. (English Summary).

Reger, R., Mullane, J., Gustafson, L., DeMarie, S. (1994) *Creating Earthquakes to Change Organizational Mindsets.* Academy of Management Executive 8 (4), 31-42.

Rekilä, E. (1994) *Millaista korkeakoulun johtamista ja suunnittelua aika vaatii. [What Kind of Leadership and Planning is Needed Today.]* Korkeakoulutieto 20 (4), 36-41.

Rekilä, E. (1995) *Contracts as Management Instrument: New Policies in Relationships between the Universities and the Ministry of Education.* Tertiary Education and Management 1 (1), 76-80.

Richman, B.M. & Farmer, R.N. (1974) *Leadership, Goals and Power in Universities. A Contingency and Open-Systems Approach to Effective Management.* Jossey-Bass Publishers, San Francisco.

Roethlisberger, F.J. & Dickinson, W.J. (1970) *Human Relations.* (First published in 1939.) In Grusky, O. & Miller, G.A. (Eds.) The Sociology of Organizations. Basic Studies. The Free Press, New York.

Rossman, G., Corbett, H.D., & Firestone, W.A. (1988) *Change and Effectiveness in Schools.* State University of New York Press, New York.

Rousseau, D. (1990) *Assessing Organizational Culture: The Case for Multiple Methods.* In Schneider, B. (Ed.) Organizational Climate and Culture. Jossey-Bass, San Francisco.

Routila, L. (1981) *Historiallisen selityksen teoriasta. [On the Theory of Historical Explanation.]* Opuscula Philosophica Turkuensia XIV. SFFS, Naantali.

Ruoppila, I (1967) *Nuorten ja varttuneiden opiskelijoiden väliset asenne-erot eräissä ylioppilaspohjaisissa oppilaitoksissa. [Attitude Differences Between Young and Advanced University and College Students.]* Jyväskylä Studies in Education, Psychology and Social Research 15. Jyväskylän yliopisto. (English Summary.)

Russell, C. (1993) *Academic Freedom.* Routledge, London.

Saarinen, A. (1995) *Rakenteellinen kehittäminen jatkuu. Lääketieteelliset alat pisimmällä. [Structural Developing Continues. Medical Sector Farthest.]* Korkeakoulutieto 22 (3), 57-59.

Sackmann, S.A. (1991) *Cultural Knowledge in Organizations. Exploring the Collective Mind.* Sage Publications, Newbury Park.

Sallinen, A. (1994) *Arviointi johtamisen näkökulmasta. [Assessment From the Point of View of Leadership.]* Korkeakoulutieto 20 (4), 16-18.

Schafritz, J.M. & Ott, J.S. (1987) *Classics of Organization Theory*. Brooks/Cole Publishing Company, Kingsport, Tennesee.

Schein, E.H. (1985) *Organizational Culture and Leadership*. Jossey-Bass, San Francisco.

Schein, E.H. (1986) *Are You Corporate Cultured?* Personnel Journal 65 (11), 83-96.

Schein, E.H. (1987) *Defining Organizational Culture*. In Schafritz, J.M. & Ott, J.S. (Eds.) Classics of Organizational Theory. Brooks/Cole Publishing Company, Kingsport, Tennesee.

Schein, E.H. (1991a) *The Role of the Founder in the Creation of Organizational Culture*. In Frost, P., Moore, L., Louis, M., Lundberg, C., & Martin., J. (Eds.) Reframing Organizational Culture. Sage Publications, Newbury Park.

Schein, E.H. (1991b) *What is Culture?* In Frost, P., Moore, L., Louis, M., Lundberg, C., & Martin., J. (Eds.) Reframing Organizational Culture. Sage Publications, Newbury Park.

Schwandt, T.A. (1994) *Constructivist, Interpretivist Approaches to Human Inquiry*. In Denzin, N.K. & Lincoln, Y.S. (Eds.) Handbook of Qualitative Research. Sage, Thousand Oaks.

Scott, P. (1994) *Divide and Rule*. In Barnett, R. (Ed.) Academic Community. Discourse or Discord? Jessica Kingsley Publishers, Guildford.

Segerstråhle, U. (1990) *Taboos and the Distortion of Academic Discourse: A Meta-Critique of Critical Reasoning*. In Elzinga, A., Nolin, J., Pranger, R. & Suneson, S. (Eds.) In Science We Trust? Moral and Political Issues of Science in Society. Science and Technology Policy Studies 2. Lund University Press, Lund.

Seldin, P & Annis (1991) *Using Teaching Portfolio for the Improvement and Evaluation of College Teaching*. A Paper Presented at Improving University Teaching Conference. 2-5 July 1991, Glasgow.

Silverman, D. (1993) *Interpreting Qualitative Data. Methods for Analyzing Talk, Text and Interaction*. Sage Publications, Wiltshire.

Silvonen, J. (1990) *Fragmentteja suomalaisesta opiskelijaliikkeestä. [Some Fragments of the Finnish Student Movement.]* Nuorisotutkimus 8 (1), 2-17. (English Summary.)

Sims, H.P. & Lorenzi, P. (1992) *The New Leadership Paradigm. Social Learning and Cognition in Organizations*. Sage Publications, Newbury Park.

Sipilä (1991) *Asiantuntija ja johtaja. Miten hallitsen nämä kaksi roolia? [An Expert and A Leader. How Can I Manage These Two Roles?]* Weilin+Göös, Jyväskylä.

Smircich, L. (1983) *Concept of Culture and Organizational Analysis*. Administrative Science Quarterly, 28 (3), 339-358.

Smith, P.B & Peterson, M.F. (1988) *Leadership, Organizations and Culture*. Sage Publications, London.

Snow, C.P. (1969) *The Two Cultures: and a Second Look*. University Press, Cambridge.

Stiles, W.B. (1992) *Quality Control in Qualitative Research*. A Paper Presented at a Postgraduate Seminar in Department of Psychology, University of Joensuu, November 1992.

Stolte-Heiskanen, V. & Alestalo, M. (1978) *Tutkimustoiminnan mikrokosmos: tutkimusryhmät ja tuloksellisuus. [The Micro-Cosmos of Research Activity: Research Groups and Productivity.]* Suomen Akatemia, Helsinki.

Summa, H. & Virtanen, T. (1995) *Tulosajattelu ja organisaatiokuvat yliopistolaitoksessa. [MBO and Organizational Images in University Department]*. A Paper Presented at the Seminar 'Strateginen johtaminen korkeakouluissa' (Strategic Management in Universities) 1. June 1995, University of Tampere.

Sundin, B. (1996) *Hyöty nuorin tieteen motiiveista. [Utility - the Most Recent of the Legitimations of Research.]* Tiede 2000 16 (5), 28-32.

Svejby, K.E. & Risling, A. (1987) *Tietoyrityksen johtaminen - vuosisadan haaste? [Leading a Knowledge-organization - The Challenge of the Century?]* Weilin+Göös, Espoo.

Taulukoita KOTA-tietokannasta 1994; Tunnuslukuja 1994. [Statistics from KOTA knowledge-base 1994.] Koulutus- ja tiedepolitiikan linjan julkaisusarja N:o 27. Opetusministeriö, Helsinki.

Taustaraportti korkeakoulupolitiikan maatutkintaa varten (1993) *[A Background Report for the Evaluation of National Higher Education Policy.]* Koulutus- ja tiedepolitiikan linjan julkaisusarja, N:o 10. Opetusministeriö, Helsinki.

Taylor, F.W. (1970) *Scientific Management.* (First published in 1911.) In Grusky, O. & Miller, G.A. (Eds.) The Sociology of Organizations. Basic Studies. The Free Press, New York.

Teittinen, T. (1994) *Tieteellinen ja hallinnollinen johtaminen korkeakouluissa. [Scientific and Administrative Leadership in Universities.]* Korkeakoulutieto 20 (4), 7-11.

Temmes, A. (1990) *Tavoitejohtamisesta tulosajatteluun, byrokratiasta tuloskulttuuriin. Johtamisen ja kulttuurin muutoksista valtionhallinnossa. [From Management by Objectives to Result Orientation, From Bureaucracy to a Culture Supporting Results. On the Changes of Leadership and Culture in Public Administration.]* VAPK-kustannus, Helsinki.

Tierney, W. (1988) *Organizational Culture in Higher Education: Defining the Essentials.* Journal of Higher Education, 59 (1), 2-21.

Tierney, W. (1989) *Curricular Landscapes, Democratic Vistas. Transformative Leadership in Higher Education.* Praeger, New York.

Tight, M. (1988) *So What is Academic Freedom?* In Tight, M. (Ed.) Academic Freedom and Responsibility. SRHE & Open University Press, Suffolk.

Traweek, S. (1988) *Beamtimes and Lifetimes. The World of High Energy Physicists.* Harward University Press, Cambridge.

Trigg, R. (1993) *Rationality & Science. Can Science Explain Everything?* Blackwell Publishers, Oxford.

Tsoukas, H. (1994) *Redefining Common Sense: Types of Knowledge in Management Studies.* Journal of Management Studies 31 (6), 761-780.

Tucker, A. (1993) *Chairing the Academic Department. Leadership among Peers.* American Council on Education. Series on Higher Education. Oryx Press, Phoenix, AZ.

Valkonen, J. (1995) *Professori-tutkija. [Professor-researcher.]* Yliopisto 43 (17), 25.

Vanttaja, M. & Ketonen, K. (1995) *Lääketieteen koulutusalan rakenteellinen kehittäminen. [Structural Developing in Medicine.]* Korkeakoulutieto 22 (3), 50-55

van Vught, F.A. (1988) *Flexibility Production and Pattern Management. Two Basic Instruments of Strategic Planning for Higher Education Institutions.* Higher Education Policy Studies no. 74. Center for Higher Education Policy Studies (CHEPS), Enchede.

van Vught, F.A. (1989) *Creating Innovations in Higher Education.* European Journal of Education, 24 (3), 249-270.

Vartola, J. (1980) *Korkeakoulujen alihallinnon uudistamistarpeesta. [On The Need to Reform the Lower Administration in Higher Education.]* Korkeakouluhallinnon uudistamistarvetta selvittelevän projektin osaraportti I. Julkishallinnon julkaisusarja B 4/1980. Tampereen yliopisto, hallintotieteen laitos.

Välimaa, J. (1995) *Higher Education Cultural Approach.* Jyväskylä Studies in Education, Psychology and Social Research 113. University of Jyväskylä.

Wakeford, T. & Walters, M. (1995) *Science for the Earth. Can Science Make the World a Better Place?* John Wiley & Sons, Chichester.

Walford, G. (1987) *Restructuring Universities: Politics and Power in the Management of Change.* Croom Helm, London.

Walzer, M. (1989) *The Politics of Michel Foucault.* In Hoy, D.C. (Ed.) Foucault: A Critical Reader. Basil Blackwell, London.

Warren, C.O. (1993) *Chairperson and Dean: The Essential Partnership.* In Bennett, J.B. & Figuli, D.J. (1993) (Eds.) Enhancing Departmental Leadership. The Roles of the Chairperson. American Council on Education. Series of Higher Education. Oryx Press, New York.

Watson, T.J. (1994) *In Search of Management. Culture, Chaos & Control in Managerial Work.* Routledge, Cornwall.

Weber, M. (1974) *Bureaucracy.* (Previously published in 1946.) In Grusky, O. & Miller, G.A. (Eds.) The Sociology of Organizations. Basic Studies. The Free Press, New York.

Weick, K. (1988) *Educational Organizations as Loosely Coupled Systems.* In Westoby, A. (Ed.) Culture and Power in Educational Organizations. Open University Press, Guildford.

Wiberg, M. (1995) *Yliopisto-ongelmat. [The Problems of the University.]* In Wiberg (Ed.) Yliopisto uusiksi! Gaudeamus, Tampere.

Willner, J. (1995) *Luokallejääneiden salaliitto? [A Conspiracy by Those Who Were Kept Down by a Year?]* In Wiberg, M. (ed.) Yliopisto uusiksi! Gaudeamus, Tampere.

Wolverton, R.E. (1993) *Chairing the Small Department.* In Bennett, J.B. & Figuli, D.J. (1993) (Eds.) Enhancing Departmental Leadership. The Roles of the Chairperson. American Council on Education. Series of Higher Education. Oryx Press, New York.

Yin, R.K. (1989) *Case Study Research. Design and Methods.* Sage Publications, Newbury Park.

Ylijoki, O.-H. (1991) *Opiskelijan akateeminen sosialisaatio [The Academic Socialization of a Student].* A paper presented in Seminar: The State of Academic Study, 12. Sep. 1991.

Ylijoki, O.-H. (1994) *Sosiaalitieteen heimo ja hyveellinen elämä. [The Tribe of the Social Sciences and a Virtuous Life.]* In Weckroth, K. & Tolkki-Nikkonen, M. (Eds.) Jos A niin... Vastapaino, Tampere.

Ylikangas, H. (1990) *Historiantutkimus lähimmässä tulevaisuudessa. [Research in History in the Near Future.]* Perko, T. (Ed.) Tiede muutoksen maailmassa. Atena kustannus Oy, Jyväskylä.

Yliopiston johtosääntöjen uudistamisesta (1993) *[On the Reform of Service Regulations within University.]* Unpublished Memo 7. Dec. 1993. Joensuun yliopisto, hallintovirasto.

Yliopistot Universiteten '95 (1995) *[Universities '95.]* Opetusministeriö, Korkeakoulu- ja tiedeosasto. Helsinki.

INDEX

A

academic context, 2, 4, 6, 9, 33, 42, 44, 52, 57, 106, 125
academic culture, 7, 55, 58, 71, 80, 88, 120, 124, 153, 159, 174
academic freedom, 43, 52, 53, 80, 92, 97, 112, 113, 122, 130, 135, 137, 138, 145, 146, 153, 155, 156, 157, 160, 161, 164, 166, 168, 173
academic leaders, vii, viii, 2, 3, 5, 6, 7, 8, 9, 27, 35, 40, 41, 42, 43, 47, 50, 52, 53, 54, 55, 56, 57, 59, 70, 72, 75, 76, 77, 78, 83, 85, 87, 88, 107, 109, 113, 114, 116, 117, 122, 123, 125, 126, 130, 132, 138, 141, 143, 147, 150, 154, 159, 160, 161, 163, 164, 169, 170, 171, 172, 173, 174
academic leadership, vii, viii, 2, 3, 5, 7, 8, 9, 27, 42, 52, 53, 54, 55, 56, 57, 59, 70, 72, 75, 76, 78, 83, 85, 87, 88, 109, 113, 114, 117, 125, 150, 154, 159, 160, 164, 169, 171, 173, 174
academic professional associations, 26
academic studies, 58, 153, 170
academical-traditional doctrine, 14, 15
accountability, 2, 5, 27, 173
achievement, 4, 24, 44, 120, 170
administration reform, 16, 19, 27
administrative authority, 27, 51
administrative bureaucracy, 18, 57, 130
administrative reform, 16, 17, 18, 57, 134
allocation of resources, 11, 14, 17, 25, 55, 68, 145, 151

B

basic research, 26
behavioral theories, 31, 41, 64
budget cuts, 22, 26, 89, 92, 102, 104, 106, 112, 115, 122, 133, 137, 139, 145, 147, 155, 165
budget funding, 1, 11, 22, 165
budgeting by results, 8, 24

bureaucracy, 18, 57, 129, 134, 148
bureaucratic hierarchy, 51

C

citizenship, 14
cognitive theories, 31, 32, 38, 124
collective values, 4
collegial control, 27, 140
collegiality, 128
commonality, 109
constructivism, 62, 63, 64, 65, 67, 102
contingency theories, 31, 33
creativity, 2, 28, 51, 52, 137, 173
critical theories, 62
cultural diversity, 26
cultural models, 40, 41, 121
cultural theories, 31, 40
cultural values, vii, 114, 121, 133, 161, 168, 169

D

decision-making, 2, 3, 5, 16, 17, 19, 21, 27, 29, 36, 45, 46, 47, 48, 56, 57, 93, 98, 114, 121, 126, 127, 128, 129, 138, 140, 145, 148, 149, 155, 158, 160, 161, 162, 163, 164, 166, 170
degree reform, 17, 18, 148, 162
degree targets, 24
democracy, 16, 18, 19, 57, 90, 95, 97, 98, 100, 103, 114, 117, 127, 129, 133, 134, 142, 145, 148, 149, 162, 168
democratic ideal, 19
democratic leadershi, 98, 128, 131, 135, 145, 147, 164, 166, 168
departmental cultures, 1, 3, 9, 16, 59, 73, 76, 94, 125, 159, 173
departmental leadership, 3, 6, 7, 9, 26, 27, 42, 55 56, 59, 88, 92, 114, 117, 119, 121, 125, 126, 132, 133, 135, 140, 158, 159, 160, 161, 162, 168. 171. 173

departmental leadership cultures, 9, 117, 119,
    126, 140, 159, 161
development doctrine, 14, 15, 18, 25, 27, 29
disciplinary cultures, 3, 6, 7, 9, 42, 72, 77, 82, 88,
    107, 114, 119, 120, 133, 159, 174
disciplinary-based leadership, 51
disciplines, 1, 3, 5, 6, 7, 9, 18, 29, 49, 50, 51, 53,
    54, 56, 69, 71, 73, 74, 75, 76, 83, 87, 88, 89,
    91, 92, 96, 97, 98, 103, 107, 108, 110, 112,
    113, 114, 116, 117, 120, 121, 122, 133, 144,
    160, 174
doctoral degrees, 73, 131, 152
doctoral dissertation, 13, 74, 111, 112

E

economic crisis, 23, 33, 69, 155
economic growth, 12, 19
economic pressures, 2, 169
educational planning, 17
educational policy, 14, 18, 20
event management model, 38
event meaning, 38, 39
expansion of knowledge, 117
extreme relativism, 68, 82

F

Finnish higher education system, 7, 11, 12, 14, 26
flow of information, 56, 138, 139, 155, 157
fragmentation, 7, 42, 43, 45, 54, 87, 102, 107,
    116, 117, 121, 124, 125
frame of reference, 45, 54, 64, 66, 76
framework for leadership, 9

G

gender issues, 80
global industrialization, 87
goals and priorities, 51, 53
good leadership, 34, 75, 87, 123, 131, 132, 145,
    154, 160, 167, 173
group work, 53, 103, 109, 112, 141, 163

H

handling of knowledge, 42
higher education policy, 14, 15, 17, 18, 19, 20,
    22, 28, 122, 128
human relations, 4, 5, 32, 57, 131, 139, 146, 147,
    162, 166
humanities, 12, 21, 53, 71, 88, 91, 99, 165

I

individual leadership, 2, 27, 52, 97, 107, 128,
    161, 164, 173
industrial production, 12

intellectual leadership, vii, 5, 110, 172, 173
interest groups, 37, 45, 48, 50, 52, 53, 121
international competitiveness, 19
internationalization, 26
interpersonal disagreements, 139

L

leadership environment, viii, 33, 50, 53, 109
leadership style, 33, 58, 92, 93, 116, 117, 128,
    130, 131, 136, 137, 138, 139, 143, 150, 152,
    156, 159, 162, 164, 166, 167, 170
leadership training, 122, 160
level of analysis, 45, 54, 84, 120

M

management, viii, 2, 3, 4, 5, 8, 14, 20, 21, 31, 32,
    33, 36, 38, 42, 43, 44, 46, 49, 51, 54, 56, 57,
    59, 80, 106, 114, 116, 121, 122, 126, 128, 137,
    138, 139, 142, 145, 147, 151, 155, 160, 162,
    164, 166, 167, 173, 175
market forces, 22

N

naive realism, 63
national progress, 14
nationalism, 101

O

objectivity, 43, 70, 83, 101
organizational culture, 3, 6, 7, 9, 39, 42, 56, 58,
    61, 71, 76, 114, 119, 121, 124, 126, 152, 159,
    160, 169
organizational effectiveness, 124
organizational leadership, 5, 110

P

point of reference, 61
political pressure, 37
positivism, 62, 64, 108
postgraduate studies, 58, 153
postpositivism, 62, 63, 64
post-war generation, 12, 19
power and influence theories, 31, 35, 64
productivity, 23, 55, 74, 136, 138, 139, 154, 167,
    168
professional autonomy, 18
professorial role, 146, 162
psychology of management, 3
public interest, 19
public relations, 50
public sector, 26

R

radical student movement, 19
recession, 8, 17, 20, 22, 23, 26, 27, 68, 76, 107, 111, 133, 145, 156, 158, 163, 168, 169
regional equity, 20, 21
research projects, 3, 23, 28, 56, 58, 77, 78, 103, 105, 111, 140, 143, 145, 149, 150, 151, 155, 163, 170, 174
researcher training, 26
responsibility, 4, 21, 34, 39, 44, 47, 51, 55, 123, 129, 139, 149, 161, 164, 168, 170, 172, 173

S

scientific power, 51
scientific/expert tasks, 57
social sciences, 12, 17, 20, 21, 53, 62, 71, 95, 97, 99, 110, 111, 114, 127, 162
specialisms, 7, 9, 50, 51, 52, 53, 83, 87, 88, 91, 99, 106, 107, 108, 110, 111, 112, 113, 114, 115, 116, 117, 120, 122, 146, 149, 152, 163, 168, 173, 174
spheres of reality, 68, 69
standard rules, 45
standardization, 18
steering policy, 8, 16, 22
structural change, 19

student housing, 20
student radicalism, 16, 19, 20, 94, 131, 162
suffrage, 16, 20
sustainable development, 26

T

Taylorism, 18
teaching staff, 12, 13, 127, 145
teaching tasks, 1, 58, 129
training of researchers, 26
trait theories, 31, 32
transformational leadership, 37, 47, 123, 168

U

unclear goals, 44, 45
uniform standards, 89, 109, 144
university business, 2
university of Helsinki, 11, 13, 15, 17
university teachers, 12
unpredictability, 45, 48

W

welfare-state, 12
work situation, 38